Bridging Three Worlds

Bridging Three Worlds

Hungarian-Jewish Americans

1 8 4 8 – 1 9 1 4

Robert Perlman

The University of
Massachusetts Press

Amherst

Copyright © 1991 by
The University of Massachusetts Press

All rights reserved

Printed in the United States of America

LC 90-11224

ISBN 0-87023-468-4

Designed by David Ford

Set in Linotype Plantin

Printed and bound by Thomson-Shore, Inc.

This book is published with the support and cooperation
of the University of Massachusetts at Boston.

Library of Congress Cataloging-in-Publication Data

Perlman, Robert.
   Bridging three worlds : Hungarian-Jewish Americans,
   1848–1914 /
Robert Perlman.
       p.   cm.
   Includes bibliographical references and index.
   ISBN 0-87023-468-4 (alk. paper)
       1. Jews—Hungary—History.   2. Hungary—Ethnic
   relations.   3. Jews, Hungarian—United States—History.
   4. Jews—United States—History.   5. Immigrants—
   United States—History.   6. United States—Ethnic
   relations.   I. Title.
   DS135.H9P47   1991
   943.9′004924—dc20   90–11224
                                              CIP

British Library Cataloguing in Publication data are
                   available.

To My Grandmother

Fannie Goldstein (1865–1940)
who traveled these three worlds
with courage and grace

★

Contents

APPENDIXES

★

Illustrations and Tables

★

Preface and Acknowledgments

The sounds of the places, spoken in the soft, lilting Hungarian of my grandparents, have remained in my ears: *Shuroshpottoch . . . Mishcolts . . . Ooey-hey*. It was many years before I saw those towns on a map as Sáros-patak, Miskolc, and Újhely, whose full name is Sátoraljaújhely. None of my four grandparents said much of their youth in those strange-sounding places or their arrival in America about 1880. Their reticence and my ignorance pulled me first into a search for the story of my own family and then, though I am not a professional historian, into this history of the Hungarian Jews who came to this country.

It is a rarity these days to step into a field of inquiry where few have trod before. Yet that is the case with Hungarian Jews in America. In the vast writing on American immigration, they are practically unknown as a distinct group. When Yeshayahu Jelinek published a paper in 1972 on this subject, he was a pioneer. No one followed him. I hope this book makes a beginning. It is addressed to two audiences: those who want to learn more about their own background as Hungarian Jews and those who have a professional interest in American immigration and ethnicity.

Many people had a part in this work. First and foremost, my wife, Bernice, has done everything from Yiddish translation, library research, and data entry to being critic and source of daily support. My children provided technical help and encouragement.

Earlier drafts of this book benefited much from the critical comments of Robert C. Binstock, David Giele, Arnold Gurin, Leon Jick, Robert Morris, and Marshall Sklare. Yeshayahu Jelinek gave generously of his time and expertise and I am grateful for the use of notes from his research in Cleveland in the 1970s.

For suggestions on the chapters on Hungary, I am indebted to Nathaniel Katzburg of Bar-Ilan University, Victor Karady of the Centre de Sociologie Européenne in Paris, and Anna Wessely of Budapest University. Ágnes

Lukács in Budapest provided much valuable help with the demography and history of Hungary, as did Aranka and István Szaszkó with Hungarian government statistics.

One cannot find material in a library or archives conveniently catalogued under "Hungarian Jews." I am therefore especially grateful to librarians in the reference and the Judaica sections of the Goldfarb Library at Brandeis University; to Nathan M. Kaganoff of the American Jewish Historical Society; to Nancy F. Becker, Archivist of the Cleveland Jewish Archives at the Western Reserve Historical Society; and to Joel Wurl at the Immigration History Research Center at the University of Minnesota.

For arranging access to Hungarian-Jewish families, whose recollections provided much rich material, I want to thank Gary Mokotoff of the Jewish Genealogical Society and Sallyann Amdur Sack, editor of *AVOTAYNU*, the International Review of Jewish Genealogy. To the many people who then sent me information about their families I am very grateful. Some thirty Jewish historical and genealogical societies around the country were more than cooperative in supplying material on local history.

I am indebted to the National Council of Jewish Women, Pittsburgh Section, for permission to use interviews from their Oral History Project. The Population Analysis Unit of the City Planning Commission of New York City gave me access to unpublished census data. Vera Deák helped with translations from the Hungarian language and Brad Hubbell volunteered aid with programming the computer.

After sifting through the thoughtful advice and recommendations of others, it was my task to decide what to accept and what to set aside. I and not they must be held responsible for the final product.

Bridging Three Worlds

★

CHAPTER I

The People of This Book

The Hungarian Jews who came to the United States between 1848 and 1914 were, comparatively speaking, few in number. They were a small proportion of all the Hungarians who came, a still smaller part of all the Jews who poured into America in those years, and a drop in the tidal wave of the millions of immigrants who reached here around the turn of the century. But numbers are not everything, and there are at least two good reasons for the writing of this book.

First, the Jews of Hungary occupied a unique position in Europe. They had achieved an understanding with the ruling Magyars that gave them rights and opportunities that Jews in other countries did not enjoy. This in turn shaped their social and cultural characteristics in a way that distinguished them from both Western and Eastern European Jews. For example, their rapid entry into the higher reaches of the economic and intellectual life of Hungary was extraordinary, as was the extent of their acculturation and assimilation.

Second, the story of these people has not been told. This is remarkable, considering that approximately 100,000 Hungarian Jews came to America before the First World War. It is the more remarkable because Hungarian Jewry was the third largest in the world outside of the United States at the beginning of the twentieth century.[1]

One scholar, characterizing the situation in Hungary from the middle of the nineteenth century to the First World War, wrote: "The Jews became a decisive factor in the formation of Hungarian social and cultural life. Their contribution to the development of their country was greater than that of any other European Jewish community . . . At the height of its assimilation . . . Hungarian Jewry succeeded in establishing social ties with the gentile society more than did any other European Jewry."[2]

These preliminary observations lay the groundwork for posing the main questions to which this book is addressed: In what ways did the Jews of

3

Hungary differ from other Jews? What were the distinctive characteristics of their history, their practice of Judaism, their language, and their community life? What was the nature of their relationships with the Gentiles around them? Can one really generalize about Jews in Hungary as though they were a homogeneous group or were there significant internal variations? To address these questions, I devote the first chapter to a very brief history of Hungary and the next four chapters to the status and life of Jews in Hungary.

The middle section of the work concerns emigration and immigration. Given the relatively favorable circumstances of Hungarian Jews and their attachment to Magyar society, why did any of them leave for America? Where did they settle and how did they make a living?

Finally, as the years went by, How did Hungarian Jews manage the adjustments they had to make in three distinct arenas? While the metaphor is awkward, so was their situation: they had a foot in three worlds. They were loyal, often chauvinistic Hungarians and it would have been understandable for them to continue their relationships with their Christian countrymen in America and to maintain their ties to the old country. But did they hold on to this Magyar connection? Clearly they needed to find their place in the Jewish community in America. Was this to be as Hungarian Jews? How strong was their bond to other Jews? And finally they were caught up, as all immigrants were, in the exciting but demanding process of becoming Americans. How easily did they pass through the door to America?

A good deal has been written about Jews' acculturation and assimilation in this country, but generally it concerns their adjustment to two worlds or two reference groups: Americans and Jews.[3] Hungarian Jews had a three-way cultural identity to juggle, similar to but not quite the same as the German Jews who had reached America somewhat earlier.

In searching for light on these questions, several influences will be explored. These seem to have acted with equal force on the Jews in Hungary and after they came to the United States. One of these is the almost ceaseless mobility of Jews over the centuries. Their movements from Germany, Austria, and Poland into Hungary roughly between 1650 and 1850 and their subsequent departure to places like the Lower East Side of New York and to Wharton, Texas, and Puebla, Colorado, were simply parts of a much larger and much older migration of Jews. Hounded from Germany, Spain, or other countries or drawn by beckoning opportunities to newly

developing areas, in time the Jews acquired the characteristics of international migrants: an ability to adapt to new conditions, a way with languages, portable occupational skills—equipment that eased their accommodation to Hungary and later to America.

Social and economic contact between Jews and non-Jews was a powerful
force in shaping the Hungarian Jewish story. In Hungary these relationships hinged largely on the occupations and the political and social status
that were accorded to the Jews. There was a sort of reciprocity in economic
roles which brought mutual advantages as well as serious antagonisms. But
deep cultural differences, religion being only the most obvious, separated
the Jews from Christians in Hungary. These differences were compounded
by the politics of nineteenth-century nationalism and they were rubbed raw
by deliberate exploitation by anti-Semites. The oppressed status of many
ethnic or national groups within Hungary exacerbated conflict with the
Jews. Not all of this was left behind by the Christians and Jews who came to
America.

Another influence impinging on the developments traced in these pages
was language. It was more than a device for communication. It was the glue
that bound people to a common set of memories, values, and loyalties. This
was particularly important in what has been called "the polyglotic monarchy" of Hungary. The languages in question—Magyar, German, Yiddish, Hebrew, Slovak, to name a few—played a significant part in the
Hungarian Jews' relationship to their environment both in Europe and
here, probably more so than with other Jewish groups who immigrated.

Some preliminary observations are in order. First as to the question
posed above: Was Hungarian Jewry homogeneous? It will be a central
argument of this book that there were, in a sense, two Hungarian Jewries.
There is a lucid illustration of this in Illés Kaczér's novel *The Siege*, in a
scene in a village tavern in northern Hungary.[4] In this scene Sholem, an
innkeeper, is reading the biblical story of Purim to his children, just as he
had every year at this time. Sholem was a devoutly religious man, and for
him serving drinks to the peasants was a regrettable distraction from his
main interest: study of the Talmud and its vast store of commentaries. This
morning the barroom was empty except for Sholem, his children, and a
nephew who was visiting. The visitor broke into the reading with a different interpretation. "Where did you learn all this?" Sholem asked. "I
read it in Polybius and also in Josephus Flavius," the boy answered. "And
who are they?" Sholem asked. The boy explained that Josephus was a

Jewish historian in Roman times. "You are mistaken," Sholem reproved the boy, "the history was written in the Bible." The visitor argued his case. "Is that the sort of books you are given to read," Sholem asked, adding with finality, "They are forbidden books and we must not read them." But the wall had been breached and Sholem's children never forgot this conversation.

This vignette makes clear the sharp distinction between two kinds of Jews in nineteenth-century Hungary, represented by the poor, Orthodox innkeeper and the middle-class, Westernized visitor. They were separated by the gap between secular knowledge and traditional Judaism. One was a villager, the other a cosmopolitan. It is quite likely that Sholem's family spoke Yiddish at home and Slovak with the peasants; his guest's language was probably Hungarian or possibly German.

There were indeed significant differences among Hungarian Jews. But can it be said that they differed as a group from other Jews? In the search for an answer to this question I stumbled across an intriguing contradiction. I think of it as the paradox of "the different, but invisible Hungarian Jew." Some people thought the Jews of Hungary were certainly different— perhaps better or worse, but distinctive. Others somehow lost Hungarian Jews in broad generalizations about "Eastern European Jews" or they folded them in with Gentile Hungarians.

Let us consider first those who saw the Hungarians as different from other Jews. When I mentioned this study to two colleagues, the responses were half-jocular, half-negative. One said: "The Hungarian Jews weren't so good on the other side and they were no better here." The other replied with a kindly smile, "as a Litvak (a Lithuanian Jew) I must say the whole question of Hungarian Jews isn't very important." A similar assessment was offered by an informant in a history of Boston's Jewish community, who remarked that there were many Hungarians but "we had no use" for them.[5] These people saw them as regrettably different: weak in their identification and behavior as Jews, snobbish, and not part of the warm world of Yiddishkeit.

From their own point of view some Hungarian Jews saw themselves as distinctive in an altogether glowing light. My grandfather solemnly explained to me more than once that the Spanish and German Jews were at the top of the hierarchy, we Hungarians came next, then the Russian and Polish Jews, with the Galizianers (natives of Galicia, Poland) at the very bottom of the pile. My grandmother, to whom this book is dedicated, stood behind him motioning to me that this was utter nonsense. For years I was convinced that my grandmother was right, so it was unsettling to read—in the presumably impartial words of the United States consul to Budapest, writing in 1886—that the Hungarian Jews "ought not to be confounded with those who during the last few years have been emigrating in masses from Russia . . . and who comparatively seem to be of a very low standard as a people."[6]

However, I am now more sure than ever that my grandmother was wiser than the U.S. consul. That there was, as Naomi Cohen put it, a "social pecking order" among Jews in America cannot be denied. It depended, she said, on the time of arrival and the geographic location from which one's forebears came. The farther west in Europe one's origins were, the better. She did not include Hungarians in her analysis of the pecking order, but we can note that geographically and culturally they occupied a mid-space between the Eastern and Western Jewish communities. One scholar, who went very far in making the case for distinctiveness, wrote that "most Hungarian Jews arrived in the United States without a command of Yiddish. Consequently the first generation Hungarian Jew also does not 'mix' readily with Jewish immigrants from other countries . . . [and] frequently stands at a distance from general Hungarian, Jewish or American experiences. They are Hungarian-Jews; a group apart."[7] Perhaps the writer exaggerated to make his point, but he was not far off the mark.

Now we come to the part of the paradox that makes the Hungarian Jew invisible. Many people at different times and for quite diverse motives have not only smudged the lines that distinguish the Hungarian Jews, but have managed to lose them entirely in either Hungarian or Jewish historiography. One explanation for this tendency is related to the quid pro quo arrangement between Magyars and Jews, the subject of Chapter 4. The Magyar aristocrats and the Jews of nineteenth-century Hungary made a mutually beneficial deal. The Magyars, just short of a numerical majority in their multiethnic kingdom, gave unprecedented political protection and economic opportunities to the Jews. In return the Jews acceded to cultural assimilation and nationalistic loyalty to the Magyar nation. Both sides in this understanding wanted to emphasize their likeness, not their differences. Hence, in some of the writing by non-Jewish Hungarians there are references to "merchants, artisans, and professionals" where it is unmistakably clear from the context that the writer means Jews. It would have defeated the quid pro quo strategy if attention were called to the Jews as a separate population. So, for example, many of the official census reports and emigration statistics counted the Jews as Magyars. In more recent times following World War II the Jewish aspect of the country's history was not encouraged as a subject for research and publication in the Hungarian People's Republic. In the last few years this has changed markedly and in 1988 Budapest University had, for the first time in the Eastern European countries, a Center for Jewish Studies.

Another explanation for "invisibility" lies in the tendency to speak of Austro-Hungarian Jews as if they formed a homogeneous bloc. In the face of the distinct politics and language of the Kingdom of Hungary—albeit within the Austro-Hungarian monarchy—this borders on the absurd, if only because "Austrian Jews" meant in effect those from Galicia. Other people have had difficulty distinguishing a Hungarian Jew from a sort of generic "German Jew," presumably because they all shared the German language and culture. Thus, we learn in a book about Morris Rich, a successful department store owner in the American South, that he was born in Hungary in Kassa in 1847. In the very next paragraph, the writer refers to him as "the German Jewish boy."[8] In a similar instance, my great uncle, who was born not far from Kassa, registered himself with great pride as "German" in the 1900 census in New York.

The writing on immigration has abetted the invisibility of the Hungarian Jew. The extensive literature on Jewish immigration to the United States and on the American Jewish community gives almost no attention to the people who are the subject of this book. Similarly the writing on Hungarian immigration to this country devotes only a paragraph here or a line there to its Jewish component and nowhere treats them systematically.[9] Taken together, thirteen standard works from these two bodies of literature do not contain as much as a dozen pages on Hungarian Jews.[10]

There has been a tendency to identify the Hungarians who arrived after 1880 as part of the mass movement of Eastern European Jews to America, and then not to mention them again. The Yiddish-speaking Jews of Poland and Russia would hardly have agreed to this classification; they looked upon those from Hungary—with little enthusiasm—as being among the "Daitchen" or German Jews.[11]

Hungarian and other writers have been inclined to incorporate the Jews in histories of Hungarian immigration. The Hungarian Jews were not alone on this score. Concerning the immigrants who preceded them, Naomi Cohen had this to say: "They were both Jews and Germans. Because of that duality some later historians . . . could not agree on how to treat them: to ignore them completely or to set them apart, either as a non-German group whose arrival happened to coincide in time with that of the Germans, or as a discrete subgroup within the larger German parameters."[12]

Here are some illustrations of the tendency on this side of the Atlantic to erase the identity of the people of this book: "More than 25,000 Hungarians live in Cleveland. There are manufacturers, merchants, industrialists, physicians, lawyers, and newspapermen among them. They are well represented in the city's social and business life." This newspaper item of 1892 goes on to name seven men. All of them were Jews.[13] In the 875 pages of Géza Kende's book on Hungarians in America, Jewish names appear frequently, but there are only a few instances in which they are identified as Jews. At the end of seventy-six pages devoted to the religious institutions of Hungarian Americans, four paragraphs are devoted to the Jews, who by 1926 had established many synagogues across the United States.[14]

An especially interesting example of the phenomenon of invisibility comes from an American novel about a Hungarian immigrant family in New York.[15] The family's name is Benton and the unusual thing about the book is the complete absence of their religious identity. It has simply been washed out. In point of fact, the author was Jewish and Mr. and Mrs. Benton were in reality Mr. and Mrs. Goldstein, Orthodox Jews. This assertion is not difficult to substantiate. The author was my aunt and the main characters in the book, except for their names, were my grandparents, my mother and father, and their siblings. How does one explain the invisibility of the Jewish identity of the people in this book? Is it reasonable to think that they were perceived as only or primarily Hungarian and that their Jewishness was unimportant or was not noticed?

That speculation would not have been very credible in nineteenth-century Hungary where everyone's ethnic and religious identity was of critical significance in a political sense. This was just as true in the United States. If all this were not enough, the steady anti-Semitic drumbeat of certain politicians and clerics in Hungary would have let few people forget that the 5 percent of the population who were Jews were "different."

We have already pointed out that the quid pro quo arrangement in Hungary had the effect of deemphasizing the Jewishness of Hungarian Jews. In addition they were looked upon as German in culture and language. On this side of the Atlantic the blurring of the identity of Jews from Hungary probably stemmed in part from devotion to the idea of Americanization and a corresponding reluctance to underline religious and ethnic differences. (This book does not attempt to present the experience of Hungarian Jews in Canada.)[16] In part the erased identity was due to the traditional division of Jewish immigration into the Sephardic, German, and East European periods. Virtually alone among historians, Peter Wiernik gives Hungarian Jews a place in the second wave of Jewish immigrants along with German and Polish Jews, as distinct from the third wave from Russia. His classification of Hungarian Jews is however very questionable.

Perhaps unwittingly the immigrants themselves contributed to their invisibility by not leaving a written history of their experiences. Their history lies buried, in part for understandable reasons. The immigrants literally and figuratively pressed forward along the railings of the ships that brought them here, straining to get their first look at the Golden Land. Once ashore, they and even more so their children had little time to look back. They concentrated their energies on getting settled here and making the best life they could. Leaving a paper trail was far from their minds.

But their grandchildren and great-grandchildren (or some of them) have made their way back to the ships and are looking astern toward the land from which their people came 75 or 125 years ago. They are trying to understand more about the kind of people who came here, about their life in Hungary and about their experiences as immigrants in this land.

We do not refer here to the well-known Hungarian Jews whose accomplishments in America have been widely trumpeted. In the movie industry people such as Alexander Korda, Adolph Zukor, William Fox, and Marcus Loew have been celebrated, along with well-known musicians, actors, and writers. And much has been written about the strong representation in the sciences by men such as Leo Szilard, Edward Teller, and John Von Neumann. But the writings about celebrities do not constitute a rounded social history of the many thousands of unglamorous immigrants who came here. Accordingly the information for this book comes from interviews, personal correspondence, questionnaires, archives, passenger ship lists, census reports, old newspapers, and the like.

A fundamental issue in all of this talk of identity is, of course, whether these people were thought of or thought of themselves primarily as Jews or primarily as Hungarians. The issue has rattled around for a long time. "Magyar Jew or Jewish Magyar?" was used as the title for an article published in 1848 and was used again in 1974.[17] What I hope to show in the chapters that follow is that culturally and geographically the Hungarian

Jews were sandwiched between the German Jews and those from the Slavic lands to the north and east. And while they shared many characteristics with their Jewish brethren, they were also distinct in several important respects.

Of equal importance, however, is the fact that Hungarian Jews of the late nineteenth century and the early twentieth century cannot be described as a homogeneous population. Streams of Jews entered Hungary from different parts of Central Europe and brought quite diverse cultural backgrounds with them. Some were close to the Yiddishkeit of the Polish shtetl; some closely resembled the Westernized German Jews. These differences among the Jews of Hungary are of prime importance in understanding the character of the immigration to America. It will be a major contention in this book that there were significant differences between those who emigrated following the failed Revolution of 1848 and those who came after 1880. Essentially they represented the two Jewries to which we alluded earlier.

It is tempting to draw parallels between the development of the Jewish community in Hungary and the one here in America. They began at approximately the same time, in the late seventeenth century. German-speaking Jews formed a large part of the early community in both lands. In Germany they had been restricted to certain occupations and most of them arrived in Hungary and the United States as artisans and petty tradesmen. In both countries they struggled for civic and social acceptance and political rights and were often greeted with the proposition that these rights would be forthcoming if they would only change their alien ways and religious practices.

And for the Jews themselves, living in two societies that were relatively free, there was always the painful dilemma of how much to assimilate and how much to preserve their Jewish heritage. In both countries, the resolution of this issue led to a religious rift in the Jewish community. Even the numbers involved in the formation of Jewish communities in Hungary and the United States were not very different. It is worth noting that in the period 1910–1915 approximately one-quarter of the population of Budapest and one-quarter of New York City were Jewish.

But the parallel is far from complete, for Central Europe was not America. And what became a thriving Jewish community on this side of the Atlantic was all but exterminated in the Hungary of the Final Solution. Before World War II there were almost half a million Jews in the territory that is now Hungary. Today the Jewish population has been estimated to be about seventy-five thousand, most of it concentrated in Budapest. Only small remnants of Jewish communities survive outside the capital.

As one winds the crank of a microfilm viewer scanning ships' manifests or turns the huge, dry pages of citizenship applications, the facts about ordinary people, not luminaries, pass before one's eyes. Each person is "summarized" in a short entry. The same names appear over and over again and become a blur—Feldman and Schwartz, Weiss and Guttman . . . Sarah, Frieda, Jacob. There are countless instances of exactly the same name, Samuel Rosenberg or Hannah Gross.

But always the realization breaks through the search for information that these were very real people, leaving homes and families to travel to another land and another life. What the microfilm and the documents cannot reproduce are the hopes and apprehensions that must have traveled with them. To address this deficit and to introduce the real people of this book I reproduce here the story of a lad who left Hungary in 1914 to come to America.

Maurice Amsel's story begins in his boyhood home near Stropkov (Sztropkó in Hungarian) in Zemplén County and ends in Simpson, Pennsylvania, where he and his wife settled. At the age of eighty-six he tape-recorded his recollections and I was lucky enough to borrow them from his niece in Israel.[18]

The Amsel family lived in the upper part of Zemplén County in a hamlet five kilometers from Stropkov, which in 1900 had 2,300 inhabitants, half of them Jews. Maurice had heard that the family originally came from Poland, but that their name was German since "maybe somebody lived there." His father combined farming and running a tavern, but could hardly make a living for himself, his wife, and seven children. Maurice's sister urged him to continue in school and not to become a farmer like their father.

They had two bedrooms, a kitchen, the tavern, and twenty-five acres where they raised potatoes, corn, and wheat for themselves and hay for their three cows and two horses. The bar served people passing by, like those who went to market on Mondays, some of whom hired the Amsel wagon for the day. The Amsels employed men to do their reaping; the threshing they did at home. The threshed wheat was taken to the mill for grinding but was not sold because it was needed for the family. One sack of flour required half an acre.

Maurice remembers his father with a beard and his mother with a shawl, people well liked in the town and known for helping others. They "had no trouble with anti-Semitism . . . the Jews and the Gentiles got along well." The Hungarian government treated Jews very well. If anyone did anything to the Jews, they were put in jail. Kaiser Franz Joseph was very good to the Jews.

In Stropkov people spoke German, Hungarian, and Slovak; at home the Amsels spoke Yiddish. The Amsels went to the synagogue, a mile from their house, on Saturdays and occasionally on other days. It was a religious family, but with some flexibility. Except for Maurice, the boys did not go to public school, where they could not wear their hats in accordance with Jewish law; they went only to the Hebrew school. Maurice was the only Amsel child to attend the public school; his father said nothing about the boy's removing his hat in school. He went there for three years, starting when he was eight years old. He had already been in a Jewish school since he was five, going every morning for six years, with his Jewish education supplemented by his father during the winters.

"There wasn't much to cook there," Maurice recalls. Potatoes were used in soup, with sauerkraut, and in borscht. They bought sugar in a cone and broke off pieces with a hatchet. A piece of sugar was held in the mouth while drinking coffee. For Shabbos his mother made *cholunt* mostly from beef. ("Cholunt," also called "Scholeth," was a combination of meat and vegetables, placed in huge black pots and carried to the communal bakery to simmer for eighteen hours until after the Saturday morning synagogue service, with each pot marked in chalk with the name of its owner.)[19]

For recreation men played cards, and during the winter evenings the women spun cotton grown in their fields. In the town drunkenness was a problem. One peasant who was constantly drunk slept in the Amsels' stable. Another had died in their tavern, with no relatives to provide a church funeral. The strong liquor stock—vodka, rum, slivovitz, etc.—had to be cut with water before it was served in the bar.

There was no doctor in town and no dentist. Maurice was told that he had been very sick as a baby and apparently given up for dead. Candles had been lit, when a doctor's daughter who happened to be visiting put feathers near the baby's nostrils and saw the feathers move. The candles were extinguished.

Maurice left Stopkov in 1909 when he was about fifteen, to go to work on a farm in nearby Grozócz to earn money for his passage to America. His brother was already in the United States and Maurice wanted to join him since he saw no future in Hungary. For several years Maurice loaded carts and delivered milk, worked in the stables, and stood watch to prevent stealing. In two years he saved some money but not enough, and his father gave him some more for the trip.

One day shortly before Maurice left for America, Archduke Francis Ferdinand, the nephew of the king, came to Stropkov, which had carefully cleaned its streets. (This was only a few months before his assassination in Sarajevo ignited World War I.) The hamlet did not have newspapers and Maurice remembers people gathering in the street in order to hear the news when they heard a "town crier" beat his drum. (Another version of this describes the local town official, perhaps a tax collector or sheriff, sounding the drum before giving information about taxes, military conscription, church news, and the sale of personal property.)[20]

When he was ready to leave Hungary, Maurice could not get a passport because he was due to serve three years in the army. He left anyway. Maurice, now about nineteen, did not want to face a crying family so he left without saying goodbye to his parents. He took only a little money so he could not be accused of theft on the way. Maurice got a ride to Kassa and a train to "Alleberg" (probably Odelberg, a Prussian transit station). A policeman came onto the train and asked for his papers. The young man had some kind of identification, which the policeman said was no good, but apparently let him go on, warning that the border police would question him again. To avoid further contact with the police, he got off the train, spent the night in a hotel, and in the morning managed to get across the border into Austria.

Once in Austria he stayed overnight in a hotel and moved the next day to Salzburg, where he got another train. His next conveyance was a cart, covered with canvas, which took him to Issenberg near Vienna. A Jew gave him directions and again he was able to walk across a border, this time into Germany. In Breslau he telegraphed home for the money he had left behind. Here he met a Jewish actor on his way from Russia to Vienna; they hit it off, and enjoyed Breslau together for two weeks. It was in Breslau that, on the recommendation of someone he met, he bought a second-class ticket to America. The stranger told him that steerage was no good. The ticket cost about $80 or $90, which included a promise of good food.

Young Mr. Amsel (at least in recollection) was not homesick; after all he had already been away from his family for two years in Grozócz. He went to Hamburg, where he waited for two weeks for a ship. While there he bought a three-quarter tailor-made coat and completed the outfit with spats, gloves, and a cane. Finally the Grosser Kurfuerst of the North German Lloyd Line sailed, with Maurice Amsel on board, seasick. The trip took about seventeen days and the ship arrived in New York on February 5, 1914.

Maurice was eagerly looking forward to seeing his brother, Charlie, who had come to America ten years earlier. Maurice left his second-class cabin and was down on the pier waiting to see his brother. Charlie, however, was looking for him among the steerage passengers. They missed each other and Maurice finally made contact with a representative of a Jewish emigrant aid society. He called someone he knew in Simpson, Pennsylvania, and was put on a train with the hope that he would eventually connect with Charlie. The brothers eventually met in Scranton, where Charlie was working in a grocery store which served miners, frequently on credit. But Maurice decided that Scranton did not look as nice as Kassa back home and he went on to short-term jobs in Simpson, Wilkes-Barre, and other places. He spoke Hungarian, Slovak, and Yiddish but little or no English. He made friends, "some Jewish, some Gentile."

Maurice had to work on Saturdays in violation of the Sabbath requirements and less and less often did he put on his phylacteries. In Bethlehem he found work running a battery-powered cart that moved heavy parts around a factory of three thousand workers who made hardware and later guns for the British in the First World War. Later he opened a clothing and dry goods store in Simpson, where he met a "greenhorn girl" who was visiting from New York. She was a milliner, making good money at piece work. They were married in 1924 and their store managed to survive the Depression of the 1930s and times when the miners were on strike.

Those relatives of Maurice Amsel who were not killed in the Holocaust today live in various parts of the United States, Australia, Canada, Czechoslovakia, and Israel.

In Hungary

★

CHAPTER 2

A Very Short History of Hungary

In the center of Europe the Carpathian Mountains rise gently to a modest height and form a half circle that embraces a great fertile plain. The land and the hills have long known farming, invasion, and fierce contention among peoples of different languages, ideas, and interests.[1]

Here the province of Pannonia guarded the northern rim of the Roman Empire until its legions were pushed out in the fourth century by Germanic and Slavic tribes. At the very end of the ninth century, the Magyars swept in from the Ural Mountains to the east and conquered the land.[2] (Magyar is pronounced as though the "gy" were the "du" sound in *during*.) They were not Germanic or Slavic or Latin. They spoke Finno-Ugric of the Uralic family of languages, related only to Finnish and Estonian. In 1001 their hereditary prince was crowned the first Catholic king of Hungary and was later canonized as St. Stephen. The crown of St. Stephen has since taken on almost mystical force as a symbol of the Hungarian nation.

The kingdom reached its greatest glory in the late 1400s; a period of instability followed. The Ottoman Turks, exploiting this weakness, invaded and in 1526 defeated the Hungarians and held much of the country for almost two hundred years. In their time of need the Hungarian nobles turned to the House of Hapsburg, the rulers of Austria. By electing the Austrian monarch as king of Hungary, the Magyars got help in expelling the Turkish armies. They also got Austrian rule.

At the end of the war against the Turks in the late 1600s, the land and the economy were devastated and the territory depopulated. The number of non-Magyar people soon began to increase, in part through immigration, in part by natural reproduction. But the influx of other ethnic groups was deliberately encouraged by the Austrian rulers and some wealthy Hungarian landowners intent on redeveloping the country. This was especially true of Germans and Serbs, but Slovaks, Rumanians, Czechs, and Jews also increased in number. The Hapsburgs had another motive in subsidizing the settlement of large numbers of Germans and others: they wanted to dilute the influence of the Magyars.

This strong brew of nationalities turned out to be important to the history of Hungary and to its Jews. The Magyars were now a minority, culturally and politically. Their language fell into disuse. The Hapsburgs were determined to make German the language of Hungary and it was in fact used for a century in commerce, government, the press, and the universities.

After the Turks left, the Magyars became restive under Austrian control. By the middle of the nineteenth century, Hungary was caught up in the surge of nationalism that propelled many European countries into the revolutions of 1848. Lajos Kossuth led a Magyar war for political independence from Austria and for cultural autonomy. The opening paragraph of the Hungarians' declaration of independence will sound more than a little familiar to Americans, for it resounds with such phrases as the "inalienable natural rights of Hungary"; the Hapsburg crown has "forfeited its right to the throne"; and "we feel ourselves bound in duty to make known the motives and reasons which have impelled us to this decision."

Ultimately the Austrians called in the Russians and quashed the uprising. Hungary returned to its position as junior partner in the Austro-Hungarian empire, which was ruled from 1848 to 1916 by Franz Joseph. Some Kossuth supporters—the '48ers—fled to the United States, a number of Jews among them. They welcomed Kossuth when he made a tour here in the early 1850s; he received much sympathy from America but no concrete help.

The Hungarians saw their chance when Austria was defeated in a war with Prussia in 1866 when Bismarck was moving to create a unified Germany without Austria. Within a year the Magyar nobles forced the weakened Austrian court in Vienna to accept an agreement, known as the Compromise or *Ausgleich*. A Dual Monarchy was established, in which the two countries shared the same king, Franz Joseph, and had a common foreign policy, military forces, and finances.

As a result of the Compromise the Kingdom of Hungary achieved independence in its internal affairs and proceeded with the cultural renaissance that had been gestating for decades. Magyar was made the official language and a process of Magyarization was initiated, using both carrots and sticks to achieve domination over a country of many ethnic groups.

In the half-century between the Compromise agreement with Austria in

1867 and the outbreak of the First World War in 1914, Hungary struggled with a conglomeration of problems. These grew out of its backward economy, its semifeudal social structure, and the tensions between the ruling Magyars and the restless nationalities under their control. The Jews found themselves deeply involved in these issues. Over time, stretching to the 1940s, the Jews were occasionally beneficiaries but more often victims of the social and economic strains within Hungarian society. Before we place the Jews in the picture, however, it is important to know more about the problems that gnawed at nineteenth-century Hungary.

For centuries Hungary had been an agrarian society, increasingly made up of large landowners and a depressed peasantry still mired in vestiges of medieval serfdom. Invasions and wars, both Turkish and Napoleonic, had blocked the growth of industry and commerce. Agriculture was primitive in its technology and its organization. The Hapsburgs, sitting at the imperial center in Vienna, wanted a subservient Hungary to be the granary for the empire, while Austria and Bohemia would develop the industrial sector.[3]

A measure of the quasi-feudal state of social and economic relations is the fact that until the middle of the 1800s, the peasants paid taxes to the state (which the landowning nobility did not), performed military service on call, and gave labor and fees to the local nobles. The Revolution of 1848 and the laws adopted in 1867 formally abolished serfdom, but did not greatly improve the living and working conditions of the peasantry. They continued to constitute a large rural proletariat living in poverty. The political life of the country was in the hands of a tightly knit, largely Catholic aristocracy, often acting in league with the Hapsburg court and just as often at odds with the local gentry and smaller landowners, many of whom were Calvinist Protestants.

Meanwhile the Slovaks, Croats, Rumanians, Ruthenians, and other minorities were responding to the same calls for national and cultural autonomy that had inspired Kossuth and his people in their fight against Austrian hegemony. What is more, these non-Magyars were concentrated in the peasantry so that the "nationalities problem" was intertwined with the conflict between social and economic classes.

Toward the end of the nineteenth century Hungary adopted a number of measures to modernize its economy. Educational reforms were instituted and literacy rose rapidly. The infrastructure of the economy was strengthened by railroad construction and flood control projects and earnest efforts were being made to develop industry. However, changes in laws regulating land tenure led on the one hand to the division of family farms into uneconomic "dwarf holdings" and to large debts for equipment. On the other hand, the new laws encouraged the consolidation of huge commercial farming enterprises. These changes aroused a new level of aspiration and people began moving about within the country, especially to the cities, to improve their situation. They also began thinking about going to America to earn enough to return and buy a farm or a shop or retire.[4]

Despite these changes, Hungary on the eve of the First World War was torn by problems that stemmed from an outmoded, essentially feudal social system strained by interethnic and economic tensions. "Its policies," Randolph Braham wrote, "reflected the interests of a landed aristocracy. . . . Unable and unwilling to solve the burning social issues and reluctant to come to grips with the urgent problem of the nationalities, the Dual Monarchy increasingly became an anachronism in the age of liberalism and nationalism."[5]

Even as an anachronism the Dual Monarchy survived through the First World War. When the war broke out in 1914, the Kingdom of Hungary occupied an area equivalent in size to the states of Indiana, Ohio, and Pennsylvania and had a population of twenty million. (See Map 1.) Approximately 60 percent of its people were Catholic, primarily followers of the Roman or Latin rite, but there were also some Greek Catholics. Almost 25 percent of the population was Protestant, mostly Calvinists who belonged to the Reformed Church of Hungary. Some 10 percent belonged to various Eastern Orthodox churches. About 5 percent were Jews.[6]

Hungary fought on the side of Germany in the First World War and emerged a serious loser. (See Map 1.) The Treaty of Trianon in 1920 stripped Hungary of three-quarters of its territory and two-thirds of its population, reducing it to its present size, approximately that of Indiana. At the end of the war Hungary had on its borders, in addition to Austria and Rumania, the new states of Czechoslovakia and Yugoslavia.

The outcome of the war roughly cut in half the Jewish population of Hungary, reducing the number from over 900,000 in 1910 to approximately 475,000 in 1920. After the war there were about 230,000 Jews in Czechoslovakia and 185,000 in Rumania. Some of the immigrants discussed in this book left towns and cities that were in Hungary before World War I but are now in one of the adjacent countries.

In the turmoil at the end of the war in 1919, leftists took power and

Map 1. Hungary before and after World War I (Map by Richard B. Gelpke)

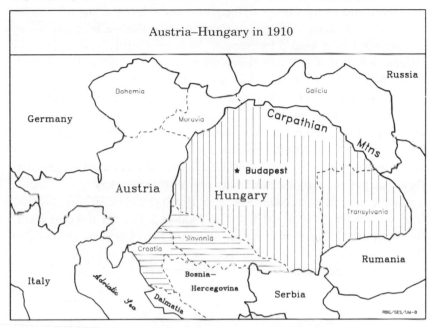

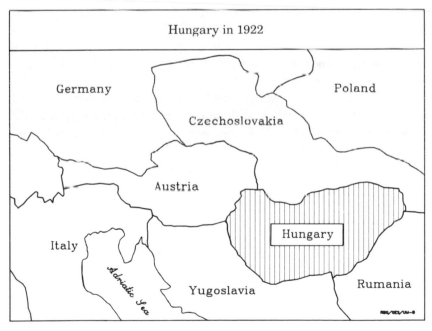

for five months the country had a Communist government. The leader, Béla Kún, and thirty-one of the forty-nine commissars in the revolutionary group were Jews. This government was overthrown by a right-wing counter-revolution headed by Admiral Nicholas Horthy, and a period of violence followed. The White Terror, as it was known, fostered a resurgent anti-Semitism. Jews were blamed for the excesses of the Communists just as they had earlier been held responsible for the dislocations of capitalism. Some 1,800 Jews were killed and 5,000 wounded.[7] Hungary was one of the first countries to adopt anti-Semitism as a national policy in the period between the two world wars. For example, a limit—a *numerus clausus*—was placed on the number of Jews permitted to enter the universities. Jews left the country in the early 1920s, though not in large numbers.

Hitler promised the regime of Admiral Horthy restoration of some of the lands Hungary had lost in the Treaty of Trianon at the end of World War I. As a result the Hungarian government joined Nazi Germany and Italy in the Second World War and did in fact receive back part of its lost territory. The German army did not occupy Hungary until almost the end of the war, when Horthy seemed to be vacillating between the Allies and the Axis powers.

In less than a year the Nazis—with the eager cooperation of Hungarian fascists—brought about the annihilation of half of Hungary's 450,000 Jews.[8] Despite the rapid ascendancy and assimilation of Jews in Hungarian society in the nineteenth century (or was it partly because of it?), the Jews shared the fate of the rest of European Jewry. Herzl was far-sighted when he wrote in 1903: "The hand of fate shall also seize Hungarian Jewry. And the later this occurs, and the stronger this Jewry becomes, the more cruel and hard shall be the blow, which shall be delivered with greater savagery."[9] Some of the survivors of the Holocaust were able to reach Israel, the United States, and other countries.

At the end of World War II Russian troops occupied Hungary, which had to give up the land that had been received from Hitler. Within four years a Communist government again held power in Hungary. An attempt by Hungarians to oust the Communists in 1956 was thwarted by additional Russian forces that poured into the country. There was again an exodus of Jews and others. Today the Republic of Hungary stands as a nation of ten million people living within the boundaries that were set at Trianon after the First World War.

★

CHAPTER 3

Jews and Magyars

Strands of Jewish history are woven into the story of Hungary, beginning with the presence of Jews in the Roman province of Pannonia.[1] In the eleventh century Jews from Germany, Bohemia, and Moravia settled in Hungary and were protected by the king from Crusaders trying to attack them. Their descendants came to occupy important economic roles. In the Middle Ages, when the country was called "The Land of Hagar" by the Jews,[2] Jewish immigration was resisted by the nobility and the church.[3] Jews were expelled from the country several times and there were collective burnings of Jews at the stake. A few, forced out by the Inquisition, arrived from Spain after 1492 and from the Balkans.

Jews enjoyed a favorable position under the Turkish occupation and they helped defend the Ottoman forces in Buda, for which they were fined by the Austrian victors. However, few remained until the seventeenth century, which saw the beginnings of modern Jewry in Hungary. Three successive waves of Jewish immigrants entered the country. Before we continue with this development, a fallacious interpretation of the early history needs to be confronted.

Toward the end of the nineteenth century a number of Jewish political leaders and intellectuals, eager to enhance their chances for genuine emancipation, engaged in a recasting of their history. They sought to prove that Jewish settlement in Hungary went back to the earliest days of the Magyar tribes. They insisted that Jews had been an integral part of the Hungarian nation for a thousand years. The assertions are unfounded.[4]

A similar piece of mythical history, with the same underlying motivation, concerns the Khazars, an ancient Turkic people who appeared in Europe in the second century. By the ninth century they had built a strong empire stretching as far west as Kiev. The king, some of the nobility, and part of the general population converted to Judaism. In the late nineteenth century the chief rabbi of the Neolog congregation in Budapest asserted that the origins of Hungarian Jews went back to the Kabar tribe of the Khazars. He wrote that the Jewish Kabars joined the Magyars in their conquest of Hungary and later became the foremost tribe among the Magyars. This view, which served the Hungarian government's Magyarization policy, was also taken up by non-Jewish historians.[5] The Khazar theory of the beginnings of Hungarian Jewry is not supported by serious scholars.

To return to the factual account of the Jews' settlement in Hungary, it is important to understand the characteristics of the three waves of immigration roughly between 1650 and 1850.[6]

1. Austrian and German Jews, mostly artisans and merchants of modest means, entered the western counties of Hungary between 1650 and 1700, when the census showed four thousand Jews in the country. The movement from Austria was precipitated when the king's advisors persuaded him that the Jews were in league with his Turkish and Swedish enemies and that he should therefore expel them from his realm.

2. Fifty years later a larger influx of Jews from Bohemia and Moravia, northwest of Hungary, was triggered when the authorities there decided to limit or if possible decrease the size of their Jewish population. To accomplish this they decreed that only one male in each Jewish family would be allowed to marry. Young Moravian Jews, usually the wealthiest, crossed the border into Hungary in considerable numbers seeking wives and homes. Incidentally this generated in the border villages a lively business in wedding arrangements, complete with cooks, musicians, and jesters. By 1735 the Jewish population of Hungary amounted to only eleven thousand, most of them German-speaking people who had settled in the northwest or "Oberland."

3. Within another fifty years the largest migration of Jews got under way from the Galician province of Poland soon after it came under Hapsburg rule. The Galician Jews were living in dire poverty, practically their only permitted occupation being the distilling of spirits. Thus economic need drove large numbers of them across the Carpathian Mountains into the northeastern section of Hungary, known to the Jews as the "Unterland." Here they engaged principally in innkeeping, distilling, rural trade and peddling, and to a large extent manual labor. The Galician phase of immigration reached its peak in the 1830s and 1840s.

There were 185,000 Jews in Hungary in 1825. In the next seventy-five years the increase was rapid, culminating in a peak population of 910,000 in 1910.[7] A small number of Sephardic Jews had trickled into Hungary from

Turkey and the Balkans, but they did not retain a distinct identity within Hungarian Jewry.

Far more important than the dates and the numbers were the sharp differences among the three groups of Jews who migrated into Hungary. It is vital to understand what the Jews brought into Hungary from Austria, Moravia, and Polish Galicia; some of these differences left their imprint on emigration to America. It is debatable to what extent the three streams merged, but it is clear that during the period in which we are interested they inhabited, to a substantial extent, different cultural worlds, despite the fact that they shared a common Jewish heritage.

The Austrian-German immigrants reflected the baroque spirit of the seventeenth and eighteenth centuries. "In the Jewish version this spirit meant the closed system of rabbinism aiming at absolute authority . . . [and] strict discipline along the narrow path of the law." These devout German-speaking merchants and craftsmen brought their rabbis with them and pursued a "rigorous conservatism" in religious matters.

The Moravians were utterly different. They were well versed in the culture of Western Europe. Conversely they were the least traditional in their adherence to Judaism, openly asserting that many of the old religious strictures were no longer valid. They were more affluent than the Austrian Jews and were oriented toward the emerging system of capitalism. By experience and interest they were well positioned to participate actively in the economic development of Hungary. They were "the pioneers of enlightenment, citizenship, and religious reform" among the Jews of Hungary.

At another extreme were the destitute Orthodox Jews pouring in from the ghettos of Galicia. These people spoke Yiddish, that modern, distinctively Jewish version of medieval German liberally salted with ancient Hebrew words. In addition, since they came from the dense Jewish settlements of Galicia they "preserved to the end their national customs and brought into being their own particular folklore. This separation also contributed to the fact that this part of Hungarian Jewry remained almost untouched by the temptation of the era of assimilation." Part of this Orthodox population consisted of the adherents of Hasidism, a religious movement that had emerged in the eighteenth century.

The persistence of traditional Jewish ways among the Galician immigrants is the dominant note in historical writing, but a rather different view of what happened appears in an account of the Grosz family, which "had arrived in Hungary sometime early in the nineteenth century, fleeing the Cossack knout and sword. Abandoning some *shtetl* surrounded by sunflowers periodically fertilized by Jewish blood, they led their wagons into Hungary leaving *Yiddishkeit* strewn along the trail behind them. Caftans and fur-trimmed hats gave way to jackets and caps; the plaintive songs of the Diaspora faded in the din of Gypsy violins and the crashing boots of the csardas."[8]

As the three types of Jewish immigrants arrived in Hungary in succeeding waves, they moved inland from the border areas, forming Jewish communities throughout Hungary. In the early stages they lived mostly in the areas inhabited not by Magyars but by Slovaks, Ruthenians, Rumanians, and other groups. (See Map 2.) In time more of the Jews settled in the Magyar areas, with a continuing concentration in the central and northeastern parts of the country.[9] It is also of interest that the Jewish population in 1910 was half that of the Slovak population and half of the German population. There were 1,946,357 Slovaks, 1,999,060 Germans, and 9,944,627 persons who identified themselves as Magyars.

The northeast section of the country was known as "Upper Hungary" or Felvidék. Today part of that area is the Slovak section of Czechoslovakia. In the period before World War I, the Jews in western Slovakia were of Moravian stock. Those in east Slovakia were originally from Galicia and were called, in a rather derisive way, "Finaks." This stemmed from the Yiddish question "Fin wo sint sie?" ("From where are you?" To which the answer might be "Fin Stropkov.") In the western part of Hungary, known as Burgenland, the influence of the German language and of ties to Vienna were strong among the Jews.[10]

Some Jews went to live on the large estates of the landed aristocracy, who gave them protection in return for fees and services. Frequently this arrangement included the franchise to operate the local tavern and inn. Generally this was not a lucrative occupation and often the innkeeper had to supplement his income with farming. The more skilled and educated Jews became estate managers and overseers. Many Jews, encountering hostility in the towns, especially from German merchants, made their homes in the smaller villages. Gradually many gravitated toward the expanding cities, especially Budapest.

With this social map of the Jews in mind, we turn now to their struggle to secure civil rights and social toleration. There has always been an ironic twist to the legal definition of "Jewish rights." Wherever civil or ecclesiastical authorities have defined what Jews are permitted to do, they have by the same act prescribed what Jews must not do, where they cannot live, or what kinds of work they must not perform. We have already encountered an example of this in the decree in Moravia which established the "right" of only one male in each Jewish family to marry, thereby taking the right of marriage away from the other men in the family and from the women they might have married.

In some parts of Hungary well into the nineteenth century Jews faced a number of restrictions. The guilds made it impossible for Jewish artisans to join their ranks. Jews, along with many others, were prohibited from acquiring real estate. The Royal Free Towns, largely controlled by German burghers, did not permit residence by Jews. In the Kaczér novel one finds Jews from the surrounding villages going into the town on market days to sell their wares and rushing to be outside of the gate before sundown when their right to be in the town expired. Some of the Jews' rights and restrictions were subject, in the best feudal tradition, to the discretion of the local estate owner.

A liberalization of the laws was set in motion by Emperor Joseph II, who ruled from 1780 to 1790. An enlightened monarch and a reformer, his goal was "to assimilate the Jews into the population, or at least to 'reform' their 'negative' characteristics and transform them into what were then considered 'useful citizens.' "[11] Joseph II repealed the ban on living in cities, and while this was annulled in practice by the assertion of feudal rights, in time the opening of the cities resulted in a major shift in Jewish population to Budapest and other large centers. He instituted general, secular education for Jews including the study of technical trades, a move that stirred controversy between those Jews who sought changes in the traditonal ways— mostly the people from Moravia and Bohemia—and those who wanted to preserve the Orthodox patterns of Jewish life.

But Joseph II exacted a price for his liberal reforms. One of his goals was to Germanize the population of Hungary and, in the end, he was better accepted by the Jews than the Magyars. He ordered the Jews to take German names, to cease printing books in Hebrew, to shave their beards, which they grew in accordance with religious law, and to make other changes that would render them more like other citizens. The monarch was persuaded to rescind the shaving of beards.

Joseph II also established regulations for the organization of the local governing body or kehillah in each Jewish community. Leaders were henceforth to be chosen by an annual election, the process and outcome of which were to be supervised by the public authorities. The local Jewish communities were further strengthened in the mid-1800s by giving them the responsibility for calculating and collecting the Tolerance Tax, so named because it was levied on all Jews for being tolerated in the country. The more liberal laws were often violated in practice.[12]

The changes wrought by Joseph II were followed by a period in which the Jews struggled to expand their civil rights. As this extension of rights took place in the middle of the nineteenth century, "it elicited massive immigration . . . [and] opened the way for the socio-cultural assimilation of the Jews."[13]

In the context of these developments, it is interesting to see how Jews were portrayed in Hungarian literature. In the eighteenth century they were often stereotyped as moneylenders. During the struggle for Emancipation in the 1830s and 1840s, hostile depictions of Jews appeared in fiction where they were presented as criminals or as exploiters and enemies of the Hungarian people. This was in contrast to the sympathetic writings of József Eötvös, Sándor Petőfi, and others.[14]

In the early part of the nineteenth century the Jewish communities were rocked by new intellectual and social trends infiltrating from Western Europe. In response the Orthodox Jews entrenched and strengthened their position. The stage was being set for a backlash effect in Hungarian society and for conflict within the Jewish communities. These were not long in coming.

A fundamental change in the status of the Jews had been under discussion in parliament and in the press. In the political debate that continued into the second half of the century, three principal approaches were taken.[15]

One position, articulated by József Eötvös, called for unconditional political rights for the Jews, in accordance with the liberals' belief in the basic "natural rights" of all people.[16] Eötvös, not unlike Joseph II in the 1780s, believed that, given freedom, the Jews would ultimately and voluntarily assimilate into Christian society.

Another view was that civic equality was not enough; the Jews had to be formally integrated, socially and culturally, into a unified Hungarian people. This, in the opinion of Lajos Kossuth, the leader of the nationalist revolution of 1848, required the Jews to accede to religious reforms as the ticket of admission to integration. Kossuth also wanted Judaism to be defined solely as a religion, with no implications of nationhood attached to it.

The third approach was one of complete opposition to the political or social acceptance of the Jews. The foremost spokesman for this position employed a remarkable simile to express his attitude: "Széchenyi (who disliked the Jews more than was customary for an aristocrat) was particularly agitated by the massive influx of the poverty-stricken East European Jewry. He wrote in 1844: 'The English or the French can afford to liberate them because a bottle of ink will not spoil the taste of a great lake, yet it would certainly spoil a plate of Hungarian soup.'"[17] The resistance to the arrival of more Jews in the country was strong among the German merchants but it "transcended ethnic and religious boundaries."[18]

While these political positions were under discussion, developments in Hungary echoed events elsewhere in Europe, which was experiencing the revolutionary movements of 1848. Steps were taken in a number of countries to emancipate the Jews.[19] In Hungary Jews took an active part in the 1848 revolution against Austrian rule, at least partly in the hopes of achieving civil rights under a more liberal government. At first Jews who volunteered for the revolutionary militia were bodily thrown out, but the poet Petőfi and another leader, Vasvári, created their own all-Jewish National Guard.[20] Later Jews served as officers in the Hungarian revolution and some, having emigrated to America, were officers in the Civil War here. "The patriotism of many Hungarian Jews was truly amazing, not explainable solely by their attraction to liberal programs . . . When war came, some Orthodox rabbis even violated the Sabbath for the sake of fighting."[21]

In each country the expanded liberties extended to the Jews gave rise to a strong counter-reaction. In Hungary measures were taken at the time of the '48 revolution to improve the Jews' legal status, but these were met by anti-Jewish riots in several cities.[22] Ten Jews were killed and about forty wounded, for example, in pogroms in Pressburg. However—and this is important in terms of Jewish attitudes toward the Magyars—the anti-Jewish pogroms were unanimously condemned by the new Liberal establishment and the Jews were physically defended by government troops.[23]

With the defeat of the Hungarian army, the victorious Austrians dispensed stern retribution to the Kossuth rebels and their allies. The Hapsburg government in Vienna imposed martial law until 1854 and made clear its intention to "subdue and modernize the feudal Magyar society."[24] One of the measures was the introduction of a modern public school system, based of course on the use of the German language. This had serious and entirely unexpected effects on the Hungarian Jews.

The imposition of secular education stirred up tensions between Jewish traditionalists, wedded to the "Winkelschule" (literally "corner school" or *heder*), and the reformers eager for their children to acquire the new ideas and knowledge of the nineteenth century. Paradoxically, Philip Adler observes, "In the end, it was the imposition of educational secularism, which the public schools demanded, that encouraged the Jews' assimilation into Magyar society, and thereby strengthened the specific element which Vienna was trying to negate." This may well have been one of the elements that led toward the quid pro quo arrangement that evolved between Magyars and Jews, which is discussed in the next chapter.

In the middle of the nineteenth century the situation of the Jews looked like this: "Excluded from most professions and from many urban areas, the Jews thrived nevertheless. They rented the taverns of the large estates; they dealt in grain and wool; they settled without permission in the cities, there to practice illegally the professions formally protected by the Christian guilds. The overwhelmingly German-speaking burghers fought this immigration tooth and nail, but nationalist-liberal public opinion and the local administrative machinery sided with the Jews. Besides, Jewish skills were badly needed."[25]

When the Compromise was arranged with the Austrians in 1867, the new, independent Hungarian national assembly granted the Jews unconditional civic emancipation. This was the first Law of Jewish Emancipation in Central Europe. The earlier legislation enacted on the eve of defeat in the revolutionary war had had no practical value. However, it made the idea of Jewish emancipation part of the legacy of the 1848–1849 period.[26] It was not until 1895 that the Jewish faith was declared a "received" religion and given equal legal standing with Christianity. However, the basis for an understanding between Jews and Magyars was established in the 1848–1867 period, when the Jews supported Magyar independence with manpower and money, and the Hungarian Liberals protected the Jews militarily and politically. In addition, Jews acquired the right to lease and even buy land for farming.

A virulent anti-Semitism emerged in Hungary in the 1870s. It erupted, as it often has, from three main fonts: economic competition; the teachings of Christian churches; and the advantages accruing to political parties and public figures. Because much of the literature stresses the generally favorable situation of Jews in Hungary, it is necessary to indicate here that there was also anti-Semitism, though it was sternly opposed by the ruling Magyar Liberals.

Anti-Semitic speeches were made in the parliament as early as 1875, but were ridiculed by the dominant political leadership. The agitation reached a high point in the blood libel trial at Tiszaeszlár in 1882—just over one hundred years ago—when Jews were accused of a ritual killing of a Christian girl before Easter.[27] While the accused Jews were ultimately acquitted and liberal Christian leaders condemned the libel, anti-Semitic disturbances continued in several towns.[28] Karoly Eötvös, a leader in Kossuth's party, defended the Jews at the Tiszaeszlár proceedings and in 1904 wrote a book, *The Great Trial*.

The anti-Semitic movement was soon crushed. "But even after this," writes Macartney, "and despite all official disapproval, many Magyars felt uneasily that the situation was dangerous which placed so many of the country's power-positions in the hands of an element which still appeared to them alien."[29] A surprisingly different and rosy view is taken by Oscar Jászi, who found less anti-Semitism in Hungary than in Austria and attributed this in part to "the sober and benevolent character of the Hungarian peasants, devoid of any religious or race fanaticism," a judgment that seems at odds with much of the evidence.[30]

The benign personal stance of Emperor Franz Joseph won for him the warm loyalty of the Hungarian Jews, who were able to balance this with steadfast, sometimes extremist devotion to the cause of Magyar nationalism which opposed the emperor. Many an immigrant to America repeated what one of them told an interviewer: "He was a wonderful, wonderful man." When he died after reigning for sixty-eight years, the Jewish immigrants in the Poale Zedeck (Workers of Justice) congregation in Pittsburgh held a special memorial service for him.

Just before 1900 anti-Semitism again assumed political form under the banner of the People's Party in its fight against liberalism and socialism. In an extensive discussion of the anti-Semitic resurgence in Hungary and especially in Budapest after 1900, John Lukács argues that this was "the result of new ideas rather than old ones. The chief attackers of the Jewish presence and influence were populist and democratic rather than reactionary and aristocratic."[31] Nathaniel Katzburg, on the other hand, writes that behind the People's Party "stood powerful elements like the Catholic Church, the pro-Hapsburg aristocracy, the wealthy landowners and the Catholic intelligentsia."[32]

Understanding the growth of anti-Semitism in nineteenth-century Hungary requires us to take a closer look at the social composition of Hungarian society and at the strains and conflicts generated by the rush to build a capitalist economy. Political power was held by a small circle of Magyar aristocrats, predominantly Catholic, whose large estates accounted for much of the productive land. Their interests were directly opposed to those of the national minorities (Slovaks, Serbs, Rumanians, etc.) and to the Hungarian peasants, while coinciding at points with the ruling Hapsburgs in Vienna. These aristocrats spurned any involvement in commerce or industry, preferring "the pursuits of a bygone feudal era."[33]

On the next level were thousands of petty nobles or landed gentry, mostly Protestants, who owned smaller and less productive tracts of land. In common with the aristocrats, the gentry employed and often exploited the serfs and peasants, but frequently were themselves hard pressed financially. In fact, while agricultural progress was benefiting the big estates, a part of the gentry and thousands of small farmers were being ruined.[34] Politically the gentry, sharing power with (but often against) the aristocracy, had a tradition of liberalism and was responsible for legislation in the 1890s which went far toward establishing Jewish rights.[35]

At the bottom of the social pile the bulk of the population consisted of the peasants—Magyar and Slovak, Croat, Ruthenian, and Rumanian. The emancipation of the serfs, beginning in 1852 and more thoroughly in 1867, had left large numbers of them landless, earning their livelihood as seasonal wage laborers or permanent farm servants.[36]

It scarcely needs to be pointed out that there was no entrepreneurial middle class in this social structure. This was the situation when two developments converged. One was a fierce determination by the Magyar leadership, after its liberation from Austrian domination, to make Hungary a great power and an economic success. The other was the entry on the scene of a Jewish population, some of whom were far more oriented by experience toward commerce and industry than they were to the land and farming. The dynamics of the convergence of these two developments are caught in these words: "It was as if the Compromise Agreement had unleashed all the hidden energies of Hungarian society: there came into being an unwritten alliance between the governing liberal nobility and the new urban bourgeoisie . . . [which] was a curious construct, made up of upwardly mobile farmers, déclassé landowners, former German artisans and tradesmen, immigrant Czech skilled workers, and, most importantly, Jews."[37]

What the aristocrats were unwilling to engage in personally—the capitalist development of the nation—Jews were fully prepared to take on. In any case, the processes that unfolded toward the end of the nineteenth century produced winners and losers and, inevitably, social and political antagonisms. It is in this context that the position of the Jews in Hungary needs to be understood.

Toward the end of the century much of Europe was seized by an outbreak of anti-Semitic activity.[38] From West to East, from the Dreyfus trial in France to the pogroms in Russia following the assassination of the tsar, the liberalism of the first half of the century was crumbling. While the numbers of Jews in Russia and Poland and the ferocity of violence against them were far greater than in Hungary, antagonism toward them was on the rise in the Magyar kingdom, where the Jews were playing a major part in the economic and intellectual life of the country.[39]

In fact it was, to a considerable extent, the conspicuous success of the Jewish bourgeoisie which figured so large in Hungarian anti-Semitism. One contributing factor was the takeover by Jews of the bankrupt estates of the gentry, some of whom were forced to take bureaucratic jobs as government officials; these displaced petty nobles viewed the Jews with hatred. Another reason was the antipathy to capitalism on the part of some of the higher nobility, though as we shall soon see, the liberal wing of the aristocracy was poised to make a political arrangement with the Jews.

And then there were the daily frictions between Jews, peasants, and Christian merchants. The burghers "had a superstitious horror of the race that had such mysterious prayers and such low prices."[40] Although many of the Jews had taken on Magyar ways, they had not given up their Jewish identity. Newcomers from Galicia, with their foreign dress and language, accentuated the resentments of some segments of Hungarian society.[41]

Toward the end of the nineteenth century, Jews in Hungary were the target of anti-Semitic feelings and actions. Not the least important of the causes of this can be found in the tensions surrounding the "nationalities question." It was essentially this problem that gave impetus to the accommodation that the ruling Magyars and the Jews arranged with each other. In that quid pro quo arrangement, something of value to the Magyars was traded for something desired by the Jews. For those with a taste for Latin, the next chapter might be called "Quid Hungaricum Pro Quo Judaico."

★

C H A P T E R   4

The Quid pro Quo Arrangement

"Before I could speak one language, I cried in three." This is how Edward Steiner, who grew up as a Jew in Hungary, begins a book about his childhood.[1]

William Scarlett, a U.S. immigration inspector working the docks of New York City in the early 1900s, had the unenviable task of finding out and recording the precise ethnic background of the Hungarian immigrants passing in front of him. In the column marked "nationality" it was easy; he simply wrote "Hungary." But then he had to place a checkmark in another column labeled "race or people," that is, "the stock from which they sprang and the language they spoke."

So on April 27, 1905, when the SS *Barbarossa* docked, Mr. Scarlett was checking his list, on which were to be found these choices for the "race" of the Hungarians:

Slovak
Croatian
Magyar
German
Hebrew
Ruthenian
Rumanian
Servian
Slavonian

It was this "nationalities question"—so keenly experienced at first hand by Steiner and Scarlett—that lay at the root of the quid pro quo arrangement between the Magyars and the Jews.[2] The Magyar side of the understanding stemmed from the need for an ally in their beleaguered situation in a country which was a patchwork quilt of hostile ethnic populations. On the Jewish side it bespoke their quest for security and acceptance.

The areas in which the ethnic groups were concentrated are shown in Map 2, adapted from Robert Kann's *The Multinational Empire*. Kann treated an area as Slovak, for example, if more than half its inhabitants were Slovak. This, perhaps unavoidably, fails to convey an important fact: most areas actually had two or more ethnic groups living side by side. This can be seen on the map in the region in the east where Hermannstadt is located. Here Magyars, Szekels, Germans, and undoubtedly Rumanians (not to mention Jews, who are not shown on the map) were living cheek by jowl. Brief descriptions of the nationality groups before 1919, drawn mostly from Kann, are given below.

MAGYARS. (8.7 million of the 19.2 million inhabitants of Hungary in 1900) This was the politically dominant group. Originally nomads from the border between Europe and Asia, they spoke a Finno-Ugric language which is utterly different from the other nationalities in Hungary. They were concentrated in the great plain in the central and eastern parts of the country and constituted about half the population of the kingdom.

RUMANIANS. (2.8 million) Historically under the control of the Romans and later the Ottoman Turks, Rumanians speak a Romance language and consider themselves Latin. They lived in Transylvania, the eastern region of Hungary, most of which today is in Rumania.

GERMANS. (2.1 million) Germans were scattered about Hungary, especially in the cities and towns where many were merchants. As members of the emerging middle class they were often in competition with the Jews in the nineteenth century.

SLOVAKS. (2.0 million) A Slavic people who lived in the north of Hungary in the western part of the Carpathian Mountains. They are close in language to the Czechs and with them today make up Czechoslovakia. Their cultural autonomy was harshly repressed by the ruling Magyars.

CROATS. (1.7 million) They inhabited the southeastern part of pre-Trianon Hungary, now part of Yugoslavia. Croatia-Slavonia, which the Croats shared with the Serbs and the Slovenes, had its own parliament and, as a result of fierce resistance to the Magyars, enjoyed considerable autonomy within the Kingdom of Hungary. They were Roman Catholics, used the Roman alphabet, and oriented themselves toward Western Europe.

SERBS. (1.1 million) They were found in the most southern parts of the country, now in Yugoslavia. While they shared the same language with the Croats, the Serbs used the Cyrillic alphabet, belonged to the Greek Ortho-

Map 2. Hungary's Multiethnic Population (Map by Richard B. Gelpke, adapted from Robert Kahn, *The Multinational Empire* [1977])

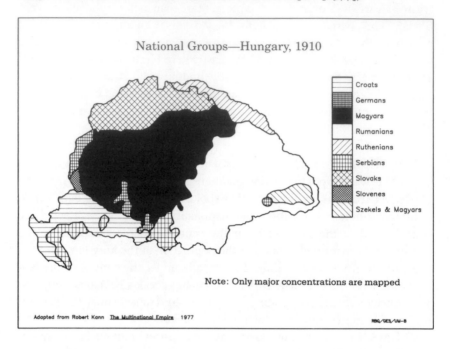

National Groups—Hungary, 1910

Croats
Germans
Magyars
Rumanians
Ruthenians
Serbians
Slovaks
Slovenes
Szekels & Magyars

Note: Only major concentrations are mapped

Adapted from Robert Kann The Multinational Empire 1977

RBG/GES/UW-B

dox Church, and were more oriented toward the Balkans and Turkey than the Croats.

JEWS. Some 900,000 Jews lived in various parts of Hungary, but were most heavily concentrated in the northeastern and central areas, especially in Budapest. Their geographic distribution was not included in Kann's map. (See Map 3.)

SZEKELS. (About half a million) The Szekels claimed descent from Attila the Hun and viewed themselves as "more Magyar than the Magyars." They lived, mixed with Rumanians and Magyars, in the easternmost part of the country.

RUTHENIANS. (400,000) Also known as Rusyns, Carpato-Ukrainians, and "Little Russians," these people were mountain dwellers and among the poorest and most neglected of the minorities. They inhabited the eastern region of the Carpathian Mountains in the north of the country. Their language is closely related to Ukrainian.

SLOVENES. (Their number was not included in the Kann data.) They lived as neighbors of Austria in the western part of the Hungarian kingdom and had fought for many centuries against the southward thrust of the Germans.

This was the mixture of peoples who in the middle of the nineteenth century were seized with nationalistic fervor and revolutionary movements. This was bound to have a profound effect on the country in two ways. The Magyars were eager to get out from under Austrian rule, and the many ethnic groups within Hungary—encouraged by the Austrians, both to revive the economy and to check the influence of the Magyars—were pressing for their own cultural and political autonomy. The 1867 agreement between the Austrians and the Magyars left the tensions among the nationality groups unresolved, except that it was clear that the Magyars were in charge.

What must be emphasized is that most of the ethnic minorities were also economically and socially the most depressed segments of Hungarian society.[3] From the Magyars' perspective, they felt pressed between Germans and the Panslavic movement, which was attracting the Slovaks and other Slavs within Hungary. What is more, the Magyars were in a politically precarious situation: their number hovered just short of 50 percent of the population.[4]

Fearful of a splintering of their nation, the Magyars were intent on control and stability, not accommodation or change in their relations with the nationalities who lived among them. Consequently they embarked on a process of intense Magyarization and forced assimilation of the nationalities. So, for instance, senior positions in government and public administration went solely to Magyars. Laws concerning education, the press, and the renaming of places and people, were passed.[5] And harsh measures were taken to suppress nationalistic challenges to the Magyar hegemony. It was also charged that the Magyars deliberately drained off (or bought off) the ablest potential leaders of the ethnic minorities.[6]

(In the early stages of writing this book it might have been possible to think that the political and ethnic antagonisms of pre-Trianon Hungary were a thing of the past. However, in the course of the work, several people who helped in the research expressed just such feelings. And they were critical of what they perceived as either too pro-Magyar or anti-Magyar a bias in the manuscript. At this writing the pent-up feelings of national and ethnic identity have exploded in Eastern and Central Europe from the Baltics to the Balkans. The Hungarian government, for instance, is complaining about the treatment of the Hungarian minority living in Rumania.)

The challenge to the Hungarian Jews was to stay afloat in this roiling sea of Magyars, Slovaks, Croats, Serbs, and others. The question has even been raised as to whether there was such an entity as "Hungarian Jewry" or whether it would be more meaningful to speak of the Jews of Slovakia, the Jews of Transylvania, the Jews of Budapest, etc.[7] For the purposes of this book, we take the boundaries of the Kingdom of Hungary as they stood before World War I and consider the Jews within these boundaries as Hungarian Jews. Apparently that is how most of them saw themselves at the time.

Out of mutual need an informal arrangement was gradually worked out between Magyars and Jews. This was not a formal, negotiated "contract" but seems rather to have evolved over time as a tacit understanding. Even before the war of 1848, the Jews had voluntarily begun in earnest their own Magyarization through which they hoped to earn emancipation. And the Magyars were making approaches to the Jews. For example, in 1840 József Eötvös commissioned a Jew to write "an encomium advocating Jewish magyarization and then to translate the Torah into Magyar."[8] The translation was made, but the translator later converted to Lutheranism, which was a grievous blow to some of the Jews. The Orthodox Jews in particular raised objections to some of these developments, but the link between emancipation and assimilation "became embedded in the minds of Hungarian Jews."[9]

In the closing decades of the nineteenth century the dimensions of the understanding between Jews and Magyars became clear: in return for political loyalty and cultural assimilation, the Jews would receive civil rights, protection against anti-Semitic violence, and unprecedented opportunities in the economic development of the country.

The quid pro quo worked, in most respects. The Magyars got what they wanted. For one thing, by counting Jews as Magyars in the census, they achieved a majority in the population. By 1900 speakers of the Magyar language comprised 51 percent of the population.[10] This was not the only time that Jews were employed in this way. In western Poland at about the same time, the Prussians, also a ruling minority, made the German-speaking minority look larger on occasion by counting the Yiddish-speaking Jews as Germans.[11]

The Jews performed certain valuable functions for the Magyar leaders "by serving as living examples of the possibility of rapid integration and by functioning as intermediaries conveying Magyarism to the non-Hungarian nationalities."[12] As peddlers, tradesmen, and shopkeepers Jews spread the Magyar language, which neither the rulers in distant Budapest nor the "Hungarian peasant chained to the soil" could achieve. The Magyars got a loyal and patriotic partner in Hungarian Jewry. In the period after the crushed Revolution of 1848, when the Austrians clamped a repressive control on the Hungarians, "patriotism became the most cherished trait of true Hungarians . . . and the Jews of Hungary felt that their greatest duty toward their homeland was to be demonstratively patriotic, which remained a major characteristic of Hungarian Jews down to the tragic days of World War II."[13]

However, the Jews' search for security via Magyarization and assimilation exacerbated conflict with the ethnic minorities. The outcome was intensified hostility toward the Jews, who were perceived as henchmen of the Magyars. The resulting anti-Semitism was found useful "not only by the minorities who wished to discredit the central government and by the reactionaries, but even by the left wing."[14] A vitriolic depiction of the role of the Jews stated that they "cunningly assumed the mask of Magyar Chauvinism, in order to gain control of the finance, the trade, and the municipal government of the country."[15] With somewhat less venom, Jászi argues that "the Jewish capitalist press took the crudest jingoist attitude in the national struggles and was the chief obstacle to a reasonable compromise among the rival nations." He points to the "intolerant nationalism and chauvinism of the Jews which accepted blindly and without criticism the most extreme ideology of the foreign nation by which they were assimilated."[16]

Take the case of the Slovaks and the Jews, whose relations were often embittered. One can sense the feelings of a fervent Slovak partisan who wrote that the Jews were "the exponents of the Magyars, an auxiliary troop of the sheriffs, of the village officials, of the gendarmerie and they are feared everywhere."[17] However, there seems to have been some Jewish sympathy toward Slovak nationalism.[18]

All in all, both Magyars and Jews seemed to benefit from the political arrangement. The Jews became super-patriotic nationalists, highly successful participants in the building of capitalism in Hungary, and prominent in the flowering of the nation's cultural and intellectual life. Some Jews who spoke Hungarian improved their social status in the more remote places where Magyars, being scarce, needed skilled and literate representatives. One writer put this "phenomenal" upward movement in this way: "Jews had established and owned most of the mines and heavy industry in the country, and in the free professions their presence was not less notable . . . They figured prominently in the ranks of the scientists, writers, poets, and artists . . . Jews were an important element among university professors, on the Supreme Court, and in both houses of the parliament."[19] Another writer places this phenomenon in the context of the capitalist development of Hungary and notes that this "had been almost entirely of their [the Jews'] making . . . The Jewish recruits to the new Hungarian society had thus achieved a position far stronger than the Germans', and even one which in many fields was stronger than that of the Magyars themselves."[20]

The upward movement was most visible in the economic sphere.[21] It took until the middle of the nineteenth century for the country to begin to shake off its feudal fetters. With its fertile plain available for modern methods of agriculture; with coal, oil, and salt ready for mining; with its rich forests, the Hungarian economy was ripe for rapid expansion. Both in terms of capital and personnel, Jews helped to fill the vacuum that existed. They supplied much of the capital, especially through their connections with the Rothschilds in Austria, for railroad construction and industrial exploitation of natural resources and they provided entrepreneurial skills. The economic aspects of the quid pro quo understanding were clearly as significant as the political ones.

The granting of noble titles to Jews was an extraordinary feature of this situation. Most of the titles between 1824 and 1918 were bestowed on Hungary's "capitalist elite," who were for the most part Jewish.[22] Upwards of 350 Jewish families received titles, some of them hereditary and used to this day. However, we should put this in its proper context: titles were held by large numbers of the rural gentry in Hungary and thus did not have the same significance as noble titles in most other European countries.

The understanding between the Magyars and the Jews also opened up tremendous opportunities in the cultural field.[23] We can see this in the entry of Jews into the field of letters.[24] The Jewish peddler and storekeeper were already a part of Hungarian folklore when the Jewish poet József Kiss began writing ballads in Hungarian and then produced works depicting Jewish peasants and workers. He encouraged a generation of Jewish writers. Most of the contributors to a weekly literary journal edited by Kiss were Jews. In the period before World War I, "undoubtedly, urban Hungarian literature possessed a distinctly Jewish flavour; this manifested itself in the wide variety of themes stressing a more general outlook than the traditionally self-centred Hungarian viewpoint."[25] Consistent with this, a number of Jewish writers chose non-Jewish themes. The playwright Ferenc Molnár was one of these, though most of his characters were Jews and his prose works dealt with Jewish problems. (It should be noted that following the Second World War there was an exodus of Hungarian-Jewish writers to Israel, where Illés Kazcér—quoted in these pages—was the dean of the group.)[26]

A revealing example of the Magyar-Jewish arrangement—and also of the extent of Jewish orientation to Western European culture in general—is furnished by the Rabbinical Seminary of Budapest, which opened its doors in 1877 in the presence of members of Parliament and Jewish dignitaries from various parts of Western Europe. The seminary was funded by the government out of the proceeds of the fine levied by the Austrians against the Jews for their participation in the Revolution of 1848. Subsequently the fine had been converted by the emperor into a fund for Jewish education. The seminary was to offer both classical rabbinical studies as well as training in modern scholarship. Its graduates "were not only to teach Judaism but also to foster Hungarian patriotism among their co-religionists by disseminating the language and culture of Hungary."[27]

The rapid social mobility that the quid pro quo made possible can be seen within the lifetime of a single individual who was born Pinchas Judah Groszman in 1869 and died in 1931 as Péter Ujvári and was known as the Hungarian Sholom Aleichem.[28] The Groszman family lived in the northeastern county of Zemplén, where the father was a rabbi. Among other things, the rabbi had learned French while a student in the yeshivah and then had been able to supplement his income as a tutor to rich Jewish families.[29]

While Pinchas was a yeshivah student, he was caught secretly studying secular books and was expelled. Soon thereafter he began writing poetry in German, but then learned Hungarian and established himself as a writer in that language. At the age of twenty he changed Pinchas to Péter and moved to Szeged, where he joined the staff of a Hungarian newspaper. Because much of his childhood had been spent in Érsekújvár, his colleagues began calling him "Ujvár," which he took as his last name, simply adding the "i" to mean "from Ujvár." Soon after he married the daughter of a wealthy Jewish merchant.

Ujvári began editing periodicals and publishing novels and took an interest in the problems of the poor and issues of social reform, like many young Jews who in those years joined socialist and radical parties. His novel *The New Christian*, serialized in a Jewish newspaper, was "the tragicomic story of the conversion to Christianity of the head of a small Jewish community, so that his son may be elected to parliament."[30] The world he had left—the provincial Jewish communities—was the setting of his novels and he offered realistic pictures of Jewish life before the turn of the century in which people were either trying to preserve or destroy those communities.

When the First World War ended, a Communist government held power in Hungary for a few months. Ujvári saw this as the end of an age of privilege and injustice and he took a post as director of the literary section of a national education committee under the Communist government, though he was not by ideology or party membership a Communist. The Communists fell from power and a right-wing government unleashed the White Terror on the country. Ujvári fled from Hungary, but eventually was permitted to return. Toward the end of his career he became the editor of a Jewish political journal and supervisor of an ambitious project, the writing of a Hungarian-Jewish encyclopedia.

To sum up the quid pro quo understanding, a social and political situation without parallel among European Jews developed in Hungary in the last quarter of the nineteenth century. Within a few decades a population that numbered less than 5 percent of the nation occupied a significant portion of the top tier of the society. Hungarians have for some time been devoted and assiduous statisticians and their figures vividly tell this story of almost unprecedented economic ascendancy.

By 1900 Jews constituted: 54 percent of the owners of commercial establishments; 62 percent of all employees in commerce; 85 percent of the directors and owners of financial institutions.[31] By 1914 Jews constituted: 42 percent of the journalists; 45 percent of the lawyers; 49 percent of the physicians.[32]

In short, some of the children and grandchildren of the stolid craftsmen from Austria, the poverty-stricken peddlers of Galicia, and the middle-class Moravian Jews who had entered Hungary experienced a meteoric rise in economic and political status. This was true enough for some of the Jews, but it projects a lopsided, distorted picture, for it seriously neglects a much larger group.

There were, in effect, two Hungarian Jewries. The picture of the highly successful businessman and the assimilated professional needs to be balanced by the "other Jewry," the artisans, the farmers, the innkeepers, and the men who continued to peddle goods in rural villages. These people were by no means as affluent or as educated or as Westernized as those represented in the statistics presented above. (Chapter 6 discusses the two Jewries.)

The statistics cited above are constantly quoted in writings about Hungarian Jews with the effect and sometimes the purpose of portraying them as essentially a bourgeois community. It must be recalled that it was a small, newly emerging middle class that the Jews were entering; there were a limited number of positions to be occupied. True, the Jews held a considerable proportion of these positions, but to focus only on this group is to perpetuate a skewed image of the Jewish population as a whole.

A main source of these statistics is Alajos Kovács, whose reputation was that of an accomplished statistician and an equally accomplished anti-Semite. He was determined to demonstrate in the early 1920s that the Jews occupied a disproportionate share of the professional and commercial occupations.[33] Kovács's figures show, for instance, what proportion of all Hungarian doctors or lawyers were Jews. They do not show what proportion of all the Jews were doctors or lawyers.

The last census for pre-Trianon Hungary was 1910 and we have reanalyzed those data to arrive at the occupational profile of the Jews. (See Table 1.) This recasting of the census information shows clearly that the oft-repeated statistics obscured as much as they revealed, as Figure 1 demonstrates. In reality, less than 8 percent of the Jews were in the professions and white-collar occupations. Specifically as to doctors, lawyers, and journalists, less than 2 percent of the Jews were in these professions.

While it was true that almost three-quarters (73.4%) of the Jews were engaged in commerce and industry, more than half of that number were employees rather than employers or entrepreneurs. Only 35 percent of all the Jewish earners were self-employed in industry and commerce and some of them might well have been craftsmen or peddlers trudging through the villages carrying a backpack. This information puts in a more realistic perspective the data that have been used so often to foster the impression of a primarily urban, upper middle-class Jewish population. Indeed, almost as many Jews were engaged in agriculture (6.6 percent) as in the professions and white collar jobs (7.9 percent).

In some parts of the country, the economic profile of the Jews was even

Figure 1. Occupation of Jewish Earners in Hungary, 1910

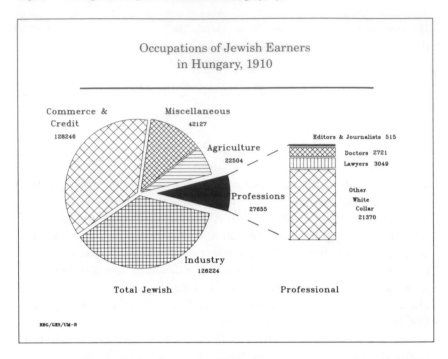

less in line with Kovács's analysis. The area of greatest Jewish concentration in Hungary spanned the northeastern section of the country. Within this region, now mostly in Czechoslovakia, was an area known as Subcarpathian Ruthenia, where about 100,000 Jews lived among six times as many Christians—Ruthenians, Slovaks, Magyars, Germans, Gypsies, Czechs, and Rumanians.[34] It was a mountainous area and the peasants scratched out a precarious living. People lived here in small, self-contained villages rather isolated from each other by the contours of the mountains.

Most of the Jews in Subcarpathian Ruthenia were also poor and were not "the commercial vanguard of Magyarization but rather the rearguard of Jewish orthodoxy."[35] Jews had been escaping into this region from Galicia since the pogroms of Chmelnitzki in 1648. Two hundred and fifty years later in 1900 the Jews here, sometimes called the "unterlander," continued to be more closely related to the shtetl world just on the other side of the Carpathians than to the city Jews of such places as Budapest, Miskolc, and Szeged.

It has been argued that the "concentration of shopkeeping, innkeeping, and small trade almost solely in Jewish hands," with Jews barred from "the agricultural and labor classes," constituted an imbalance that had ill-effects on the Jews in Hungary.[36] This view that most Jews played primarily if not exclusively a commercial or service role is widespread. Paul R. Magocsi, for example, writes that the social center of the village in Subcarpathian Ruthenia was the tavern (*korchma*) and store (*sklep*), "both likely to be owned by Jews. The Rusyn peasant turned to the Jews for credit to sustain himself physically and for alcohol to soothe himself psychologically."[37] He notes also that the peasants "whether of Rusyn, Slovak, or Magyar nationality . . . remained economically and socially immobilized and in debt to the large landholders or, more often than not, to the local Jews."[38]

A more complete picture of Jewish occupations in the Subcarpathian region does not support the notion that most of the Jews were sellers, middlemen, or lenders, though again it must be recognized that most of the middlemen were Jews. A study was conducted in this area in 1921 by the American Joint Distribution Committee immediately after the end of World War I. It was a time of difficult postwar economic readjustments and the extent of poverty may have been greater than at the turn of the century, though in general "until the late 1920's, the economy of the region remained essentially unchanged."[39] It is worth reporting the survey in some detail since it is one of the few available studies of its kind. There is an additional reason to look at this area: it was the home of many of the Jews who came to America.

The Joint Distribution Committee found that 48 percent of the 11,860 Jewish families surveyed were supported by "agricultural workers, shepherds, village laborers, unskilled workers, and wagoners." Only 21 percent were found to be shopkeepers, businessmen, and manufacturers. Another 10 percent were skilled workers. It should be pointed out that the survey accounts for only the 60 percent of Jews who were gainfully employed—the other 40 percent being "presumably beggars, paupers on public dole, religious attendants and miscellaneous others."[40]

To give him his due, Kovács would have been correct if he had pointed out that the 2,400 shopowners and businessmen in the table below were probably a very high proportion of all the shopowners and businessmen in Subcarpathia. What he never seemed to recognize was that they made up only one-fifth of the employed Jews, fewer than the number of Jewish agricultural workers and shepherds in Subcarpathia. The JDC data are presented below in full.

Professions	Families	Individuals
Agricultural workers, shepherds	2,500	12,500
Village laborers, unskilled workers	2,000	10,000
Wagoners	1,200	6,000
Skilled workers (tailors, shoemakers, carpenters, tinsmiths, etc.)	1,380	6,900
Tavern-keepers	1,180	5,900
Shopowners	1,500	7,500
Businessmen	900	1,500
Professionals (physicians, lawyers, engineers)	200	800
Butchers	100	400
Manufacturers	100	400
Teachers	800	4,000
	11,860	55,900

To return to Hungarian Jewry as a whole, before World War I slightly more than one-third of the Jewish earners were engaged in "commerce and credit." This fact was important not only in economic terms; it had tremendous significance for social relations between Jews and Gentiles. We need to put the commercial activities of Hungarian Jews in a larger context. Unlike Western Europe, the countries of Eastern Europe were still inching their way out of feudalism and toward a modern economy of mechanized agriculture and industry and of expanding markets for the exchange of goods, labor, and money. A new role was emerging in this nascent capitalism, that of the facilitator of exchanges, the trader, the middleman. Many Jews, but not a majority of them, having been blocked from tilling or owning the land, found their way into this new economic role. Zemplén County offers a useful illustration of this.

Jews in that wine-growing area were generally forbidden to buy a certain kind of grape, known as asu, since this was the nobles' prerogative. However, from the peasant's point of view "it was more advantageous to sell to whoever offered the highest price. The landed gentry sought to lower the prices, whereas the Jews always offered higher prices." The restrictive regulations protected the local nobility but were clearly not in the interests of the peasants or the Jews. In time this feudal prohibition, enacted specifically against the Jews, eroded and gave way to free trade, which was one of the factors resulting in an increase in the number of Jews in Zemplén County.[41]

Throughout Central and Eastern Europe the Jew was perceived as the ubiquitous storekeeper, trader, source of credit. The popular perception was that of a middleman, often an exploiter, locked with the peasant in a set of reciprocal roles in which each bought and sold from the other. In the local Jewish-operated taverns, the peasants ran up bills for their drinks. A moment's digression is appropriate here to describe the accounting system that was used in the taverns, as explained in the Kazcér novel, *The Siege*. The innkeeper and the peasant split a stick down the middle, each keeping one half. As each drink was served, they would put the two halves together and make a notch with a knife that nicked both halves of the stick in the same place. At the end of the week or month, they would compare the number of notches and arrive at the bill. The simple ingenuity of the system must have avoided the "down-time" of computers in today's banks and stores.

Ewa Morawska has produced a finely detailed picture of not only the economic but also the social and psychological relations between Jews and Gentiles in Eastern Europe, including Hungary. She notes that Jews were heavily involved both in trade and related commercial operations and in manufacturing and handicrafts, all of which were carried out on a small scale.[42] She explains: "Jews functioned both as buyers of peasant produce to be distributed across the region and exported outside and as sellers to the rural households of services and manufactured goods prepared by local artisans or brought from city factories. . . . Set in close physical proximity and a long historical tradition, this economic symbiosis bound the two groups in daily interactions and allowed for considerable familiarity." We must keep this description in mind when we come to see the Jewish storekeeper and peddler performing much the same role in America.

This economic relationship, which was frequently disadvantageous to the moneyless peasant, was overlaid in Hungary with ethnic hostilities toward the Magyars and their presumed agents, the Jews. Even among the Magyar peasants, the Jews' economic role was seen as exploitive, despite the fact that the Jewish storekeeper might himself be barely able to make a living. This tight minisystem of complementary roles provided some of the ingredients for tension and conflict.

Emily G. Balch notes that many Slavic peasants were "really living largely in the pre-commercial age, where there is no fixed scale of values, and where every possession has its own incommensurable worth to its owner, who has never bought or sold it, or thought of doing so."[43] While her presentation of the Jews is hardly sympathetic, she does make it plain that their experiences in Europe had prepared them for the market economy that was developing.

Commenting on the financial exploitation of Slovaks, she notes that "the local reputation of the Jews seems to vary with the credit situation. Where credit institutions have been established, lending money at 5½ or 6 percent instead of at the Jewish rate of 8 or 12 percent or more, the Jews are often respected and not disliked; but in too many places, where the simple, drink-loving peasants are wholly at their mercy, the Jews are accused of getting them into debt, often through tavern bills. There is especial complaint of the way they contrive to get control of the woods, which are the only valuable asset of the region, and which are being recklessly cut down by speculators."[44]

The frequent, often daily interactions between Jew and Gentile in Eastern Europe and their physical proximity did not diminish "mutual strangeness and distance" between them. Morawska writes that in everyday contacts the Jew represented to the peasant "the pursuit of things 'other' than those characteristic of their own agricultural existence: namely, commerce, money, and profit . . . They were also, and contemptibly, thought to have been physically and 'characterologically' incapable of engaging in agriculture." Jews were seen as "treacherous and exploitative by nature and, by extension, all Jews were considered deceitful, cunning, and greedy." At the same time they were perceived as intelligent, competent, and given to solidarity among themselves.[45]

In religious terms, Jews were assigned by this belief system an essentially destructive role in Christian theology. They were "God's betrayers, tormentors, and crucifiers" and therefore deserving of contempt and even physical retaliation. They were sinners and somehow connected with both good and evil spirits, people to be held in awe. Here too, however, the peasant was ambivalent, admiring the Jews' studiousness and religiosity and holding the rabbi in high esteem even as a source of advice. Within the structure of European society, the peasant felt secure and superior to the Jew, who was fair game for all manner of harassment and torment, especially when the peasant was drunk.

These pejorative perceptions were reciprocated in Jewish attitudes toward the Gentile peasant. The peasant was grudgingly acknowledged to be the source of the Jews' material livelihood. But always he was perceived with "disdain, uneasiness, and suspicion" as being different from the Jew—as backward, primitive, uncultured, instinctual, ignorant, and mentally slow. The peasants were dirty and lazy. They embodied none of the things the Jews valued most: spirituality, learning, intellectualism, the ability to deal in abstractions and to avoid physical force. Rather than a passionate hatred, the Jew felt pity, since he felt his own life to be better than the peasant's.

Together with these feelings was a pervasive insecurity and fear of the Christian peasant, of his "physicality" and excitability. His was a menacing presence, harboring the possibility of violence. This generated an outward appearance of accommodating demeanor on the part of the Jews, a desire to appear submissive and compliant, balanced by an inner sense of superiority over the peasant. This superiority stemmed also from the surety that Jews as the Chosen People were followers of the one and only God and the Christians were heathens and idolators. What is more, in biblical terms, harking back to the destruction of the First and Second Temples, the Gentiles were viewed as bent on the destruction of the Jews.

The stark and bitter feelings that Morawska describes in the paragraphs above may well have been the underlying attitudes of the two groups toward each other. But they varied in intensity from place to place in Eastern Europe and within Hungary. As a whole Jewish-Gentile relations in Hungary have been described by both Jews and Gentiles in somewhat more favorable terms than Morawska employs.

Consider, for example, the statements of a number of Hungarian Jews who emigrated to America. Whether they saw the past in more benign colors or whether their assessments were subject to the vagaries of memory, it is difficult to say. Of fourteen immigrants interviewed in Pittsburgh most of them spoke about good or very good relations with non-Jews, though some acknowledged the presence of anti-Semitism. A few statements will give the tenor of these immigrants' recollections.[46]

One person said that his father and mother were loved by the Gentiles but that still there was anti-Semitism, which was against the law under Emperor Franz Joseph. He added that people, particularly teen-agers, were inflamed by what they heard from their priests. The most negative comment was from a woman who said that Gentiles "didn't like Jews," but she added "I got along well" with the Christians. Her town, incidentally, had a Jewish mayor. Another town, where the Jews seemed to have "full rights" and good relationships with Gentiles, had a Jewish "justice of the peace."

The experiences of Edward Steiner, sociologist and writer on ethnicity and immigration, are vivid, but before presenting them we must take note of his change of religious identification. Steiner's boyhood was spent as a Jew in a small Slovakian town. He received the traditional Jewish education along with secular studies and then attended a Jesuit school. From early on Steiner was engaged in a wide-ranging ideological search. He became a personal friend of Tolstoy and an admirer of his brother's friend, Theodor Herzl, one of the founders of modern Zionism. Steiner turned to Christianity as a young man and was ordained a Congregational minister the year he came to America. His account of his experiences as a Jewish boy, however, show a directness and candor that spared no one.

Steiner played with peasant children and formed close friendships. He had "boyhood love affairs with Slovak girls" and helped a Slovak boy ring the Catholic church bells, attended mass, and listened to Lutheran hymns.[47] But before long both adults and other children were calling him "Christ-killer" and "Schid," a Slavic term for Jew that "had a contemptuous and menacing sound." His family forbade him to play with Gentiles and he was estranged from his former friends.

Feeling against the Jews, Steiner remembers, was especially strong in certain villages, and this was heightened by "periodical Easter raids" on the Jewish community. One incident burned itself into his memory. It was Pesach (Passover), which comes close to Easter each year, and the family was holding a seder. His mother, a widow, was apprehensive because the whole Gentile community was agitated over the disappearance of a young girl. The Steiners had bolted their door and barred the windows. As they were arranging the ceremonial objects on the table, a stone hit the shutters and broke several windowpanes. Then his uncle and his three sons arrived to begin the service that commemorates the Exodus of the Jews from Egypt. They told of a mob gathering in the streets and of stones crashing through the synagogue windows. As the Passover service proceeded, the crowd outside their house swelled and they could hear a crowbar straining at the hinges of the door. A strong voice addressed the mob: "Is this the way the risen Lord has taught you to treat your neighbors?" "Your Reverence," one replied, "they have slaughtered Anushka." Their pastor's response was to send the mob home.

Gentile-Jewish relationships in Hungary, as well as the status of Jews, varied from region to region and from estate to estate. The relatively favorable position of Jews in the fertile and comparatively prosperous Croatian and Slovenian areas in the southwest is attributed to their small numbers there.[48] In Transylvania, economically one of the richest areas, Rumanian-Jewish relations were also somewhat better than in other places. In short, Jewish-Gentile relations presented a mixed picture, summed up rather well by the comment of an immigrant who grew up not too far from Steiner's town. Her guide for a prudent Jewish attitude toward Gentiles was: "respect and suspect."

Looking back over the whole course of the quid pro quo understanding, it too was a mixed picture. It gave the Magyars a political and cultural ally in their confrontation with their "nationalities problem" and a willing partner in the economic development of the country. For the Jews it brought protection and legal rights. For some of them it meant unheard of opportunities to rise in the financial, professional, and cultural spheres of Hungarian national life.

These advantages did not however bring social acceptance, as this observation makes clear: "And while they had concluded a mutually beneficial alliance with the Hungarian ruling class according to which they were to be regarded as Hungarians of the Jewish faith, just as there were Catholic and Protestant Hungarians, this did not mean that they were able to integrate fully into Hungarian society and thus fulfill their assimilationist expectations."[49]

The economic and cultural opportunities that this "alliance" opened up were seized by a minority, primarily the urban, Westernized Jews of Hungary. For the "other Jewry"—by far the larger number—life in the small towns and villages was simpler and harsher. For them, swimming in a sea of ethnic groups in conflict, there were strains and dangers in their relations with Christians, despite the protection of the government. But while these Jews had to be keenly aware of their Gentile environment, they cultivated an inner, Jewish life.

We look to this now, not only to fill out the picture of Jews in Hungary, but also to pick up clues as to characteristics that influenced the settlement and acculturation of those who emigrated to America.

★

CHAPTER 5

Religion, Languages, and Folklore

In order to determine what was distinctive about Hungarian Jews it is necessary to examine their culture as it evolved out of the history just recounted. That history saw rapid and far-reaching changes in the nineteenth century. This was reflected in the conflict between traditional Judaism and the secularism which had begun with the Enlightenment.[1] The changes were seen in the shifts in the languages used by the Jews and in the names they chose. In fact the changes were so swift that a group of scholars banded together to rescue a disappearing Jewish folklore. In addition, there was a substantial movement of population from the periphery of the Kingdom of Hungary to its center, especially to Budapest.

These changes and tensions ought to be seen in the light of Hungarian Jewry's relatively short history. When the century opened, the modern Jewish community was less than 150 years old, younger than the communities in Russia and Poland and much younger than the well-established Jewries of Western Europe. The ideological and political frameworks surrounding the Jews of Hungary were changing quickly, almost before they could get their feet firmly planted on the ground. Much like their descendants who came to the United States, they had to find ways of accommodating to different worlds—to the insecure world of the Magyars and the minorities and to the world of European Jewry, which was itself in ferment. William O. McCagg calls the Hungarian-Jewish community an "ad hoc structure," lacking a past and "fragile in proportion to its newness."[2] He goes on to say that "it lacked staying power; it lacked the hold that might have ensured religious stability in the face of an onslaught of 'modernism' which began earlier than in Poland." We begin our review of Jewish life in Hungary with the religious sphere.

RELIGION

The religious issue requires a consideration of developments in Eastern and Central Europe beyond the borders of Hungary. For centuries Judaism had been a complete system of living and thinking, a self-sufficient body of knowledge, faith, and daily observance of commandments. But in the seventeenth and eighteenth centuries new ideas were abroad in Western Europe and were beginning to impinge on the intellectual foundations of Jewish belief and practice. Rationalism, notions of universal morality, and freedom of thought were spreading through Western society and profoundly unsettling the equilibrium of its Jewish communities.

The winds that brought these new values and ways of thinking—which Jews called Haskalah or the Enlightenment—also carried the promise of Emancipation and civil rights for the Jews. Both Emancipation and Enlightenment, however, entailed increased contact between Jews and Christians, and this meant for the Jews either opportunity or threat, depending on one's point of view about the traditional way of life. The Haskalah confronted Europe's Jews, individually and collectively, with wrenching choices as to how they would relate to the Christian world and to their own past.

The Jewish response varied greatly.[3] Early in the 1800s there were many conversions to Christianity, especially in Hungary. These constituted total rejection of the Jewish tradition and expressed the view that "Judaism is not a religion, it is a catastrophe." Conversions were undertaken in order to gain access to universities, to more desirable jobs, and to social acceptance in the upper class, as well as being a means of expressing solidarity with the Magyars.

McCagg, commenting on twenty thousand Jewish conversions in the period 1867–1918, is of the opinion that these not only were the "product of opportunism" but also constituted an adjustment to the "rational, scientific, and democratic ideas" of the day. This adjustment, he writes, could more easily be made by Christians than by people who had no land or state and whose identity was "overwhelmingly theological." Despite all this, he concludes that the Jews showed "a remarkable degree of resistance" and that in fact the conversion rate remained low before the First World War. The number of those who left the Jewish community through intermarriage and conversion has been estimated at less than 2 percent.[4]

There were of course throughout this period many who firmly rejected all changes in the traditional practices of Judaism. But increasingly Jews were attracted to an accommodation or a synthesis of tradition and modernity. They sought to balance participation in the Haskalah with adherence to the fundamentals of Judaism, though not to all its observances. This called for religious reform, a movement which began in Germany.

There a new type of rabbi, educated in the university, was introducing changes in the ritual and was conducting scientific, historical studies of Judaism. These men concluded that there was a priceless moral and spiritual base to Judaism, but that over time, customs and requirements had been added that were not essential. Indeed, they found some of these man-made accretions to be unsuited to living in the modern world and therefore disposable or at least subject to modification. Such was the case, for example, with the hitherto strict dietary laws or the prohibition of work on the Jewish Sabbath.

The new wave of thinking and behavior was also expressed in the ritual. The vernacular was introduced into religious services; in Hungary this meant first German and later Hungarian. Moreover, increasing numbers of Jews turned from immersion in the Hebrew texts to contemporary literature of all kinds. Much of this was an expression of the thrust of the rising Jewish middle class. They were pressing to enter the contemporary world in all its manifestations: science and art, journalism and politics, universities and industry. They did not want to appear too alien; but more fundamentally they were attracted to the ideas and knowledge of the secular world.

Among both Christians and Jews in Central Europe were those who fervently believed that secular education would reshape the ghetto Jew by abolishing his "outlandish" style of dress, his Yiddish jargon, his "addiction to trade," and his practice of an "irrational" religion.[5] Many Jews became infatuated with German culture. In both Germany and Hungary Jews were loud in their assertions of patriotic attachment to the fatherland, claiming that Judaism was only a religion, not a culture or a people. This movement echoed the hopes of both liberals and reactionaries who expected that Emancipation and Enlightenment would bring the Jews into the Christian fold. There were conversions and defections of Jews, but the dominant reality was otherwise. The more the Jews pressed for entry into the main institutions of the society, the greater the resistance from Christians who felt threatened.

The efforts to modernize Judaism made almost no headway in the Russian-Polish Pale where ghetto living severely restricted the Jews' interaction with Christians, but the Reform movement spread quickly and deeply into Hungary. At the same time it generated vehement opposition from the Orthodox community. Chief among the opponents early in the century was Moses Sofer (1762–1839), the rabbi in Pressburg, now Bratislava. He was born in Frankfurt and had come to Hungary as part of the early influx of Austrian-German Jews. From the acrostic of the title of the most acclaimed of his hundred books, he became known as the Hatam Sofer.

Rabbi Sofer was a leader in Central Europe of the uncompromising opposition to any changes in ritual or the religious commandments. In 1819 he wrote that excommunication should apply not only to Jews who became Christians but to those who broke the Oral Law and rejected rabbinic authority, for example, by profaning the Sabbath. Rabbi Sofer made his city a center of Orthodoxy. He built up in Pressburg "the greatest yeshiva of the age."[6] He also encouraged his disciples to go to Eretz Israel, or Palestine.

During the same period of time, an early and radical advocate of change was Rabbi Aaron Chorin (1766–1844). In 1803 he published an attack on customs he deemed to lack a basis in the Talmud. He was tried and stoned and his book was ordered by a rabbinical court to be burned. Chorin appealed to the government, which set aside the verdict. He went on to give his approval to such serious changes as writing or riding on the Sabbath. The corollary of his religious radicalism was that he became "a fanatical fighter for secular education."[7]

A few decades later Rabbi Leopold (Lipot) Loew, originally from Moravia, took up the struggle for reform.[8] He was "army rabbi to the Hungarian freedom fighters of 1848–49" and later enriched Jewish scholarship through a journal he edited and through the first writings in Hungary on Jewish archaeology and folklore.[9]

The clash between the two main streams of Judaism in Hungary was a serious one by the middle of the 1800s, despite the fact that some Orthodox rabbis no longer called for the excommunication of religious reformers.[10] The advocates of accommodation, the Neologs, soon achieved a numerical majority among Hungarian Jews over the Orthodox. Their reforms, however, were less extreme than those in Germany.[11] The situation reached a critical point, in fact a breaking point, not long after the Jews received full civil rights.

A congress was convened by the government in 1868 on the initiative of the Neologs with the purpose of establishing an autonomous Jewish body with which the government could negotiate, particularly with respect to education. The expectation was that the Neologs would determine the outcome of the conference, but the Orthodox delegates walked out, rejecting the decisions taken by the majority. They set up in many cities and towns their own kehillah or community organization. In passing, we note that two men whose names were to become well known as rabbis in America took an active part in the congress. One was Alexander Kohut, a friend of Lajos Kossuth, and the other was Aaron Bettelheim, who would become Kohut's father-in-law after they had both emigrated.

After the congress the Hungarian-Jewish community was thoroughly and bitterly polarized, more so than in any other country. "The division between Orthodox and Reform Jews was so great," writes Solomon Poll, "that there was a ban against intermarriage among them."[12] Beyond the basic break between the Orthodox and the Neologs, there was a moderate group eager to return to the situation before the schism took place. They formed "Status Quo Ante" congregations. The government had little choice but to accept these divisions among the Jews. On numerous occasions the traditionalists as well as the reformers appealed to Emperor Franz Joseph for favorable rulings in their disputes.[13] In some communities, such as Újhely, three separate central organizations or kehillot existed: Orthodox, Neolog, and Status Quo Ante.[14]

Despite these acrimonious disagreements, Hungary saw a rich development of Jewish learning and scholarship by both traditionalists and reformers. A number of Hungarian rabbis received recognition throughout Europe and a literature in German, Hebrew, Yiddish, and Hungarian flourished.[15]

A significant element in religious life in Hungary was Hasidism, a movement that had developed in the Ukraine and Poland in the second half of the eighteenth century. It stemmed from a rejection of what was perceived as the rigidity and the cold, abstract quality of the prevalent practice of Judaism with its emphasis on study of the authoritative texts. In advocating a more intimate and direct connection between God and the individual and in developing a joyous and spontaneous form of worship, Hasidism had a strong appeal to poverty-stricken Jews in Eastern and Central Europe. As their movement developed, the Hasidim clung fiercely to their own ways, their manner of dress, and a whole lifestyle built around the hereditary "court" of their leader or rebbe.[16] When the Galician part of Poland was taken into the Austrian Empire, Hasidism spread into Hungary.[17]

The development of Hasidism in Hungary differed from that in Poland.[18] The founder of the movement in Hungary, according to Andrew Handler, was Rabbi Eizik (Yitzhak) Taub, known as the Kalever in the late eighteenth century. He was a simple and pious man, given to mixing with Jewish and Gentile shepherds, innkeepers, and fishermen. He was a wanderer and something of a musician, using Hungarian folk tunes in his religious services. One of the Kalever's tunes will turn up in a later chapter as the favorite at Hungarian-Jewish weddings in McKeesport, Pennsylvania. The song was "Szól A Kakas Már" and it is about the rooster who is already crowing, but the Hasidic rabbi used it in an allegorical sense "to express the messianic longings of the Jew in the form of a love song. . . . It was both Hungarian and Jewish. Both secular and religious.

> The cock crows the morn.
> A new day is being born.
> In the green sward, in the meadow
> A bird walks all alone."[19]

In Hungary Hasidism did not meet violent opposition from the Orthodox rabbis. Rabbi Moses Teitelbaum (1759–1841), for one, attempted to bridge the differences between traditional Orthodoxy and the new Hasidism. Born in Galicia, he settled in Újhely, where he founded a dynasty which was later active in Siget and in Munkács. He wrote a four-volume work, *The Rejoicing of Moses*, and was highly esteemed as a "zaddik" or saintly man. Many non-Jews came to him in Újhely for blessings, advice, and aid. Today his grave is maintained as a memorial in Újhely.

There were, then, serious divisions among the Jews—divisions that would persist among the immigrants to America. The Hasidim joined with the traditional Orthodox in fierce opposition to the reform movement. The changes that were creeping into Jewish life are evident in a folk song addressed by a marriageable girl to her mother. It was sung in Yiddish, except for the last line which was in the Magyar language. Here is the first verse (payess were the long ear-ringlets and sideburns worn by very Orthodox men):

> Oy, mama, what kind of news is this!
> I don't want a groom with long "payess."
> Not for any money do I want him,
> Because I'm a young woman of today's world.[20]

Although there were many more Orthodox than Neolog "communities" or congregations, the number of people who were observant Jews constituted a distinct minority. Jacob Katz estimates that "a third of the 900,000 Jews at the turn of the century, i.e., 300,000, were fairly observant, at least to the extent that in the eyes of the observer their Jewishness was clearly apparent in their outward religious behavior."[21] The observant Jews, however, were well represented among those who left for America.

The congregations were not only the focus of worship; they were also the locus of community organization and the source of services for the Jewish community. Early in the eighteenth century long distances for the horse and wagon separated the small Jewish settlements, and until 1848 the traditional authority (kehillah) was responsible for the governance of these Jewish communities.[22] It was organized on a county basis and took charge of internal discipline, decision making, and the collection of taxes for the government. After the congress in 1868 at which the religious factions split, the local kehillot were no longer responsible for tax collections.

The Jewish communities grew in size in the latter part of the century, though it was still necessary in some places for a "circuit-riding" rabbi to supervise religious functions in several communities. Lines of communication were shortening and interaction among Jewish communities was increasing. More and more localities had at least two synagogues and a network of religious functionaries and institutions. It is important to grasp the scope and purpose of these communal programs because the immigrants tried to re-create them, in one form or another, when they reached America. Typically a community would provide for at least some of the following functions:

A *Hevra Kaddisha* or society concerned with burial and comforting the bereaved
Bikur Holim, visitors of the sick
Gemilut Hesed, a free loan and charity fund
Hevra Shas, the Talmud study association
Shochet or ritual slaughterer of animals
The *mohel* who performed circumcisions
The *mikveh* or ritual bath
Sometimes there was a "Frauen Verein" or women's organization

The most weighty responsibility of the kehillah was the children's schooling. In the 1780s Joseph II had required Jewish children to study a secular curriculum which included Latin, Hungarian, and German. In the middle of the nineteenth century the overwhelming majority of Jewish children attended schools under Jewish auspices; about 10 percent went to Catholic or Calvinist schools. As time passed, more children attended public schools and studied traditional Jewish subjects after hours. In 1884 school enrollment for Jewish children in Hungary stood at 75 percent, though it was lower in the rural areas.

Recalling his boyhood schooling, one of the immigrants interviewed in Pittsburgh gave this as his daily schedule:

> 4 A.M. to 8 A.M.—Hebrew school
> 8 A.M. to 3 P.M.—public school
> 3 P.M. till dark—Hebrew school

Six months before he was thirteen, the age at which he would become a full-fledged member of the Jewish community, he was sent to a yeshivah for advanced Jewish studies.

Further insight into the situation of Judaism and into the world of the Orthodox is provided by the yeshivah, which constituted the primary institution in which teenage boys and young men studied the Talmud and Jewish law.[23] Yeshivot were present in Jewish communities throughout Hungary. There were in pre-Trianon Hungary more than two hundred yeshivot with ten thousand young men studying twelve to thirteen hours a day. These schools existed not solely for the training of religious functionaries, but for the instruction of much larger numbers of men who, as they later became tradesmen and artisans and farmers, remained pious and learned Jews. The purpose of the Hungary yeshivah was training in the practical application of Jewish law and customs to everyday life, in contrast to the more scholarly and abstract approach of the yeshivot in Lithuania. The yeshivah was a rampart of Orthodoxy, fighting off attempts to include secular subjects and occupational training, though eventually many yeshivot adopted Magyar as the language of instruction.

The Hungarian yeshivah was closely tied to its Jewish community. The head of the yeshivah also functioned as the local rabbi. Integration with the community was reinforced by the practice of having the students take their meals as guests of Jewish householders, sometimes in exchange for tutoring the children in the family. This arrangement, known as "teg essen," often meant eating each day of the week with a different family. The students, in addition, had to go "schnorring," knocking on doors to collect alms to support themselves and the yeshivah. This was resented as an indignity by the students, who formed an organization and undertook a campaign to have the fund-raising responsibility taken over by the community; their efforts were unsuccessful. A description of the horrendous lack of food, clothes, and decent housing that some yeshivah students suffered appears in Victor David Tulman's account of his own experiences in *Going Home*.

The profound differences between the Orthodox and the Neologs were clearly expressed in the existence of two competing seminaries for the training of rabbis, which were mentioned earlier. At the Seminary in Budapest classical rabbinic studies were combined with training in modern Jewish scholarship. Moreover, no student would be admitted to the written and oral examinations for ordination unless he had also pursued a four-year program at a secular university leading to the degree of doctor of philosophy. The seminarians graduated from universities in Prague, Vienna, Breslau, Berlin, and other cities.

In Pressburg the seminary founded by Rabbi Moses Sofer was the training ground for the Orthodox, conducted in the time-honored traditions of rabbinical education. It was the very antithesis of the Neologs' seminary, which was seen by the Orthodox as the carrier of assimilation.

Each of these seminaries sent rabbis to America, where they continued to engage in debate and controversy, as did members of their congregations. A member of a synagogue in Cleveland, writing anonymously in 1891, had this to say: "The mighty schism [in the Old Country] had left father opposing son, brother against brother . . . The Jews who emigrated to America continued the old battles, and the chief pleasure at the holding of services was fighting and quarreling."[24]

There is an aspect of Hungarian Jews' relationship to the larger body of Jewry, both in Hungary and later in America, that calls for discussion at this point—Zionism. An oft-repeated view of this is that Hungarian Jews never really took to this movement of Jewish nationalism at the turn of the century. Here we cite only two examples. Emil Lengyel called the Hungarian Jews "the most anti-Zionist Jews on the surface of the globe until the Second World War."[25] The *Encyclopaedia Judaica* notes that the movement "only seriously attracted a limited circle of the academic youth, the intellectuals, and a minority of Orthodox Jewry, while assimilationist circles and the overwhelming majority of the Orthodox were sharply and firmly opposed."[26]

The Orthodox rabbis in nineteenth-century Hungary stormed against Zionism at the very time that it had a powerful appeal to desperate Jews in

Russia and Poland. And yet, Hatam Sofer in the early 1800s urged his disciples to go to Eretz Israel. Clearly the Neologs, with their strong attachment to Hungary, had little interest in the notion of a Jewish homeland in Palestine. One writer exclaimed: "We do not need Jerusalem! Budapest is our Jerusalem! The Danube is our Jordan!"[27] Still, Theodor Herzl and Max Nordau, two of the towering figures in Zionism, were both born in Budapest.

A study of this subject points out that the Hungarian Zionist Association, the Makkabea (a student organization), and the first Zionist newspaper in Hungary were all launched in 1902.[28] But these efforts had to take into account the apathy and opposition to Zionism of the bulk of Hungarian Jewry. So they fashioned, as a first step, a cultural and educational program with the emphasis on study groups, Hebrew language courses, and sports clubs, rather than aggressively promoting emigration to Palestine.

Joseph Patai was a founder of the Zionist organization of students in Budapest in 1903, against determined resistance from other Jews. His son's comments are illuminating. "One must remember that Hungarian Jewry in the early twentieth century was living withdrawn into a state of self-isolation from world Jewry in general and from the Palestinian *yishuv* in particular. The Jews of Hungary were fearful that any expression of interest in what the Jews in other countries were doing . . . would be taken by the powers that be in Hungary as a sign that the Jews were not good patriots."[29] There was, in short, limited interest in Zionism, but enough to send a group of engineers and technicians from Hungary to Palestine in the early 1920s and to set down a base for an upsurge in interest as Hungarian Jews encountered more and more antagonism in their own country between the two wars.

LANGUAGES AND NAMES

Until the nineteenth century, Yiddish was "the mother-tongue and the colloquial speech" of Hungary's Jews.[30] When the Hapsburgs achieved control of Hungary, they insisted on the use of the German language and, with the Jews specifically, on their adoption of German names. In fact German was becoming the dominant language among Jews in Central Europe at that time and had "assumed an almost holy status" in their eyes because it had been the vehicle for their acquisition of the fruits of the Enlightenment.[31] After the Hapsburgs ceded internal control to the Magyars in 1867, the Jews were under pressure to use the Hungarian tongue and to take Magyar names.

The results of successive periods of Germanization and Magyarization were apparent for many years in the speech and the names of Jewish families. Despite these pressures, however, Yiddish continued to be spoken.[32] Moreover it was used by the traditionalists as "one of the major instruments which strengthened the social separation between Orthodox and non-observant Jews in Hungary."[33] Some prayers were written in Hebrew using Latin letters and Hungarian orthography. The Kaddish or prayer for the dead, for example, appeared as "Jiszgadal wejiszkadas." Unlike Jewish women in Poland who used prayer books in Yiddish, the women in Hungary usually had books in Hungarian or German.

A convincing piece of evidence of the continued usage of Yiddish comes from the area that was northern Hungary in 1918. Only three years later this area was in Czechoslovakia and the new government's census showed 130,762 Jews, of whom 70,480 said they spoke Yiddish.[34] In pre-Trianon Hungary Jews did not have the option of naming Yiddish as their mother tongue, since it was not a "recognized language."[35] One historian asserts that the Hungarian census of 1910 counted Yiddish as German.[36]

In this connection it is instructive to look at the United States census of 1910. Immigrants in that year were asked what their customary speech or "mother tongue" was before immigrating to this country. Of the 495,600 persons born in Hungary, 19,896 said that Yiddish or Hebrew was their mother tongue and 73,338 said it was German.[37] It is reasonable to assume that many of the German speakers were Jewish.

We asked the relatives of a group of immigrants to name the languages spoken in their families' homes in Hungary. According to their recollections, Magyar was mentioned twenty-seven times, Yiddish twenty-one times, German thirteen, and Slovak four. Often there were combinations of two or three languages. It should be kept in mind, however, that many of the immigrants came from the Yiddish-speaking parts of Hungary.

Despite the persistence of Yiddish, in the latter half of the nineteenth century and the first decades of the twentieth century more and more Jews adopted Magyar as their everyday language. Based on Hungarian census reports, the use of the Magyar language by Jews increased from 63 percent in 1890 to 73 percent in 1900 and reached 78 percent in 1910.[38] Small percentages chose Slovak, Croatian, and Rumanian.

The use of German even by pro-Magyar Jews was resented by the

Magyars, and the Jews' use of Hungarian was resented by the Slovaks and other minorities. In point of fact, however, a Jew frequently spoke several languages in order to communicate with neighbors and customers. As a young girl, Esti Pollack, who lived in the Croatian-Slavonian region, was at home in German, Hungarian, Croatian, and French. The knowledge of various languages on the part of Hungarian Jews turned out to be important when they came to the United States, for it was often the key to their communication with Magyar or German or Slovak or other groups here. Also, it is no wonder that a number of Hungarian Jews served as interpreters in courts in the United States.

In general, the languages used most commonly by Hungarian Jews followed the earlier lines of Jewish migration into the country. In the northwest, those of Austrian and Moravian origin spoke German or a "western dialect of Yiddish." In the central area of the country, including Budapest, the overwhelming majority spoke Hungarian. In the northeastern districts, Jews who had originally come from Galicia tended to speak Yiddish, but even there it was heavily German in its vocabulary and grammar.[39] However, it was spoken with a decidedly Magyar accent.

The source of words in the Hungarian dialect of Yiddish is interesting. There were of course many Hebrew words but fewer than in the more standard Yiddish spoken in the Slavic lands. These words tended to be related to religious use. A few words of Magyar crept in, replacing the more widely used Yiddish words, such as *utca* instead of *gass* (street); *bácsi* in place of *fetter* (uncle); *úr* instead of *herr* (mister). In Slovakia and Máramaros, some Slovak words were incorporated. Only a few Yiddish words made it into Hungarian—*cholet* from the Yiddish *cholunt*, a tasty dish, or *nebech*, meaning "unfortunately" or "a weak, helpless, hapless person."[40]

What were the attitudes toward Yiddish among Hungarian Jews? Poll presents an elaborate analysis of eight different attitudes, a spectrum ranging from the Neologs' outright rejection to the Hasidic Jews' insistence on the "exclusive use" of Yiddish. Patai drew from his experiences the conclusion that "contempt for Yiddish was the general attitude of the majority of Hungarian Jews, whether Orthodox or Neolog."[41] His own great-grandfather had entered Hungary from Kurland with Yiddish as his mother tongue.

Two incidents separated by only a few years but by many thousands of miles illustrate, in remarkably similar circumstances, the dislike that some

Hungarian Jews had for Yiddish. When Patai was a student in the seminary, he picked up a bit of Yiddish, which was never spoken in his home. Once when he used a Yiddish phrase in talking with his grandmother, she slapped him and said " 'Never again dare to say a Jargon word to me!' " When the writer of this book was a small boy he learned a few songs in Yiddish and proudly sang them for his grandparents, who did not use that language. They greeted the performance with dour faces and remarks to the effect that he should forever drop this outlandish tongue.

We come now to the fascinating subject of names. When Joseph II set out to Germanize his subjects in the 1780s, he found that a Jew was called by his first name followed by his father's first name. Thus a man might be David ben Moshe (David son of Moses). The emperor decided that the Jews must take on family names and that these must be German. This was also being done in other countries in Central Europe as a way of expediting the collection of taxes and the drafting of men for the army. Sometimes surnames were assigned, but considerable leeway was permitted the Jews to select their own names and they drew on Hebrew and Slavic as well as German to designate their families.

Some, following the ancient pattern, took their fathers' name and added the Slavic suffix "vics" (or "witz" or "vits" or "vitz") to indicate "son of," as in Hymovitz (son of Chaim).[42] Some incorporated the name of their mothers or wives, such as Pearlman (Pearl's man). Still others based their new names on their occupation: Schneider (tailor). Other names came from a physical characteristic—Kurtz (short). Patai reports that often, especially in the case of newcomers to a locality, the name of the town or place from which a man came was taken as a last name; thus from the time his own great-grandfather arrived in Nagyvárad he was known as Raphael Kurlander since he had come from Kurland, an area that is now part of Latvia.[43]

It was said that "in many communities in Hungary, the Jews were divided into four groups and each group was assigned the name Weiss (white), Schwartz (black), Gross (big), and Klein (little) respectively."[44] I can only say that among the almost two thousand names of immigrants collected for this book, these four names appear with more than random frequency.

The authorities once assigned the name "Weltner" to a family in Slovakia whose breadwinner was a peddler, but a peddler without a license. The man was making his rounds one day when he was haled into court and asked his name. Terrified, he could not remember "Weltner" and stammered something that no one was able to understand. The impatient magistrate barked: "The fellow is as stupid as a *kohut* (rooster). Put him down as Kohut." The peddler left thinking this was his new name and it stuck to him and his family.

That account is told by Rebekah Kohut, and her comment on the incident is as interesting as the occurrence itself. "Certainly no resentment toward government officials resulted from the incident." In the Kohut family four girls were named after Austrian princesses and a fifth after the empress herself. The children had been brought up to revere the royal family. In fact, Emperor Franz Josef had visited their synagogue in Grosswardein. The son was originally named Rudolph after the crown prince, but this was later changed to George.[45]

After the period of Germanized names, the Jews took to Magyar names—both first and last—often with enthusiasm.[46] One writer with a strong anti-Jewish bias illustrated the Magyarization of Jewish names this way: "Weiss, Kohn, Loewy, Weinberger, Klein, Rosenfeld, Ehrenfeld, Gansl, Gruenfeld conceal their identity under the pseudonyms of Víszi, Kardos, Lukács, Biró, Kis, Radó, Erdélyi, Gonda, Mezei."[47] Ferenc Molnár, for example, was originally Neumann. Another writer suggests that most Hungarian Jews had German names but a third or more had Magyarized their names during the last quarter of the nineteenth century.[48] The custom, according to Patai, was to give babies two sets of names: "one or more Hungarian names, which were entered into the municipal birth register and then appeared in all personal documents, and one or more Hebrew names, which were used only in an inner-Jewish context, especially in the synagogue."[49] Usually the names were of recently deceased relatives, but I found in examining the records of people who immigrated to America that both girls and boys sometimes had the same first names as their parents.

Changes of name were often correlated in the course of Hungarian-Jewish history with shifts in the political winds and the rise and fall of anti-Semitism. At times the adoption of new names was done under duress or even government compulsion. At times Jews chose new names, more or less voluntarily, as one aspect—and a very visible evidence—of their desire and their need to become more like the German-speaking Austrians or the Magyars. Whichever was the motivation—and often it must have been mixed—a change in name was for many Hungarian Jews the donning of a protective coating.

FOLKLORE

As the nineteenth century ended, the erosion of Jewish culture was alarming to a number of scholars who began to take an active, almost frantic interest in collecting and preserving Jewish folklore and the Yiddish language in Hungary. A Folklore Commission undertook this task of "rescuing" Jewish culture in the face of what they perceived as the rapidly progressing assimilation of Hungarian Jews.[50] Decades later Alexander (Sándor) Scheiber wrote extensively on Hungarian-Jewish folklore, primarily in terms of legends and literary and religious references.

The Folklore Commission projected an ambitious study of the origins of Hungarian Jews—their language, proverbs, and jokes; their customs through the life cycle; and their folk literature, foods, and artifacts. Here we reproduce only a very few items from the extensive materials they published in *Magyar Zsidó Szemle*, the Hungarian Jewish Review, from 1900 to 1936.[51] The material quoted here appeared either in Yiddish or German, with approximate translations or equivalent ideas expressed in Hungarian, Hebrew, Latin, German, and French. First, a few sayings and proverbs.[52]

> A poor person lives like a lord: every day fresh bread . . . since he can never buy a bigger supply at one time . . . and every Shabbos a new pair of pants . . . because for the money he can afford, one pair won't last more than a week.
>
> A rabbi is a noble.
>
> Don't pay attention to the dog, but to the one he listens to.
>
> Children and fools speak the truth.
>
> For suffering and for joy, you need people.
>
> A mother is only a mouthful, a wife is a bedfull.
>
> For borscht you don't need teeth.
>
> Prosperity keeps away all plagues.
>
> A good name goes far; a bad one even farther.
>
> Every gypsy pleases his horse.

A number of Hungarian folk songs were taken over into Jewish folklore. Here are a few examples.

> 1. Yellow colt, yellow bells.
>   The girl is an orphan, alas.
>   Not long will she remain an orphan,
>   For after the grape-picking, I'll be her bridegroom.

2. My poor head, my poor head is wet.
   I drink wine, Slivovitz when I can.
   Whether I drink wine or not,
   I get from my wife a good scolding.

3. Look over there. What is that
   That shakes there in the grass?
   I thought it was a rabbit, a rabbit,
   But it is a girl with the master of the house.

4. My dear friend, don't tell my husband
   That I sold the poultry pot.
   When he asks, [tell him]
   That the dog dragged it away.

In the Hungarian version of song #4, the woman has sold her rooster to a Jew and is afraid that her husband will beat her if he finds out.

The following notes give an idea of folk customs.

Pregnant women's husbands tried to take part in removing the Torah from the Ark and putting it back as many times as they could. This was regarded as a miraculous help during the difficult hours of labor.

When the *havdala* candle burnt down at the end of Sabbath, the women could ask for a new dress from the man of the house.

On erev Yom Kippur all the relatives would gather at the home of either their parents or their most respected relative to receive his blessing. They asked him to forgive them their sins against him and then said farewell in tears.

After Sukkot, they gave the etrog (esrog) to pregnant women, who bit the top to have a successful birth and to have boys.

In some of the Hasidic villages until the day of the berit (bris) or circumcision, they hid the circumcision knife in the baby's crib to scare away bad spirits.

Side by side with traditional religion the village folk held on to their superstitions. Take Certizne for example. The name of the town, which in Hungarian was Nagy Csertesz, refers to the Devil and the place was indeed rife with legends and superstitions, a few of which warrant repeating. One Certizner recalled an incident that her grandmother supposedly witnessed. According to Jewish tradition, it is forbidden for a newborn male child to be left alone for even a short period of time until after the circumcision and name giving. In this story, dating from the 1850s or 1860s, a child was left alone and when the mother returned she found that it was not her child at all, but a Gentile child with a cross around its neck. The antidote prescribed by the rabbi was to take the child to the cemetery, where he was placed in a shallow grave. Everyone turned away, while a prayer or incantation of some sort was said, and when they turned back to the grave, the original Jewish child had returned.

Another incident during the same time period involved a young girl who became deathly ill from a snake bite. The folk doctor who was called in went back to the place where she had been bitten and somehow lured the very same snake out of the grass. The snake was caught, cut up into several pieces, and placed on the bite, which was then wrapped with an old sock. "Of course, the 'evil eye' was once again diverted."[53]

A favorite figure in Hungarian-Jewish folklore was Yosele Tégláser, whose name begins with the diminutive of Joseph and ends with a place called Téglás.[54] He was better known as Yosele Kakás, which means rooster. Yosele's fame rested on his great strength. One day, challenged to break twenty panes of glass at one stroke, he stacked them tightly together and hurled a coin that shattered them all. Another folk hero of the Till Eulenspiegel stripe was David Cigány or Gypsy David, a cesspool cleaner. He went about his work singing cheerily, for no discernible reason. At the end of the day, he washed thoroughly, doused himself with a full bottle of eau de cologne, and was ready for any adventure.

As one reads descriptions of the folklore of Hungarian Jews, a few themes emerge. Clearly these people built much of their lives around religious observance. Equally apparent is the impact of poverty on their lives. The sayings and songs serve up the folk wisdom and the daily round of living as well as the important occasions in their lives. They bespeak a devout, but earthy, sometimes lusty outlook on life. It is the life of the Jews in the villages and towns of Hungary, but not that of the urban sophisticates. The differences between the two Jewries were important not only in the Old Country, but in America as well.

★

CHAPTER 6

Two Jewries

Historical circumstances—political developments within Hungary and intellectual currents in European Jewry—led to important social, cultural, and religious divisions among the Jews of Hungary. The outcome was in effect the emergence of two Jewries. There was the world of Sholem, the innkeeper in the Kaczér novel—a world of poor, provincial, devout people. And there was the other Jewry—the middle-class, predominantly urban Jews, most of whom looked beyond the Jewish tradition for ideas and knowledge. Obviously these categories do not represent air-tight compartments. It is an oversimplification, for example, to think that the poor people were all Orthodox and the affluent were uniformly Neologs. But despite this qualification, there were two kinds of Jews in Hungary and it is important to take a closer look at this phenomenon, for each type contributed its own, distinct wave of immigrants to America.

We begin with the cosmopolitan, Westernized people for whom Budapest was the center and symbol of their culture. Here was the main stage on which the Jewish bourgeoisie and intelligentsia played out their parts. Also, together with Vienna, it was where Jews formed a majority of "the social democratic parties of the monarchy."[1] Budapest was the showpiece and pride of the new Hungarian nation in the closing decades of the last century. The Magyars were determined to have a first-class capital, complete with the world's largest parliament building, national museums, an opera house, and spacious boulevards and parks.[2]

Budapest was also the center of Jewish population, institutions, and wealth, having grown from 10,000 Jews in 1830 to 203,000 eighty years later. In 1910 Jews constituted one-quarter of Budapest's inhabitants and they made up almost one-quarter of the country's Jewish community, a situation that encouraged Vienna's anti-Semitic mayor to call the city "Judapest."[3] In 1900 they comprised 40 percent of the city's voters.

The Budapest Jews consisted "mainly of those who could trace their

71

genealogy on Hungarian soil for generations, along with newcomers from Bohemia and Moravia."[4] It was primarily in Budapest and the other cities that the Jewish bankers, lawyers, journalists, and academics entered so fully into the Hungarian economy and society. Some enjoyed an upper-class lifestyle, participating fully in the cultural activities of what has been called the Paris of the East. Just as the Magyars sought to surpass other European capitals, the Jews of the city were striving for prestige and for social respectability. Steve J. Heims has described this scene and the pressures it placed on a vulnerable Jewish upper middle class.[5] In 1859 they built the imposing, Moorish-style synagogue on Dohány Street. With its three thousand seats it was the largest synagogue ever built in Europe. Liszt and Saint-Saëns came here to play the organ. The Budapest Jews maintained an extensive education and welfare establishment: several hospitals, orphanages, a home for the blind, and an elaborate network of day schools. Here are a few examples of urban, middle-class Jewish people.

We have already taken note of a development in Hungary without parallel in other countries: the granting of titles of nobility to hundreds of Jews, who were in essence the cream of the Jewish financial and intellectual elite. McCagg studied 346 Jewish families who were ennobled between 1824 and 1918 and almost two-thirds of them were in Budapest.[6]

One of the ennobled Jews was József Körösy.[7] He was born in Pest in 1844 into a family that had come from Moravia. His father had been a merchant and later a farmer. József did not complete a university education; he worked first in an insurance company and then as a journalist writing on economics. In 1869, when Hungary assumed responsibility for its internal affairs after the Compromise with Austria, Körösy was appointed to establish the Budapest Statistical Bureau. The bureau gained international recognition especially for its research on the relationship between poverty and illness and death. Körösy became a member of the Hungarian Academy of Sciences, a professor, and an international figure. He was a patron of many Jewish organizations and he also established a foundation to promote the Magyar language among the non-Hungarian minorities. In 1896 he was given a noble title and his name was changed from Körösi to Körösy. Descendants of his today sometimes use as their last name "de Korosy."

Probably typical of many Budapest families—and a corrective to the notion that all of them were adherents of Reform Judaism—was that of Endre and Aranka Löwy. They were looked upon as "pillars of Budapest's worthy, upstanding Orthodox Jewish community." Mrs. Löwy's father had arrived in the capital from Poland in the late 1860s as an orphan with traditional *cheder* training, that is, beginning Jewish education. He developed a china and glassware business which by the end of the century was one of the largest in Central Europe.[8]

There were middle-class families in the other cities and larger towns as well. One of these in Miskolc traced its genealogy back to the fifteenth century.[9] The father had been a professional soldier who felt he could not rise above the rank of lieutenant because he was Jewish, despite the fact that he had changed his name when he entered the army. He left the military and went into the flour milling business and apparently prospered. They lived in a large house with gardens and servants. The daughter recalls going to a fine kindergarten and then to a Jewish elementary school, after which she studied music in Vienna. The grandparents were religious, but she and her parents never went to a synagogue in Hungary.

A fairly well-to-do family—probably on the border between the two Jewries—made their home in Bonyhád in the southern part of the Hungarian kingdom in the 1870s.[10] This was a town of about six thousand people, one-fifth of whom were Jewish. Croatian was the main language in this area, now part of Yugoslavia. The family owned a shop and one of the three daughters, Katherine, managed it. "She liked beautiful furniture, clothes, and bedding . . . was well educated and devoted to her religion. Also she had a good singing voice and her father took her to Budapest to hear Wagner's operas." Along with such secular and worldly interests, the family was deeply Jewish in a traditional sense. Katherine said after her father died, "Never again would there be a house that supported so many people. Never will there be such seders, Yom Kippur or Pesach" as when the young yeshivah students sat at the rich table loaded to overflowing with all good things.

Another daughter, Rose, married an older man who was rich in land and also had a store and an inn. She would carry eggs and poultry to market in her carriage, in order to have dowries for her small daughters. Her husband collected the fares for the livery service they operated, "but she did the work." About the third daughter, Selma, it was said that "the Turkish gypsies played their violins" when the family brought her to be named. The gypsies said she would be rich and beautiful "because she is dark like a gypsy." They put the baby on a pillow on which people threw money for her dowry. Selma, spurning a judge who said "I will put all my ducats before you . . . only be my wife," married a tinsmith. He was a "man with big arms and tough hands, but well-mannered" and a respected master of his craft. He built church towers and it was said that there wasn't a tower in the whole district that he had not covered. In 1913 he sailed for America and worked and saved until his wife and their children could join him after the First World War.

In contrast with these middle- and upper-class families were the lives of the large majority of Hungarian Jews. Life for people like Sholem in the Kaczér novel was not as benign as it was for these families in Budapest, Miskolc, and Bonyhád. Some of them knew extreme poverty and harsh deprivation, as one can read in Victor David Tulman's account of his own family.[11]

It was not by pure chance that Kazcér made Sholem an innkeeper, for this occupation was common among Jews. There were 18,012 Jewish tavern keepers according to the 1910 census—along with many thousands of butchers and shoemakers, tailors and carpenters, peddlers and farmers. We turn our attention now to these people, most of whom at the end of the last century lived in towns and villages where life was simpler and harder than in the heady atmosphere of Budapest.

We have a good description of the kind of house in which many of these people lived. This family was struggling to make a living from the town tavern and a small farm. They had a two-room house with a stable adjoining.

> Their combined bedroom and living-room had a wooden floor, raised three or four feet above the street, from which a few steps led down into a room with a hard packed dirt floor, which did duty as a kitchen-dining room. In one corner of this room was a large built-in brick oven which not only heated the kitchen but also the adjoining living room on one side and the stable on the other. The top of this oven also served as a warm bed in the winter time. Running along the walls of the kitchen–dining room was a plate shelf [upon which] was placed colorful Hungarian pottery of the time. The rest of the furniture was of the simplest kind.[12]

A striking characteristic of the Hungarian Jews we are describing is that they came from localities with small Jewish populations. This can be seen in Table 5 and below in the birthplaces of a sampling of passengers who came to America in 1885, 1895, and 1905.[13] The Jewish population of these 116 cities, towns, and villages as of 1900–1910 was as follows:

Jewish Population	Number of Localities Represented in Sample
0–25	22
26–100	31
101–250	18
251–500	13
501–1,000	15
1,000 and over	17

Almost three-quarters of these localities had fewer than five-hundred Jewish inhabitants. Almost half had less than one hundred Jews! There could in fact be only a few Jewish families in a village.

In Bosnyicza in Zemplén County, for instance, the Hungarian national census of 1869 showed a total of twenty-three families living on two streets. The innkeeper Lipót Goldstein, his wife, and four children were the only Jews. Twenty years earlier there had been 13 Jews living among 242 Roman Catholics, 112 Evangelical Protestants, and 27 Greek Catholics.

Bosnyicza was obviously one of the smallest Jewish "communities" but it illustrates an important feature of Jewish life in Hungary. The pattern of Jewish settlement differed from the shtetl of Russia, Poland, and Austrian Galicia. In her study of Eastern European Jews in Johnston, Pennsylvania, Morawska found that the towns from which they came were, on the average, 60 percent Jewish. These places were "little predominantly Jewish towns dispersed throughout the countryside."[14] In contrast, the Jews in Hungary lived as a minority in towns and villages where typically they formed less than a quarter of the total population, occasionally a third and rarely half. By comparison with the shtetl, this may have brought them into more frequent and close interaction with the Gentiles among whom they lived—a fact that affected their relationships in Hungary and in the United States.

For some appreciation of the life of the poorest and the most religious Jews in Hungary, the Hasidim, Leopold Greenwald's book written in Yiddish offers a picture of the people of Máramaros and Carpaten-Russland in the northeastern part of the country.[15] This has been called the cradle of Hasidism inasmuch as its founder, the Baal Shem Tov (Master of the Good Name) came here and gathered his first students from this area. These people lived in great poverty, their lives centered upon the study of the Torah and the preservation of a way of life that was unique in its devotion, its rituals, and its garb. Because Greenwald's description is so vivid and so rich in detail, we quote it at length as one of the best available depictions of Jewish life in a Hungarian village.

In their ramshackle houses with broken doors and windows, writes Greenwald, there are religious articles on the walls but "no clocks; no one hurries; no one is too late for anything." The one exception to this disinterest in time is Shabbos, which begins precisely at sundown on Friday, preceded by all manner of preparations. After noon on Friday

it is suddenly quiet . . . Trade in the villages and streets stops; the horses are in their stalls. Jews hurry to the mikveh [the ritual bath] with a clean shirt under their arms, holding their children by the hand. The whole atmosphere is filled with Shabbos. All the Gentiles know it is Shabbos. It is Shabbos in the village, in the field, on the hills, in all of Máramaros.

The Jews march out of their houses with their "streimlach," [broad, fur-bedecked hats worn by the men], their cloaks torn, patched and wrinkled, with a belt around them and a bit of snuff between their fingers, right into the synagogue. The children, big and little, run after holding on to their father's "caftan" [a long coat] and rush ahead with long steps.

They sing, they dance, they leap! . . . When a rebbe or his grandson comes for Shabbos, the streets are jammed with Jews and then the whole village takes on a Jewish face. They form a circle and do a little dance in the grand style . . . one puts his hand on the other's back and the other hand under his ear, though some put their hand under their belt.

Everything is ready and suddenly a little Jew emerges from the crowd and places himself in the middle of the street with his hand under his ear and, with his eyes closed, sings his own rebbe's melody, in a fiery way filled with meaning. The men sing with him; they cry with him. The houses, the stones, the trees all cry with him. The Gentiles stand and watch with amazement at how beautifully the Jews serve their God and how great is their love for the Sabbath.

Once a week they cook a large pot of borsht and vegetables. In the winter they eat cabbages and beans or sourkraut until Shabbos.

They sit thinking, pondering their bitter struggle for a livelihood. There are few stores in Máramaros. Many Jews are engaged in agriculture. They plow, they dig, they weed. In Máramaros there are a lot of Jewish peasants and shepherds. There are also a lot of tinkers who go around the whole week looking for business. They fix earthen pots . . . or patch broken utensils. They work for a bit of vegetables or beans; they chop wood, they shake pears out of the trees, crack nuts, pick apples, cut cabbage, sell hot corn, delicious plums, soda water, syrup-water and lemonade sweetened and colored green, red, and yellow.[16]

Many of the children go long distances to yeshivot for their Jewish studies. The railroad station after the holidays of Pesach and Sukkoth is filled with young men from Siget and nearby places with their suitcases.

Dressed in their holiday clothes, their mothers and fathers stand there waiting for the train which will carry their youngsters off to study Torah. Their faces shine with pride when the train moves and you can hear the mammas still calling: "Chaim, you must come home for Sukkot" or "Joseph, you must not swim in the Theiss, the Samash, or the Danube."

With the Gentiles and the local noble they lived on friendly terms. They had been neighbors for generations. The priest and the rabbi or sage had a good relationship—each respected the other's beliefs. The noble too was friendly to the Jews; he helped with the building of a synagogue or a mikveh. He knew the Jews' customs and holidays.

Most marriages were arranged through *shadchanim* [match-makers] . . . a wedding in the village was an event! Friends from far and wide came together to the joyous occasion. Without a jester or master of ceremonies, there could be no wedding. He sweated all day to put together verses for each guest and especially for the parents of the couple. A big part was taken up by singing over the bride and in one song there was the wish that "your groom will not be a widower or you a young widow." The klezmer musicians helped out the master of ceremonies with a fiddle and other instruments. . . . A wedding lasted eight days . . . It took years for the bride's father to pay off all the debts from the wedding.

Perhaps more typical of Jewry in the provinces is the town of Újhely; its full name is Sátoraljaúhely. Today as you drive into the town, a regional agricultural center near the border with Czechoslovakia, you may catch sight of reminders that there was once a thriving Jewish community here. Now there is barely a handful of Jews left in the town. Újhely can serve as background for comments on the relationship between Hungarian Jews and those from Galicia and, more broadly, on the social hierarchy among Jews. Just on the other side of the Carpathian Mountains from Újhely was Polish Galicia, ruled by the Austrians in Vienna. For many decades destitute Jews had been entering northern Hungary from Galicia. The influx was resented by the Gentile peasants. The Hungarian Jews extended assistance to the newcomers but they also resented them though for different reasons. This may be the origin of some of the coolness between Hungarian and Galician Jews in America.

It seems axiomatic that any marginal, socially vulnerable and insecure group reacts with fear and hostility when some of its own people—superficially different and "alien"—appear on the scene. The mere fact of the newcomers' arrival seems to threaten the delicate equilibrium in which the old-timers live and to jeopardize their acceptance by the dominant population. And so it was with the settled Hungarian Jews and the incoming "Galizianers." As is usually the case, the Hungarian Jews' attitude toward the new arrivals was buttressed by a mythology and a set of stereotypes: the Galizianers were horse thieves, dishonest, uncouth. The reciprocal sentiments of Galizianers are not hard to imagine. These attitudes did not diminish among the immigrants to America. In New York, marriage by a Hungarian Jew to a Galizianer, if not quite heresy, was frowned on.

How often these attitudes have been repeated! When the first Jewish settlers in America, the Sephardic Jews, saw their coreligionists from Germany coming ashore and settling, they greeted the "tedescos" with two contradictory attitudes. One was disdain and annoyance at the newcomers who appeared so different and foreign. The other attitude was to extend help to them as fellow Jews in need. This apparently contradictory pattern was repeated only fifty years later when the German Jews, by then comfortably settled in cities and towns all across the country, saw two million Eastern European Jews crowd into New York and other large cities. The German Jews resented them and simultaneously gave them tremendous assistance in getting started in America.

We return to the questions of how, if at all, the Jews of Hungary can be distinguished from Jews in other lands, and to what extent were Hungarian Jews a unified body or were there significant differences among them. Modern Hungarian Jewry is younger than most of its neighbors in Europe, having begun with an influx of Jews from Austria, Germany, Moravia, and Poland in the seventeenth and eighteenth centuries. By the middle of the nineteenth century it had been transformed in ways that clearly marked it as different from other Ashkenazic Jews. In Hungary Jews achieved a measure of political rights and governmental protection that cannot be compared to the oppression of Russian and Polish Jews and to the tenuous civil rights of German Jews.

But it was in the economic and cultural spheres of Hungary that the Jews—though only a minority of them, it is true—attained a level of participation and a status that no other Jewish community in Europe experienced during the later part of the last century and the beginning of this century. The upper class played critical roles in the capitalist development of the country; the intellectuals occupied a central position in the professions, journalism, and the arts. Certainly their social status distinguished them from Eastern European Jewry.

These advantages, which were more substantial than the German Jews had achieved, were the outcome of an exchange with the ruling Magyars that had profound effects on the Jews. For one thing, they became patriotic supporters of the Magyar regime and its culture. More significantly, these openings into Hungarian society, coupled with the spread of the Enlightenment, generated deep fissures among the Jews. At the risk of creating an oversimplified dichotomy, two kinds of Jews emerged. One type, responding eagerly to the opportunities opened to them, moved away from traditional Judaism and embraced the Reform movement; some opted for near or total assimilation.

In contrast, the bulk of the "other Jewry" were poorer people living mostly in rural areas. These people remained religiously observant and more conservative in their thinking and in their relations with the Gentile world. Some of them clung to Yiddish, a language that was rejected by the cosmopolitans who spoke German and later Hungarian. But even they were beginning to lose their Yiddish-based folklore by the end of the century.

Certainly this categorization can be overdrawn. There were, for instance, Orthodox Jews who were rich and deeply engaged in the economic business of the country and some were as nationalistic and chauvinistic as the secularized Jews. By the same token, the Neologs did not believe in dismantling Judaism nor were they all concentrated in Budapest.

But there were strong differences and these could be seen in the towns and villages of the northeast particularly—the source of most of the immigrants to America. They were a stronghold of tradition. The currents of thought—Jewish and secular—that were swirling through Central Europe barely touched them. Enlightenment (Haskalah), nationalism, Zionism, socialism were not embraced by them. For decades, even before the fractious Jewish Congress in 1869, the rabbis of this area fought against modernism and against the Neologs. After the congress each group insisted on maintaining its own community institutions.

The distinctions between the two Jewries were partly ideological, partly social. In important respects these were carried over to America. The social class differences, for example, had an interesting echo on this side of the Atlantic. In Cleveland's Jewish community there was a tendency for "the Budapest sophisticates to look down upon tradesmen and farmers from the provinces."[17]

There was, as we shall soon see, a sharp division between the two waves of Hungarian Jews who emigrated to the United States. Those who came after the Revolution of 1848 and before 1880 were for the most part secular, Westernized people. They were small in numbers compared with the working class people and petty tradesmen, mostly Orthodox Jews, from the small towns and villages who arrived here around 1880.

Migrating and Settling

★

CHAPTER 7

The '48ers

Two central issues in our inquiry concern the emigration of Hungarian Jews and their adjustment in America. Given their relatively comfortable circumstances in Hungary, why did some leave? And once they reached the United States, how did the immigrants deal with their three-way loyalties or identities as Hungarians, as Jews, and as new Americans?

The answers to both questions depend on which Hungarian-Jewish immigrants one is discussing: those who came before 1880 or those who arrived after that date. The characteristics of the two groups not only diverged, they corresponded remarkably well with the two Jewries in Hungary described in the previous chapter. Their reasons for leaving were quite different, on the whole, as were their adjustments to their new country.

The Jews' departure from Hungary was part of an almost ceaseless movement of Jews across the centuries and the continents. This larger migration suggests a flow of water finding its way across the world, now turbulently, now calmly. The stream moves into inlets and sets up eddies, part of the water remaining in these places, part moving on to rejoin the main flow. It was surely thus with the people of this book.

Jews were settling in Hungary at the beginning of the nineteenth century when a few adventurous ones were already leaving for the new United States of America.[1] Well before that, however, there is a mention of Hungarian Jews as members of a New York synagogue in 1712.[2] One of the earliest arrivals was Benjamin Spitzer, a native of Buda who had become a ship's captain in Hamburg. After circling the globe twice, he settled in New Orleans in 1798. He opened an import-export business and in 1820 was advocating American trade with Hungary.

Glowing descriptions of America began to appear in travel books in Hungary in the 1830s, and a few Hungarians, Jews among them, ventured to the New Land. But the first substantial movement of Hungarians came here after the defeat of the Magyars' Revolution of 1848–49. These were the '48ers.

The revolt in Hungary was one of a number of revolutions that broke out in Europe in 1848–49, beginning in France and spreading to Germany, Italy, and the Hapsburg empire. These revolutions were crushed and, in the reaction that followed, conservative forces rescinded liberal legislation and created a climate in which anti-Jewish violence erupted. In response, the defeated liberals—with many Jews among them—turned away from Europe in disillusionment and frustration and cast their eyes toward America and the freedoms they had heard about in that young country.

In Hungary the Hapsburgs took harsh reprisals against the political leaders of the rebellion and its army officers. Kossuth, the commander of the Magyar forces, and some of his staff escaped to Turkey, where they were imprisoned by the sultan. The United States and England interceded and offered the refugees asylum. In September 1851 the U.S. Navy steamer-frigate *Mississippi* brought Kossuth and sixty of his followers out of Constantinople. Some of these men and their families, including Jews, arrived in America in the years immediately following 1848 and were joined by other refugees from the defeated army and the short-lived government of Kossuth.

A much larger number of Jews was affected by the anti-Semitic outbreaks associated with the revolution. In the same edition of the Jewish journal in Vienna that carried the news of attacks on Jews in Bohemia, there appeared a poet's anguished call, "Auf nach Amerika" (On to America).[3] Posthaste, Jewish emigration societies were formed in a number of Central European cities. There had been earlier efforts to organize the emigration of Jews from the Hapsburg empire, but these had foundered on their inability to involve the Rothschilds.[4]

In the midst of the revolution there had been talk of Jewish emigration to America—and opposition to it. Those who firmly believed that they were simply "Magyars of the Mosaic faith . . . insisted that Jews need not emigrate to America because their historical roots were in Hungary, a land which in spite of the excesses committed by murderers and plunderers, was going to become the country of liberty, equality and fraternity."[5] Conversely, those Jews who were unwilling to buy emancipation at the cost of religious reform said they preferred to move to America, whose "most liberal constitution is world famous" and where "we shall return to agriculture and animal husbandry, the occupations of our pious forefathers, where we shall be a free and strong people, and where we shall escape humiliation and oppression even if we shall have to face a thousand natural hardships." But they also felt compelled to add that, in addition to remaining Jewish, they would "further diligently the Magyar tongue and nationality amongst themselves in their new country."[6]

Jewish emigration committees were set up in Pest and in Pressburg. In the latter city the association issued an appeal: "We no longer have any security of calling and livelihood, of person or property," the statement said.[7] Those who are lucky enough still to be secure must help their "ruined coreligionists," a group of "many skilled artisans and persons experienced in farming from Pressburg and other districts of Hungary." The spokesmen included Philip Korn, a bookseller, later a captain in Kossuth's army and one of those who escaped via Turkey and England to America. The chief rabbi of the Pressburg Orthodox congregation, a son of the Hatam Sofer, endorsed the enterprise. Some fifty-three Jews left Pressburg for America in 1848.

In Budapest a committee, at first mixed but later entirely Jewish, announced plans. In 1849 six families from the capital settled in Philadelphia and one in Cleveland, where "the number of Hungarian Jewish families rose so rapidly that about 1855 they established the General Hungarian Relief Society with 120 members."[8] Elaborate plans were promulgated in several European cities for the selection, transportation, and support of the emigrants.[9] But the movement sustained a serious blow when the editor of the Vienna newspaper promoting it took his own advice and left for New York.

The numbers of émigrés from Hungary in the 1850s were not large. Neither Hungary nor the United States kept much by way of statistics before 1870, but there is an estimate that in the fifty years between 1820 and 1870 the Austro-Hungarian Empire sent only eight thousand people to America.[10] There is no way of knowing how many of them were Hungarians, much less how many were Hungarian Jews. According to Stephen Bela Vardy up to four thousand Hungarian emigrants reached America in the years 1849 to 1851.[11]

Even in the years from 1871 to 1879 there were fewer than eight thousand Hungarians admitted to the United States.[12] However, they spread all across the land. As early as 1859, a Hungarian writer, John Xantus, was less than enthusiastic about the situation in San Francisco: "Thirty Hungarians now live in San Francisco alone. I should say, people *from* Hungary, because two-thirds of them are Jews. Very few of them speak Hungarian and they have boasted of being Hungarian only as long as being Hungarian was advantageous."[13]

Bertram W. Korn estimates that there may have been as many as four thousand Jews—probably most of them from Germany and Austria—who left for America after the 1848 revolutions. He makes a useful distinction among them. By far the largest number were people seeking "the personal opportunity, economic freedom and political equality" denied to them in Europe.[14] These people Korn sees as part of the continuing movement of fifty thousand Jews from Central Europe to America in the period 1848–1860.

A much smaller group were those who felt "compelled to leave because of their own participation" in revolutionary activities. These were the real refugees, fleeing for their personal safety. Korn discovered forty German Jews who fit this description, but it is not clear whether he included German-speaking Jews from Hungary. We found eleven Hungarian Jews who were "real refugees" of this type. They included two rabbis, two journalists, two physicians, and a lawyer. They were a fascinating lot.

Clearly the most prominent was Michael Heilprin, who made a significant mark as an intellectual, a writer, and a political activist both in Hungary and the United States. Moritz Eisler had been the editor of a radical Hungarian newspaper and was a surgeon in the Kossuth army. He fled first to Leipzig, where he worked as a journalist and also collected songs of the revolution, and then became a physician in New York.

A reference has already been made to Philip Korn of Pressburg, active in the emigration society there. He got out of Turkey on the American warship and tried to arouse support for Kossuth in the United States. He returned to Hungary in 1863 and converted to Christianity. The '48ers were in general liberal and free-thinking people and they have on occasion been characterized as atheists. This was hardly the case.

Two rabbis were among the Hungarian '48ers. Rabbi Benjamin Szold, father of the well-known Henrietta, was studying in Vienna when he joined the anti-Hapsburg revolution and was expelled from the city; he settled in Baltimore. Rabbi Adolph Huebsch had been a student at the university in Prague before he served in the revolutionary army. He came to New York and established a place as a scholar and organizer.

Louis Schlesinger, also a veteran of the Kossuth military forces, stayed only a short time in the United States. He soon joined the brazen but unsuccessful attempt by William Walker, an American military adventurer, to become the ruler of Nicaragua in 1860.[15] Schlesinger must have broken with Walker, because after a few battles he was fighting on the side of the legitimate government. He later became a plantation owner in Guatemala.

A more well-known military figure was Frederick Knefler. To describe his place in history, we must digress a bit to the role '48ers played in the American Civil War. Many Hungarians enlisted in the Union army, with only a few entering the Confederate forces. It has been estimated that eight hundred Hungarians out of three to four thousand then in the country fought in the Civil War. A book entitled "Lincoln's Hungarian Heroes" lists fifty-eight veterans of the Hungarian war of independence who also fought in the Civil War.[16] Seven names on the list appear to be Jewish.

A surprising number of the '48ers became senior officers in the Union army. Among them was Frederick Knefler (originally Knoepfler), the son of a Jewish doctor in Arad.[17] Knefler had enlisted in the Hungarian army when he was fifteen, along with his father. The family fled to New York after the revolution and then moved to Indianapolis, where there was a community of German Jews. At the outbreak of the Civil War here, Knefler, then twenty-seven, enlisted as a private in the Indiana Volunteers and soon earned not only a commission but the respect of the men under his command. He was given the rank of brigadier general for his leadership in the Chickamauga campaign. After the war he practiced law, married a non-Jewish woman, and was appointed U.S. district attorney in Indianapolis.

Emanuel Lulley, his wife, and five children were on board the USS *Mississippi* when it left Turkey.[18] He was forty-three when the family settled in Washington, D.C. When the Civil War began he was one of the founders of the "Kossuth Corps" in the Northern army. Bernard Loveman, married and the father of five children, joined the revolutionary army and served as scout and courier. His family first settled in Owosso, Michigan. Joseph Black had studied law in Budapest before he came to Cleveland as part of a family that achieved prominence and financial success in that city.

Leopold Elsner, a physician, led a body of two thousand students in Kossuth's army in 1849. At the close of the war he was forced to flee from Vienna to Italy. His family followed and together they went to America. Dr. Elsner practiced medicine in New York City and later in Syracuse. His son, John E. Elsner, became a well-known surgeon in Denver and wrote several books on natural history.[19]

These eleven men were, to repeat, part of that small group of refugees who came here to escape severe treatment at the hands of the victorious Austrians. Beyond them was the larger group who came for economic opportunities and political freedom. At least 250 Hungarian Jews came here for these reasons in 1848 and 1849.[20] Several thousand followed, but it is difficult to estimate the number.

From 1848 to 1870 the Hungarian Jews who arrived were predominantly middle- and upper-class people. They were well educated, ideologically committed to self-government, and trained in a range of usable skills. Some were "plain people" like the group of "craftsmen and small businessmen" who left Bremen for the United States in June of 1848.[21]

The newcomers found America in a state of turbulent growth. Fundamental economic and technological changes were under way. Canals and railroads, steamboats and the telegraph were altering transportation and communication, drawing the country together into a single market.[22] Population, industrial production, and agriculture were growing apace and feeding each other. It was a time of greater citizen participation in governing, ferment in ideas and in the printed word, social experiments and utopias. Above all, Americans were hitched to progress and to improvement in the human condition, both for industrial workers and slaves.

The nation was only seventy-five years old and it needed all the people and talent it could attract. The émigrés from the revolutions in Europe brought ideas, skills, and convictions. The times were right for the '48ers and they were right for the times. Probably—as happened again in the big migration after 1880—the Hungarian Christians expected to return to Hungary and the Jews came here to settle. In any event, realizing that they would not soon be going back to take up the fight in their homeland, the '48ers were "scattered all through the free states as farmers, engineers, journalists, lawyers, merchants, teachers, clerks etc."[23]

A few of the immigrants who came before 1880 went to Cuba to fight in its struggle for independence; others headed for the gold rush in California. A number of "young Hungarian Jews who had come, unburdened by families, to seek their fortunes in the West" were to be found throughout Colorado. One was Sam Butcher, who arrived about 1875 and became a railroad worker and miner. He was known for having killed a bear in a cave with his knife and for being the only one to come out alive from an Indian raid. He worked "among Jew-hating miners" but eventually won their respect.[24]

A handful of the political émigrés were given land in Iowa and tried to found a Hungarian colony known as New Buda, but the attempt failed. A more successful settlement was established in Davenport, Iowa, where "the first recorded Hungarian-Jewish settler, Samuel Hirsch," made a permanent home with his family.[25]

The most significant Hungarian colony emerged in New York City, where two to three hundred '48ers laid the first foundations for what would become the largest Little Hungary in America.[26] Jews were actively engaged in its beginnings. The *New York Tribune* of May 28, 1849, reported that a meeting was held to establish the first sick benefit association, which seems also to have had the task of securing good will in America for Hungary's cause. Within a few years the Hungarians had established a church, a newspaper, *The Journal of Hungarian Exiles*, a club, and a restaurant, "To the Three Hungarians." Apparently the Jews did not establish a synagogue at this time.

The small Hungarian community in New York was soon called upon to welcome Kossuth to the city and to help him launch his whirlwind tour of the United States in 1851–1852. The revolutionary cause had received strong support in America before and after its defeat. Most of the country's political leadership spoke out for Kossuth's cause: President Zachary Taylor, Secretary of State Daniel Webster, Henry Clay, and Abraham Lincoln, then a congressman.

Lajos Kossuth was a charismatic, flamboyant, and impetuous leader and a riveting orator. When he arrived in this country he evoked wildly enthusiastic welcomes from Americans from New England to Washington, D.C. In New York he received an almost hysterical welcome. In the course of his tour of the country, Kossuth delivered four hundred prepared speeches. He met with the president of the United States and spoke in eloquent English to the Congress.

In New York City, however, there was a sour incident in the Kossuth tour, considering how unreserved was the support he had received from Hungarian Jews in this country as well as abroad. Moreover, his sisters were frequent visitors at the home of Michael Heilprin, the Jewish intellectual and writer. In December 1851 the political leaders of New York City tendered a banquet to Kossuth and among the three hundred guests invited, not a single Jew was included.[27] *The Asmonean*, a Jewish newspaper, exploded with indignation that Jews had been excluded from the dinner.

The paper pointed to the twenty-five thousand Jews in New York City, among them "Capitalists of high standing, Physicians of great skill, Lawyers deeply learned, Ministers eminently pious" as well as merchants, tradesmen, and mechanics. The writer calculated that on a percentage basis there should have been at the least fifteen Jews at the banquet. The whole affair was "a farce, a fraud, a delusion . . . a gross insult." However, the writer of this fuming editorial, Robert Lyon, fundamentally believed that the fault for this insult was the Jews'.[28] He thought that their previous behavior "had convinced the city fathers that Jews were too weak politically to show resentment over slights." Noting that an election was not far off, Lyon urged the Jews of New York to "unite to make their weight" felt in the political arena.

In time Americans reached the conclusion that Kossuth had come here not to settle but to raise funds and arms to continue the struggle in Hungary. In Boston, for instance, Kossuth and the men who came with him were welcomed and some of the Hungarians stayed on after he left, but the Catholics branded Kossuth a "disappointed manufacturer of humbugs."[29] By the end of his tour Kossuth had succeeded in alienating large segments of the American public and he left discouraged and disillusioned.

Going beyond the handful of political refugees to the larger group of Jews who came in the 1850s and 1860s, they included merchants, journalists, artists, and artisans. With a knowledge of languages, some were appointed to diplomatic posts around the world. A few who had been officers in Kossuth's army and in the Union army had knowledge of artillery and military campaigns and this helped them to become surveyors of the new lands on America's frontiers. Jakab Janos Loewenthal became a professional chessplayer.

They were an active and enterprising lot. Some moved directly into business. The Civil War "was a great inducement for Hungarian tradesmen and manufacturers," and following the war the distillery business of New York was almost exclusively in the hands of Hungarian Jews, as was fur manufacturing.[30] But enterprising businessmen were spread across the country. Morris Richter had landed in New Orleans in 1850 and married a young woman from Austrian Poland.[31] They worked their way up to Dubuque, Iowa, where both listed themselves in the city directory as milliners. In 1860 Morris was in business and ran the following "special advert":

INTERESTING TO THE LADIES

I have received a Large Assortment of Spring and Summer
MILLINERY GOODS! Consisting of BONNETS, SILKS, RIBBONS, RUCHES, FLOWERS, LADIES FANCY GOODS, Etc.

The Ladies will find it to their advantage to give me a call, and compare Goods and Prices with those who Advertise to sell at half price.
MAIN STREET, NEXT TO DR. FINLEY'S, BETWEEN SEVENTH AND EIGHTH.

The immigrants brought skills and the knowledge of handicrafts with them. Charles Louis Fleischmann was the son of a Budapest distiller and yeast maker. First he worked in Cincinnati developing new devices for distilling and then began to make yeast as he had learned it in Hungary. After difficulties getting started, he and a partner put on an ambitious demonstration at the Philadelphia Centennial Exposition of 1876. They showed the making of the yeast, how the dough set, how the bread was baked—and then in a nearby restaurant they served the bread.[32]

Joseph Loth was an industrialist in New York.[33] He knew the weaving trade when he arrived about 1849 and got a job in a carpet factory in Connecticut. He moved back to New York, entered the wholesale trade in dry goods, and later became a manufacturer of silk ribbons. Loth was active in philanthropy and in the beginnings of B'nai B'rith and of the American Jewish Historical Society.[34] Others entered the white collar occupations. Joseph Grosner arrived in 1866, eventually worked for the Metropolitan Life Insurance Company, and was an active district leader in Tammany Hall, the Democratic party's organization on the Lower East Side of New York.

Doubtless the best-known Hungarian-Jewish immigrant of this period was Joseph Pulitzer. Pulitzer did not identify himself as a Jew, but a recent inquiry established that as fact.[35] We find him, an eighteen-year-old Civil War veteran, living among the garment workers in New York.[36] Young Joseph was contemplating his next move when he heard the call to "Go West." He went to St. Louis, worked on a ferry, read avidly in the public library, and got a job as a reporter on a German newspaper, and studied law. It was a time of breathtaking growth in the American economy and also a time of widespread corruption and venality in public life and in business. Pulitzer bought the *St. Louis Post-Dispatch* and made it into a hard-hitting newspaper that exposed graft and corruption and also appealed to the needs and interests of immigrants. Pulitzer was, as well, a man of action and was elected to the Missouri legislature and later served as a police commissioner. His place in American history comes from his contribution to a new kind of fighting journalism. He advocated, for example, taxing large incomes, and he fought against the monopolistic practices of the new octopuslike corporations. He established a journalism school at Columbia University and is known today as the founder of the Pulitzer prizes for artists and writers.

By no means were all the Hungarian Jews who came here prior to 1880 middle-class businessmen and intellectuals. Many followed the German Jews and became peddlers, both in rural and urban areas, and small shopkeepers. We must note here the striking similarity between this role and the function the peddler performed in nineteenth-century Hungary. Both were bridging the marketing gap between the rural countryside and the new manufacturers of ready-made clothes, household utensils, tools and the like. It was a quintessentially capitalist function they performed and in many ways it prepared the peddlers and shopkeepers for finding their way into the American economy.

That way was not easy, however; nor was it unobstructed. The fragile financial base of some of the early peddlers and "salesmen" in and around Cleveland is illustrated by an 1877 credit report on Ignatz Mandel, a Hungarian Jew who was a "married pedlar about the country." "The trade who knew him and sell him say he has no respons. whatever. Manages to eke out a living & they sell him C.O.D. only. No basis whatever for cr." Within three years he was out of business.[37] Others had better luck or more skill and moved into retail stores and other enterprises.

Another report in 1869 concerned a store on St. Clair Street in Cleveland and noted that E. Golden, a German Jew, was selling his store (liquors and boots and shoes) "to his former partner 'A. Hartman' & a man named 'E. Grossman', two scheming looking Hungarian Jews who had no visible means but their stock of liquors."[38] It was the practice at that time in writing credit reports such as these to state explicitly that the person under investigation was a Jew or an "Israelite."[39] Today this might well be considered illegal discrimination and anti-Semitism; in the 1870s it was an expression of the nativist bias that many Americans had toward the Jews in their midst.

The reality of discrimination, as well as the abundant possibilities of that time and place, can be appreciated in the family history of Emanuel Lulley, one of the '48ers mentioned earlier. After arriving from Turkey, he settled his family in Washington, D.C. There at various times Emanuel operated a cigar store, a restaurant, and shops where dry goods or secondhand clothes were sold. His family was poor throughout these years. At one point he became a secret service agent for the Department of Justice.[40] He was a signer of a petition to the U.S. Congress to establish a Reform synagogue in Washington. On one occasion "Major Lulley carried all his little children picturesquely dressed in Turkish costume to see the

President, who gave him a splendid silver medal, and closely questioned him to ascertain whether Kossuth had been fighting for Independence or to wear the Kingly Crown."[41] A portrait of the Lulley family was sketched by Mary Howard Schoolcraft, the wife of the "world-renowned historian and Christian philosopher, H. R. Schoolcraft." As a close friend of the family she reported that the Lulleys lived "in sorrow and poverty" in Washington for five years. She noted that "this family were Israelites and therefore prejudice followed them."

At the outbreak of the Civil War Emanuel helped organize the Kossuth brigade in the Union army and one son rushed to join the navy; another went into the army. "A little one, named Julius Caesar, only eight years of age, ran away from his father and followed the army, too" but after five months was brought back. One of the eight children was adopted by the Schoolcrafts and later was a very successful merchant in Washington. Another son, Mark, went west to Arizona in 1875 and became a successful mining entrepreneur and acquired the nicknames of "The Wandering Jew" and "The Prospector Pioneer."[42] Mark was a colorful character. In 1900 he captured two bear cubs and took them to Washington. It was an election year and Mark Lulley was a supporter of William Jennings Bryan. He wagered that if Bryan won, he was to be driven from the Capitol to the White House by a team of white horses; if Bryan lost he would walk with the bears to the executive mansion. He ended up walking and was received by President McKinley at the White House—and was given a medal.

Louis Wirth observed that the post-1848 influx of Jews from Austria-Hungary, Germany, and Poland came in such numbers that they soon outstripped in influence the older Jewish settlers. They were, he noted, "sophisticated city people . . . less inclined to stress the religious, and more the social and political issues of the time."[43] This was the case with some but not all of the mid-century immigrants.

A number of the pre-1880 immigrants were rabbis and some of them played an active part in the debates about the direction Judaism should take in America—Aaron Bettelheim, Adolph Huebsch, Solomon H. Sonneschein, Benjamin Szold, Leopold Wintner, and Aaron Wise. These rabbis fit a general pattern: educated first in Jewish schools, they went on to study in both a rabbinical seminary and a secular, German-oriented university, such as those in Prague, Breslau, Vienna, and Berlin, where they were awarded the degree of Doctor of Philosophy. When Sonneschein died, a newspaper in Des Moines called him "the greatest German orator in the

United States, not excepting Carl Schurz," and added that his English was equal to his German.[44]

Few of these rabbis were Orthodox. They tended to be Reform (Neolog in Hungary) or to occupy a middle ground between Reform and the emerging Conservative movement. Except for short stays in New York, most of them settled in smaller Jewish communities in the East, the Midwest, and the South. They took positions in synagogues where German was the language of the members. To what extent these congregations included Hungarian Jews is not clear.

There is no evidence that the rabbis who came as '48ers formed Hungarian congregations; that developed later. The first synagogue established exclusively for Hungarians was founded in Cleveland in 1866, followed by one in New York five years later, but these were not congregations of typical '48ers. They reflected the early arrival of a different kind of Hungarian Jew in the United States. After the Civil War, on the Lower East Side of New York City and the West Side of Cleveland, there were forming colonies of working class people who were forerunners of the mass immigration of the 1880s.

The rabbis who did come here with the '48ers were writers and social activists in addition to their religious functions. Szold and Huebsch had carried their convictions to the point of volunteering for Kossuth's revolutionary army. Szold as rabbi in Baltimore took the unpopular position of advocating freedom for the slaves. Bettelheim worked for prison reform in California. Rabbis wrote for newspapers here and abroad and several of them edited new journals. Consistent with their training in Europe, they published scholarly analyses of biblical texts and Jewish law.

One of the earliest arrivals was Rabbi Mordecai Tuska. He brought his family to Rochester, New York, around 1849. To that community which he served as rabbi, reader, ritual slaughterer, and circumciser, his "most admired accomplishment was his encouragement of cordial relations with non-Jews," and many distinguished Christians visited his synagogue.[45] The rabbi's son Simon is of particular interest.[46] The young man was admitted to the university in Rochester and, while an undergraduate there, wrote a booklet on "The Rites and Ceremonies of the Jewish Worship." It was designed for Christians and had a foreword by the rector of St. Luke's Church. Isaac Leeser gave it a mixed review in *The Occident,* but Isaac M. Wise praised it in *The Israelite.* Wise took a personal interest in young Simon, who wanted to become a rabbi who could give sermons in English rather than German. Simon was appointed professor of Hebrew at a Protestant seminary in Rochester, but left there to study theology at the Jewish seminary in Breslau, where he qualified as a rabbi. He took a pulpit in Memphis on his return and fulfilled Isaac Wise's hope that he would be the first graduate of an American university to become a rabbi in this country.

As for the body of Hungarian Jews in the 1850s and 1860s, little has been written about their practice of Judaism. There are hints here and there. Some joined German Jews in Reform synagogues. Some drifted away from Judaism, marrying non-Jews or converting to Christianity as many of their social group had done in Hungary. An extreme example of this was Gideon R. Lederer, "the forgotten forefather of the Hebrew-Christian church in the United States."[47] Educated by two prominent Czech rabbis, Lederer became a religious functionary and then a businessman near Pest. He was attracted by Protestant missionaries and converted in 1842. Eight years later he came to New York and went to work for the American Society for Meliorating the Condition of the Jews. Lederer became a Protestant missionary to the Jews and published a magazine, but he turned out to be a marginal man, rejected by Jews and not really accepted by Christians.

Before we leave the '48ers, it would be well to look in on Atlanta, where we can gather some impressions of one community as this period came to an end in the 1870s. Hungarian Jews were arriving in that southern city "in substantial numbers" between 1870 and 1880, according to Hertzberg.[48] Most of the immigrant Jewish population were German in origin. In 1870 some eighty-six German Jewish immigrants constituted 35 percent of all Jews in Atlanta whose birthplace was known to the researchers. The Hungarians, numbering twenty-three at the time, made up 9 percent.

In 1866 the German and Hungarian Jews living next door to each other joined in establishing the Concordia Association for recreational purposes. It comprised mostly "successful but not wealthy men" in their twenties and thirties who wanted "to foster the *gemutlichkeit* and cultural heritage of their fatherlands." Their activities, which were "German forms of sociability," included dramatic performances, literary and musical evenings, debates, dances, and cards.

Many of these immigrants had previously lived in other American cities where they had "learned English, acquired knowledge of American ways, and in some cases accumulated sufficient capital to enter business." Among these was William Rich from Kassa in Hungary who opened the first Rich clothing and dry goods store in 1865. Over the next thirty years, as his three brothers joined him, this became one of the largest stores in the Southeast and one of a chain of stores.

In response to the question of why Hungarian Jews left their country for America it can be answered that a small number who arrived shortly after 1848 came as political exiles, fleeing the Austrians, who gripped Hungary with vengeance after the revolution. These refugees came out of fear and conviction. For a larger group—perhaps as many as two thousand—with much the same ideological commitments, there was a desire to enjoy full civil rights as Jews and to improve their material circumstances through the opportunities that America offered. Together the two groups of '48ers came almost entirely out of the middle class Hungarian Jews of the early nineteenth century. They were cosmopolitans and well-educated.

How did the immigrants juggle their identities as Hungarians, as Jews, and as Americans? In general they retained their Hungarian identification. They continued to support the revolutionary movement of Kossuth. They participated in Magyar organizations in New York and were very much a part of the small Hungarian colony there. Several joined other Hungarian colonies in Iowa. But there was also a pull in another direction. The Hungarian-Jewish '48ers did not establish their own institutions. This may have been partly due to the fact that there were too few of them to sustain their own synagogues and societies. But there was another factor that could account for this—the attraction of a German-speaking community already well established in America. That community consisted not only of Gentiles but of German Jews, who by mid-century had created an institutional foundation of their own.

It must be remembered that for the most part the pre-1880 Hungarian Jews spoke German. They had however more than language in common with the Jews and the Gentiles from Germany. "Originally the Hungarian intelligentsia were so closely identified, culturally and politically, with the German element in the United States," Carl Wittke writes, "that an accurate differentiation of the two nationality groups is extremely difficult." Whatever their country of origin, he concluded, Jewish '48ers "became part of the German-American community."[49]

This involvement with Germans must have diluted the strength of the Magyar connection, especially in the Midwest, where there were many Germans and few if any Hungarians. Thus, while some of the Jews held on to their Hungarian connection, they also merged to a considerable extent with the German immigrants. As Jews, the Hungarian newcomers were particularly drawn to the German Jews. They joined the existing German synagogues, and the few rabbis among them were invited to pulpits in those synagogues. By this and by affiliation with organizations, such as B'nai B'rith, established earlier by Jews from Germany most of them retained a bond to their Jewishness. A minority among them ceased to be Jewish in belief and practice and moved off either into Christianity, into the "free-thinking" movements of the day, or into a way of living without formal religious affiliation.

Speaking of all the Jewish '48ers, Korn concluded that this small group "had no concerted, significant influence upon the life of the American-Jewish community or the German-American community. Their personal, individual achievements and influence, on the other hand, were extremely important, for they were an exceptional group of men."[50]

What is clearest is that the Jewish '48ers from Hungary plunged into the business of turning themselves into Americans. Though social acceptance was not always their lot, quite a few of them moved out of New York and made their homes in smaller cities and towns around the country. Some started as peddlers and worked their way into retail and wholesale enterprises. A substantial percentage of them were professionals—journalists, writers, lawyers, physicians, college teachers. Some used handicraft skills they had learned at home and applied them to America's fast-growing industry. And they jumped into the political controversies that were engaging Americans in the second half of the century, including the issues of slavery and the Union.

Before we take leave of the '48ers, we pause to tell the story of three families who in many ways epitomize this remarkable group of people.

★

C H A P T E R   8

Three Families

Much of the quiet drama of the Jews who settled here after the 1848 revolution in Hungary is to be found in the stories of three families: the Heilprins, the Blacks, and the Lovemans. The accomplishments and hardships, the moments of courage and of humor of the '48ers appear in these accounts. Their stories also give us glimpses of middle class Jewish life around the time of the Civil War and illustrate important characteristics of these early immigrants: the speed of their adjustment to America and their rapid rise up the economic and social scale. To facilitate these changes the immigrants made full use of strong, supportive webs connecting them with family and friends. The Heilprins, Blacks, and Lovemans had such a network among themselves, based on common origins in Hungary, friendship, marriage, and financial ties.

These names appeared in the previous chapter, for in each family there was a "true refugee" who left Hungary because he had joined Kossuth's cause and was persona non grata to the victorious Austrians. We begin with Michael Heilprin.[1] His father, Phineas Mendel Heilprin, was born in Poland in 1801—a merchant by necessity and a Jewish scholar by choice. He was a thoroughly Orthodox Jew who studied not only Maimonides but also Arabic and Greek philosophers and Kant.[2] Michael Heilprin studied mostly with his father and by the age of twelve was writing poetry in Hebrew, Polish, and German. This was the beginning of his acquisition of fifteen languages. The family lived in Russian-controlled Poland and in 1842, in the words of Michael's son many decades later, the family decided to move "from the atmosphere of depression that weighed upon downtrodden Poland to that of sunshine and hope in which Hungary was bathed."

The Heilprins went to Miskolc, where Michael opened a bookstore which became a meeting place for liberals. He learned the Hungarian language and began writing poetry that dealt with the Jews' lack of political rights and the Magyars' oppression at the hands of the Austrians. Michael established a reputation as a philologist and Hebraist and simultaneously was well received in the highest political circles of the Magyars. During the revolution he had a post in the Kossuth government, but when the revolt was crushed Heilprin barely escaped capture by fleeing to Paris.

Michael and his wife and children came to Philadelphia in 1856 and he taught for two years in the Hebrew Educational Society. Louis Wirth's comment that the post-1848 Jewish immigrants were more interested in social and political issues than in religion is illustrated in Heilprin, who never joined a synagogue but immediately plunged into American politics. The year he arrived, he turned up at an anti-slavery meeting which was being disrupted by a rowdy bunch of Copperheads. Heilprin mounted a chair in one of the front rows and delivered a scathing denunciation of the disruptors. Accounts vary as to whether he did this in the English he had taught himself in Hungary or in vigorous German. He was assaulted by the ruffians, but his friends were able to rescue him. Four years later there was a less physical but more widely known exchange between Heilprin and Rabbi Morris Jacob Raphall, who had published a pamphlet which marshalled quotations from the Bible to defend slavery. Heilprin wrote an article for the *Tribune* demolishing the rabbi's arguments. After the Civil War he spoke out against a spirit of vengeance toward the South.

The Heilprins' next stop was Brooklyn, where they lived in close association with other Hungarian exiles, including Kossuth's sisters.[3] Their home again became a gathering place for Hungarian liberals. Michael brought a high level of intellectualism and unbounded energy into the beginnings of Little Hungary in New York City. For several years his phenomenal knowledge of history, literature, and other subjects was utilized by the editors of *Appleton's Cyclopaedia*, then undergoing revision.

One of the early points of contact involving these families has been remembered as an anecdote. About 1860, Morris Black and his wife, who had settled in Cleveland, went to visit Hungary and brought back with them twenty relatives and friends. When they reached New York, they took their charges in an open wagon to their friends, the Heilprins. This was only a few years after Commodore Perry had forced Japan to grant an "Open Door" to the United States. When the children of the neighborhood saw this wagonload of oddly dressed foreigners, they screamed that the Japanese were coming. After the immigrants reached the Heilprin home, they unpacked in the backyard and—since they had been permitted to cook on board ship—proceeded to do just that in the Heilprins' back-yard. This proved to be quite embarrassing to the young Heilprin daughters.

In New York Heilprin embarked on a twenty-three-year career as a scholar, journalist, and social activist, and for the second time he learned to write in a new language. Many of those years were spent on the staff of *The Nation,* where he became a respected commentator on political and military affairs in Europe. But his interests were wide ranging. He interviewed General Paez of Venezuela in fluent Spanish; wrote an article on the Ethiopian language; translated Petőfi's Hungarian verses; and published a book of scientific criticism of biblical poetry. For a few years, in Washington, Michael ran a very unsuccessful bookstore, but became friendly with leading intellectuals and diplomats.

The family returned to New York. Heilprin's eyesight was failing and members of the family had to read to him so he could continue with his writing. Though not an observant Jew, Heilprin was deeply stirred by the outbreak of pogroms in Russia in the early 1880s and it was to this cause that he devoted his last years. He threw all his energy into efforts to resettle the Russian Jews in America. Michael was persuaded that they "needed the air of a free country to become successful tillers of the soil" and toward this end he worked through the Montefiore Agricultural Aid Society. He wrote promotional articles, raised funds, worked directly with the immigrants, and tried to establish agricultural colonies in Oregon, the Dakotas, Kansas, and New York State. His efforts on this project exhausted him and he had to withdraw into retirement.

Michael Heilprin counted among his friends Horace Greeley, Carl Schurz, and several professors at Harvard University and maintained a correspondence with Jewish scholars in Europe, such as Heinrich Graetz, Abraham Geiger, and Leopold Zunz. After Heilprin's death, Rabbi Benjamin Szold of Baltimore, a friend and another veteran of the '48 revolution, edited his biblical notes.

Just as Phineas Mendel Heilprin had prepared him for the life of an intellectual, so did Michael transmit to his sons, Angelo and Louis—by very much the same method of home teaching—the intellectual wherewithal for their careers in the worlds of science and letters. Although less is known about their sister Adassa, she was a writer on politics in her own right.

As a young boy in Újhely, Angelo became fascinated with the study of nature and by the time his father was working on the *Cyclopaedia* in New York, the young man was contributing articles on scientific subjects. He returned to Europe to study biology, geology, and paleontology under the leading scholars of the day. By 1880 Angelo was a professor at the Academy of Natural Sciences in Philadelphia and had become a well-known explorer. He worked closely with Robert E. Peary and went with him on expeditions to Greenland. Angelo Heilprin's study of volcanic activity in the Caribbean Basin had a direct and decisive impact on the United States Senate's choice of Panama over Nicaragua as the location for the Canal. In 1900, having achieved a wide reputation as a scientist, Heilprin advocated an international university in which students would undertake cross-national studies as they moved from one country to another.

It was a time of accumulating, categorizing, and disseminating vast stores of new knowledge, and Louis Heilprin followed his father by becoming an encyclopedist. In 1884 Louis was engaged in writing the *Historical Reference Book*, despite the fact that throughout his life he too had weak eyesight and needed his sisters to read practically everything to him. He took on the work of being "general reviser" of the *New International Encyclopaedia* and apparently had an extraordinary ability to correct historical, geographic, and biographical information. Louis had a particular interest in public mass transit and his article in 1892 caused a sensation when he criticized the planning for New York's subway system as being utterly inadequate. He argued for a much more extensive system of underground transportation than the planners projected at that time.

Michael's nephew, Fabian Franklin, was a mathematician and writer, serving as editor of newspapers in Baltimore and New York. Walter Heilprin Pollak, a grandson of Michael, was a lawyer for the "Scottsboro boys" in that famous case in the 1930s involving the legal rights of Negroes.

Michael Heilprin's significance as a writer, encyclopedist, and man of action owe much to the experience and skill he brought with him to America. In common with many other '48ers, he was primed for success in this country.

The ties between the Black and Loveman families go back to the early 1800s when they lived as friendly neighbors in the town of Somos in Sáros County. Five generations of the two families are buried there.[4] The Blacks were well off; for years they had been managers and overseers of an absentee noble's estate and lived in his castle. They were known as "free-thinkers," interested in the revolutionary ideas of the mid-nineteenth century. Across the street in a small two-room house lived the Lovemans, who barely made a living from the town tavern and a bit of farming. They were religious Jews. The Blacks were wealthy enough to have tutors for their children and they invited the Loveman children to study with them. One of their tutors was Adolph Friedlander, who much later came to America, and married into the Black family.

About 1850, when half-starved, defeated Hungarian soldiers were moving about the land, Morris Black and his family decided to leave. Despite their comfortable circumstances, they were unwilling to accept a return to the injustices and repression that the victorious Austrians were reimposing on the country. They left for America with a group of Hungarians under Kossuth's leadership and settled in Cleveland. Morris's brother David and his family also emigrated.

When the Blacks took up residence in Cleveland, Morris and David went into market gardening on the outskirts of the city. Morris's home became a meeting place for visitors and immigrants, among tham Lajos Kossuth and Remenyi, the famous Gypsy violinist, and he became a leader among the growing number of Jewish families from Hungary. One example of his leadership was the work he did in helping to settle new immigrants. In the late 1850s the immigration authorities on Castle Island in New York "learned that Morris Black would look after Hungarians arriving in Cleveland." It was the practice at that time to give identification tags to immigrants and "batches of them [immigrants] were sent to him here, he being named on each card as 'next friend.'" When they arrived, Morris did indeed look after them.[5]

Perhaps the number of arrivals was beginning to exceed his ability to care for them, or it may have been a desire to put this philanthropy on a community basis. In any case Morris Black decided to institutionalize his immigrant aid work. A few people met in his red brick home at the corner of Hamilton and Erie Streets on October 5, 1863, and set up the Hungarian Aid Society. His brother David was among the founders, as was Herman Sampliner, whose name denotes Zemplén County in northeast Hungary.[6]

The Hungarian Aid Society, much like its counterpart being set up at the same time in New York, was based on "the Jewish spirit of humanity, the Hungarian spirit of liberty, and the American spirit of loyalty and patriotism." Its aims actually went beyond assisting newly arrived immigrants; the society was to help the needy, bury the dead, console the survivors, and provide death benefits to widows and orphans. Quarterly dues were thirty-five cents.[7] The society clearly had staying power; in 1913 it was celebrating its fiftieth anniversary.

The early history of the Hungarian Aid Society suggests some limited contact between the '48ers and the "other Jewry," that is, the poor, working class Jews who were beginning to arrive in Cleveland at this time. As happened so often, the settled Jewish community—by now well established and with more resources—assisted the newcomers in getting started. Morris and David Black represented the established Hungarian Jewish '48ers. They saw themselves in this light, judging by two statements in a newspaper account of the founding of the society. One referred to "the political enemies of our exiled Hungarian patriots of '48." The other was the expression of a noblesse oblige sentiment: "The more influential have always aimed to come in personal contact with the beneficiaries and have given them many words of kind advice which have served as an inspiration to them."

In the ensuing years Morris and David Black and their children and grandchildren moved into prominence in Cleveland's economy and polity. In 1874 David began making "cloaks," an enterprise that before long made the Blacks financially successful clothing manufacturers. He died soon after and his two nephews, Joseph and Louis—Morris Black's sons—carried on.

Joseph Black, who had fought in the 1848 revolution and had studied law in Budapest, was active in Hungarian and Jewish activities in Cleveland. In 1887, at a gala festival of all Hungarians in Cleveland, Joseph issued a call for a national federation of Hungarian organizations in the United States; he remained active in the successive, but ineffective efforts to bring this about. The significance of this and his role in financing the largest Hungarian daily newspaper is that the Blacks were serving as leaders for both the Gentile and Jewish Hungarians in Cleveland. Some years later President Cleveland appointed him United States consul-general in Budapest. The younger brother, Louis, had joined the Union army in the Civil War. Before the turn of the century, he and an associate established the Bailey Company, a major department store in Cleveland.

A member of the third generation in the Black family, who bore the same name as his immigrant grandfather—Morris Black—was now on the scene. Born in this country and educated in the law at Harvard, young Morris took a lively interest in the civic affairs of his city. The story of his political activity is told by a close friend, Frederic Howe, who met him when they were both young lawyers in Cleveland bored with routine legal work.[8] At that time the city was beginning to plan a whole new complex of public buildings. Black and Howe saw the possibilities of creating a "splendid civic center" of the kind they had seen in European capitals. As a first step they organized the Beer and Skittles Club, to which they invited journalists. The club met in an obscure Hungarian restaurant, with excellent food, to plot the campaign. In the end they were successful in having their urban planning ideas accepted and implemented. They seem to have attributed some part of their success to a drink they concocted, called "Slivowitz punch," which "seemed harmless but as the dinner progressed, it worked wonders." They served it to the political figures and newspapermen they invited to the club to discuss their proposals.

With one success behind them, Howe and Black talked about running for Cleveland's city council. They flipped a coin and Black entered the election campaign and beat the incumbent, a Republican political boss. Once in the city council, Black was "always on his feet, delivering vitriolic attacks" on the mayor.[9] Or as another writer reported, as soon as Black was elected to the "shabby" city council "he promptly began to air embarrassing questions effectively."[10] His political career was short; he died suddenly while still a very young man. Meanwhile his cousin—Morris Alfred Black—also a Harvard graduate, was beginning a career in Cleveland that brought him to the top of the garment industry as well as to activity in voter registration and city planning.

The Blacks, in short, had moved within fifty years from vegetable farming to the ownership of department stores and garment factories and to significant positions of leadership in the Jewish community, the Hungarian community, and the civic life of Cleveland.

In Sáros County, the Lovemans had been a deeply religious and a poor family. As a boy Bernard Loveman had been the most religious of the children, but then he studied at the university in Kassa and was influenced toward agnosticism by a traveling Polish Jewish philosopher. He longed to be in a land where even free-thinkers could live in peace. Bernard was disturbed by the conditions of the serfs and the peasants and became involved early in the revolutionary movement. When he was in his late thirties, married and the father of five children, Bernard became a scout and courier in the Kossuth army.

When the war was over, there was a price on his head and he left for America. (Bernard's experiences in the Revolution of 1848 were used as the basis for an historical novel, *The Revolt,* written by Leonora Loveman, a great-granddaughter of Morris Black.) His family came later and brought their total capital, a little bag of uncut Hungarian opals. A land huckster got hold of the Lovemans and took their opals in exchange for a piece of property in Michigan on the Owosso River. They lived there in a log house for several years, not well prepared to be pioneers.

In 1854 Bernard Loveman's brother Morris, experiencing financial difficulties in post-revolutionary Hungary, wrote asking for help in getting started in America. Bernard and his wife invited him to come to Owosso. Morris Loveman and his family did not have the money for a night's lodging in Hamburg, so the family took out their bedding—which somehow the immigrants always managed to bring with them—drove their wagon out of town and slept on the ground. Altogether it was a hard journey of three months, during which their youngest child died. At their first meal in America in a boarding house, Morris Loveman, accustomed to the European practice, warned his hungry family that each biscuit or slice of bread would add to their bill. Their money was running short, so each child took only one biscuit. They learned after the meal that slices of bread and biscuits were not counted in America and that they could have had as many as they wanted.

Fortunately members of the Black family came to New York from Cleveland to meet Morris, Eva, and their children and to help them get to Owosso in Michigan. When Morris and his family arrived in Owosso, Bernard was only able to arrange for them to sleep in a wigwam. Morris worked in a logging camp, one daughter found work in the household of a neighbor, and one son found a job in a lime kiln. Bernard and his sons, successful peddlers, initiated the newcomers into the ways of peddling.

A few years later Morris and his family moved to Cleveland, where they tried their hand at the bakery business and manufacturing firecrackers. Following a disastrous explosion in which Morris lost the sight of one eye and hearing in one ear, their next move was to Mt. Pleasant, Tennessee, where they ran a more successful dry goods and notions store. Because of conditions during the Civil War, the Morris Loveman family moved again, this time to Nashville.

Morris opened a wholesale dry goods business, which became the headquarters for immigrants coming from their part of Hungary. Morris would give them a stock of goods, usually without cash payment or any kind of security, and they would be off peddling in the countryside. According to the family's recollections, of the hundreds of people he trusted, only one, a relative, failed to repay his confidence and his loan. By now financially successful, Morris was active in Jewish affairs in Nashville. In 1871 he was engaged with others in organizing the Hungarian Benevolent Society of Nashville.[11] Ultimately he became so well known that a letter addressed to "Morris Loveman, America" found its way to his Nashville address. His son David established a small factory for the manufacture of hoop skirts and corsets. The enterprise prospered and in time he developed a large department store in Nashville.

The Loveman family also illustrates the extent of intermarriage with Gentiles that was occurring among middle class Hungarian Jews. There were apparently Christian Lovemans in Hungary at the time of the '48 revolution and they and two Jewish branches of the family took part in the war.[12] All three branches came to America and kept in touch with each other through weddings and funerals. Some parts of the family, including the one in Nashville, continued as practicing Jews, but there was "a great deal of intermarriage with Christians . . . If they were not observant Jews, they were at least devout believers in Jewish ethics . . . Scholarship and education were of supreme importance."[13]

As the years passed Lovemans could be found in several southern cities. From the beginning they had intermarried with the Blacks of Cleveland and the two families were now joined by close ties of family, financial dealings, and business partnerships. The bond of friendship between the Lovemans and the Heilprins also resulted in a marriage. Adassa Heilprin, the daughter of Michael, married into the Loveman family. Before her marriage she did some writing for the press. Like her father, she wrote political commentaries and in 1872 her articles were published in the *Week* in New York.[14]

In addition to their ties with the Blacks and the Heilprins, the Lovemans united with other families, most of them Hungarian. By the 1880s they formed a large, extended family in Nashville, with relatives throughout the South and the Midwest. Adolph Friedlander, a teacher and scholar, who had been the tutor to the Black and Loveman children in Somos, came to America and married a member of the Black family; their daughter married a Loveman.

Two of the young people in the group that Morris Black and his wife brought to America in 1859 were William and Morris Rich. They were among those thought by the neighborhood children to be Japanese people invading the quiet Brooklyn street of the Heilprins. After the Civil War the Rich brothers, augmented by two more who had followed them to this country, opened stores in several southern cities. The one in Atlanta was a particular success and became a major retail enterprise.[15] The Rich clan mingled with the Lovemans in the ensuing decades.

In short, as one looks over the genealogical chart of the Lovemans, the page is liberally sprinkled with Blacks, Riches, Friedlanders, and a Heilprin. Fannie Loveman, for example, married Joseph Black of Cleveland, described by a member of the family as the very wealthy man who was named an ambassador (actually consul in Budapest) and who endowed Fannie's generation of Lovemans "with high social standing in New York, Washington, and the European capitals."[16]

The same array of names can be seen in the personal papers of Rose Loveman. She kept a gushing, blushing young woman's diary in the late 1860s and a "signature album" that covered the years from 1866 to 1914.[17] One finds in those documents the names of young Riches, Friedlanders, and Lovemans visiting and courting each other and marrying into this expanding web of relationships. It was a sprawling, extended family, one of whose members observed that the large and frequent gatherings meant "great security in being constantly surrounded by loving aunts, uncles and dozens of cousins."

Possibly the largest and most far-reaching gathering of this clan was the fiftieth wedding anniversary of Morris and Eva Esther Loveman held in 1883. The opulence of the new Delmonico Hall in Nashville makes a startling contrast to the wigwam in Owosso, where this couple had lived during their first months in America. "Every Loveman cousin with whom they had kept in touch . . . every countryman, 'landsleute,' in this country . . . all the related Blacks, and those not related, were invited," according to the family memoir.[18] The description of the grand event continues with a translation of a long article in German that appeared January 31, 1883, in "the only Austrian-Bohemian and Hungarian paper in the United States." The paper was published in New York, but its name was not given. About two hundred invitations were sent out. Guests who traveled long distances to Nashville "were lodged and fed in royal manner at their host's expense, until their departure long after the festivities." "Tokay wines, Havana cigars, and carriages were there in abundance."

The Lovemans were escorted to their seats of honor by Louis Black of Cleveland, D. A. Falter of Chicago, and I. Noa of Chattanooga. About one hundred and fifty telegrams were read; a "masterpiece" was received from Gustav Pollack of New York, an author who subsequently wrote a biography of Michael Heilprin. The list of the "most distinguished guests" is lengthy and cities and towns from Atlanta to Milwaukee were represented.

It seems fitting to end this description of the immigrant generation of the Lovemans with the tribute that Michael Heilprin paid Morris Loveman in the epitaph he wrote: "To leave behind an honored name, Forever was his only aim." In reality, Morris and the other immigrants in the family left behind much more. Here we mention only a few of the better known descendants.[19]

Several made names for themselves in the literary world. Amy Loveman, editor and critic, carried on in the tradition of her grandfather, Michael Heilprin. She was a founder and editor of both the *Saturday Review of Literature* and the Book of the Month Club in the 1920s. Robert Loveman, the poet, was known as the "Sweet Singer of Georgia." Dr. Celia Rich, a graduate of the 1898 Vanderbilt Dental School, was the daughter of William Rich (one of the "invading Japanese"). She was one of the first women dentists in the South.

Leonora Loveman has already been noted as the writer of *Revolt: A Story of Hungary for Boys of All Ages*, based on the exploits of Bernard Loveman as a courier in the 1848 revolution. The book was privately printed. According to a member of the family, Leonora was "quite rich and spent most of her adult years globetrotting" and living among intellectuals in Europe and in her "base" in Cambridge, Massachusetts.[20]

David Bernard Loveman Noa was graduated from West Point in 1900. A year later he was leading a landing party on a small island in the Philippines, when they were surrounded. He ordered his men back to their boat; he remained and was captured and killed. A destroyer was named for Noa in World War I; it was sunk off Okinawa in 1944 and a second destroyer bearing his name picked up Lt. Col. John Glenn after his flight through space.

What can be said about the families whose stories are sketched in this chapter? How do they illuminate the immigration and settlement of the Jewish '48ers from Hungary? Heilprin exemplifies those intellectuals who rather quickly moved from the Hungarian world of writers and social activists into the American counterpart. The Blacks came as middle-class people who, despite hardships at the outset, quickly reached the social and economic status they had left in the Old Country. They become leaders in the Magyar and Jewish communities and in the civic life of Cleveland. The Lovemans, poor and religious people in Somos, within one generation had moved from peddling to the ownership of significant commercial enterprises throughout the South.

Critical to much of this upward movement were the mutually reinforcing connections that were built within and between families. Both marriage partners and business partners emerged in this constantly growing web of relations. There is more than one instance of capital funds flowing through these conduits to enable a young cousin or a new immigrant to start up a business or expand an existing one. Moreover, all three families had extensive contacts outside the Jewish community, moving with ease among writers and businessmen, politicians and the upper middle class society which they in effect had joined. In fact, many of them married Christians. Finally, they gave birth and education to an American born generation that found its place in the middle class in the closing decades of the nineteenth century. By that time, however, a very different kind of Hungarian Jew was beginning to arrive in New York in large numbers.

★

C H A P T E R   9

The Big Migration

The arrival of Hungarian Jews following the 1848 revolution was tapering off when a completely different type of immigrant began landing in New York and other ports. This was the beginning of a mass immigration which was gathering momentum even before 1880. Because the two groups of Hungarian Jews were so different, it is important to ask who were the newcomers and how did they differ from the '48ers? Why did they come and how did they get here?

The advent of more than ninety-five thousand Hungarian Jews between 1880 and 1914 can only be understood in the larger context of the massive European movement to America in those years and, within that, the large Jewish migration to the New World. Several important changes converged to bring millions upon millions of Southern and Eastern European immigrants to the United States toward the end of the last century.

Economic dislocations in Europe were displacing large numbers of agricultural workers and creating widespread unemployment. This coincided with a rapid increase in population due primarily to improved health conditions. To these "pushing" forces must be added the stirring of national sentiments and the desire—certainly the case with Hungary's minorities—to be free of political and cultural control by another ethnic group.

A major "pull" factor was the attraction of a country urgently seeking brawn and brains for its proliferating factories, mines, railroads, and offices—offering wages and a standard of living far above that of the rural areas in Europe. The magnetism of America was all the more powerful because this new land, much less encumbered by social and economic rigidities than Europe, offered the hope of greater personal freedom.

American wages were "about five times those of Hungary by 1900."[1] John Kovács spoke for many in the large contingent of Hungarians in Cleveland when he said: "I loved my native country and had no intention of settling here. But after working six days at my first job, I had changed my mind. I had nine dollars the first week, more, much more than the amount I received for one year's service as a farmer's hand in the old country. This was indeed the country of golden opportunity for me."[2]

The rural settlement of America had essentially been accomplished by the end of the nineteenth century. An American historian writes that "by 1900, the first great waves of immigrants, primarily from Britain, Ireland, Germany, and Scandinavia, had reached into the American heartland, and were now yielding to another huge tide of newcomers mainly from eastern and southern Europe."[3]

While these newer immigrants were becoming Americans, what was America becoming? The country was fast taking on the stature and stance of an economic giant. Its farms and factories and commerce were on their way to being the most productive and efficient in the world. By 1870 its manufactures equaled the combined output of France and Germany; by the First World War the United Kingdom could be added to this list.[4] What is more, the United States was moving into position as a major player on the world scene, both in trade and in influence overseas. The Great Powers had divided up the world. America was a late comer to this game of imperial monopoly, a game which was one of the factors edging this country and its allies toward the first of the world wars. Hungary and the United States were to be on opposite sides of that war.

Economic expansion had created families of great wealth and a working class living in deprivation and slums. Industrial growth was punctuated by depressions, unemployment, and industrial unrest. Mine owners in Pennsylvania, finding their Irish workers hard to deal with, were looking to Central and Southern Europe for "cheaper and more docile material" and were actively recruiting workers in Hungarian towns and villages.[5] These conditions were straining America's political system, not yet a hundred years old and barely recovered from a devastating and divisive civil war. The country's ability to govern itself was being tested by huge aggregations of economic power, by the miserable conditions and corruption of its cities, and by dissatisfaction and protest among its urban workers.

The immigrants came with high expectations, but many native Americans were wondering whether the country would be able to fulfill the promises of democracy. And yet conditions in this land must have been far better than in Europe, for more than 22 million people settled in the United States between 1861 and 1920. One tenth of this vast influx consisted of European Jews. The same forces that influenced millions of Christians to leave for America—economic dislocation over there and opportunity over here; population pressure in Europe; and a yearning for social and political freedom—influenced Europe's Jews to emigrate. Two million Jews quit Europe and came to the United States in the space of thirty-five years as a result of these conditions.

The rate of increase in Jewish population in Europe far exceeded that of the non-Jews. For example, the number of Eastern European Jews shot up from 1.5 million in 1800 to 6.8 million in 1900. On the economic side, "industrialization and modern agriculture began to displace the petty merchants, peddlers, artisans, teamsters, factors, and innkeepers."[6] In addition, physical attacks, legal restraints, and restricted economic opportunities drove Jews out of Europe. The devastating pogroms in Russia in 1881 and 1882 following the assassination of the tsar increased the flow of Jewish immigration to this country, though the assumption of a direct correlation between pogroms and emigration seems not to be warranted.[7]

What about the Hungarian Jews? Given their relatively secure and favorable life after the constitutional changes of 1867, why would any of them leave for America? They were not fleeing for their physical safety as was the case with some of the '48ers. The Jews in Hungary did not find it necessary to escape from the same harsh legal disabilities that oppressed Jews in Germany and Russia. Speaking of the Austro-Hungarian monarchy, Oscar Handlin writes that "persecution alone drove no one away . . . On the other hand, when the volume of emigration increased after 1870, it was as high in Austria-Hungary, where there were no pogroms and where government policy was by then relatively liberal, as in Russia where the reverse was true."[8]

In the last quarter of the nineteenth century Jews began to emigrate from Hungary to seek improvements in their economic situation and opportunities for "a better life," a phrase much used by the immigrants. The contrast between their circumstances and those of the Russian and Polish Jews is striking. The poverty and misery of Jews in the lands of the tsar had given rise to a revolutionary outlook, "a passion for transformation . . . yearnings for deliverance."[9] Their suffering had produced an outpouring of ideological movements: Haskalah, Yiddishism, socialism, folkism, Zionism. Amid the dreams of liberation was the hope of help from the Rothschilds and resettlement in the United States or in Palestine. These stirrings of the mind and soul barely brushed against Hungarian Jewry. The misery of Eastern Europe's Jews evoked a strong response from Jews on the Continent and in America and they mobilized their financial and political resources when the worst pogroms erupted in Russia. There was no such intervention in the situation in Hungary; there was no need for it.

Certainly there was anti-Semitism in Hungary. "The new antisemitic movements in Austria-Hungary and Germany . . . drew encouragement from the pogroms."[10] This must have figured in the motivations of some Jews to get out of Hungary. Undoubtedly in 1881 and 1882 they had heard of the events in Russia and in 1894 of the Dreyfus affair in France. But the Hungarian Jews did not have to look that far afield, for in 1882 the disappearance of a Christian girl in the northeastern town of Tiszaeszlár led to the imprisonment and torture of a group of Jews for a year and a half. The story of Tiszaeszlár was widely known. In 1913 it became the subject and the name of a play on the Yiddish stage in New York. Overall, however, anti-Semitism was not perceived by the departing Jews as a significant factor in their decision to emigrate.

Improving one's economic situation was the main driving force behind the departure of Jews from Hungary. This motivation was, at the close of the nineteenth century, also generating a substantial exodus of Gentile peasants, unskilled workers, and miners from Hungary. This stemmed largely from the strains of an underdeveloped economy that was especially depressed in the northeastern area of Hungary. Nearly one-third of all emigrants to the United States from 1899 to 1913 came from eight counties in the northeast, and this concentration was even greater just before the turn of the century.[11] This exodus resulted largely from the "economic and demographic pressures that weighed on the region's population." Much of the northeast was mountainous, poor in natural resources, and low in productivity. Toward the end of the century population growth and improvements in farm technology were creating a surplus population that could not be absorbed—a population that was much attracted by reports from family members and friends who had already encountered some success in America.[12]

Overwhelmingly the Gentiles who left were agricultural workers. Following the enactment of new legislation, everybody wanted to be an independent farmer, and they borrowed money to build houses and acquire equipment and livestock for their small plots of land. These "dwarf holdings" were in part the result of the laws of inheritance, which divided the land among the surviving children. But tax policies and farming methods "could not accommodate these new individualistic aspirations. Indebtedness to tavern keepers, to Jewish moneylenders, and local Protestant and Catholic clergymen mounted relentlessly."[13]

In 1880 the poorer Slovaks of northern Zemplén County began emigrating to America. The Magyars, witnessing "the startling wealth of the Slovaks who returned," soon followed them. For Slovaks, Ruthenians, and other minorities in that area there were, additionally, ethnic-political reasons for leaving the Kingdom of Hungary. In fact, these non-Magyars predominated in the early emigration; for example, in 1899 only one of four emigrants spoke the Magyar language. The year 1880 was a bad year for farmers in Hungary and many Slavic people in the northern mountains left Zemplén County, which was at the center of the heaviest out-migration, and headed for America.[14]

Economic changes were undermining the old patterns. The new railroads, for example, "brought into the countryside new manufactured goods, which destroyed the market for peasant handicrafts. Efforts by political reformers to modernize the Hungarian economy touched even the remote northern and eastern areas, awakening aspirations . . . [and] encouraging the notion that by moving out, a hard-working individual could move up in the world."[15]

The Jews were so thoroughly integrated into this agricultural economy that the out-migration of the peasants left many Hungarian Jews with little choice but to leave. Some were renters of small farming plots and some owned larger holdings.[16] Some were traders or processors of agricultural products. Others were shopkeepers, peddlers, and skilled workers such as carpenters or locksmiths, who were directly or indirectly dependent on the peasants for their livelihood. The same was true for the Jewish professionals—doctors, lawyers, journalists, etc.—in these rural counties.

As the regional economy deteriorated, the economic base of the Jews worsened and the lure of America increased. Julianna Puskás points out that "the first to venture on the great trip were not peasants. It was the shopkeepers and artisans, whose livelihood was threatened by emerging capitalism, who were most receptive to the idea of emigration."[17] Her description clearly fits many of the Jews in Hungary.

Who were the Jews who left and how did they differ from their predecessors, the '48ers? The newcomers were less educated in Western ways. They were poor or lower middle class and more traditionally Jewish in thought and behavior. They were coming not for political reasons, but almost entirely to improve their economic situation. There is little evidence of any interaction between the highly ideological and political refugees of the 1850s and the early working-class settlers. The contrast between the first two waves of Hungarian Jews is caught in Marshall Sklare's characterization of the Jews who came to this country at the end of the last century. He refers to the unsophisticated "little people" from the villages as the "proste yidn" (the common Jews) in contrast to the "sheine yidn" or "genteel" Jews who did not come in large numbers.[18] The new Hungarian immigrants were mostly "proste yidn," though only a minority of them would have used a Yiddish phrase to describe themselves.

That the Jewish emigrants came most heavily from the rural, northeastern part of Hungary can be seen in Map 3. This map shows the distribution of the Jewish population in Hungary in 1910 and the birthplaces of 772 Jewish emigrants to the United States.[19] Tables 2 and 3 give the numbers and the percentages that are represented by the maps.[20]

Hungary was at that time divided for census purposes into nine regions. The northeast and east central regions accounted for 36.5 percent of the Jewish population in 1910, but 70.5 percent of the emigrants in our samples. It is equally clear from our study that Budapest is under-represented among the emigrants. With roughly one-fourth of the Jews, the capital sent only one-seventh of the immigrants to America, and these were not doctors, bankers, or journalists. Nor did the other cities and large towns send many immigrants.

The Jews who left Hungary were, for the most part, from communities where both the general population and the Jewish population were small. Among the 1905 passengers, for example, three out of five came from places with a total population of two thousand or less. As for the size of the Jewish population, Table 5 shows that 71 percent of the 614 passengers we studied came from places with fewer than 1,500 Jews. The table also presents information on the sixteen places with Jewish populations in excess of 1,500.

The Jewish emigrants were essentially a working-class and lower-middle-class group. To test this, we examined the occupations of 102 Jewish passengers from Hungary who arrived in New York in the 1885–1905 period. The largest group consisted of unskilled people—forty-nine "laborers" or "workmen" and four female servants. The next group comprised thirty-nine skilled workers, including five shoemakers, two bakers, several carpenters and butchers, a locksmith, and a sign painter. To these can be added seven male tailors and a seamstress. One man listed himself as a farmer.

Map 3. Areas of Jewish Population and Emigration (Map by Richard B. Gelpke)

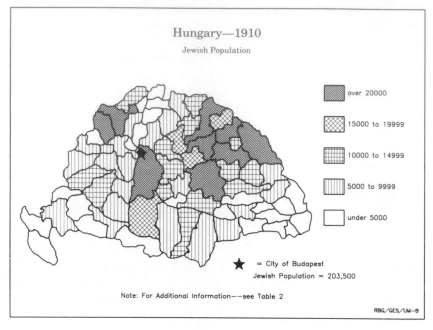

Hungary—1910

Jewish Population

over 20000

15000 to 19999

10000 to 14999

5000 to 9999

under 5000

★ = City of Budapest
Jewish Population = 203,500

Note: For Additional Information——see Table 2

RBG/GES/UM-B

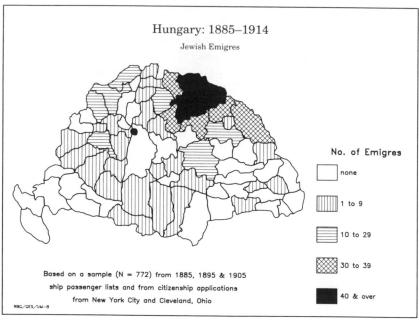

Hungary: 1885–1914

Jewish Emigres

No. of Emigres

1 to 9

10 to 29

30 to 39

40 & over

Based on a sample (N = 772) from 1885, 1895 & 1905
ship passenger lists and from citizenship applications
from New York City and Cleveland, Ohio

RBG/GES/UM-B

There were in addition eleven merchants or dealers, who tended to be older men, but we do not know who might have been a desperately poor peddler from Hommona, a comfortable storekeeper in Kassa, or a wealthy wholesale dealer in Munkács. Seven more men were listed as clerks and of course there was an innkeeper, who emigrated when he was sixty-eight. Professionals barely turned up in the sample. One was a twenty-six-year-old physician and the other at nineteen already classified himself as a writer.

Nor were the Jews emigrating from Budapest different occupationally from those leaving the northeast. Of the eight whose occupations we know, three were skilled workers and two were garment workers. One was a merchant, one a clerk, and one an unskilled worker. None of the Budapest emigrants was a professional.

This information on the occupations of the arrivals refutes the stereotype of the Jewish immigrant as a "merchant." A similar pattern of occupations was found, overall, for Jews who came to America in the 1900–1925 period. "In general merchants comprise only a small proportion of Jewish immigration—Jews brought to America not only six times as many skilled workers as traders, but also more menial laborers and domestic servants."[21]

This is not to say that the flow of middle-class and professional people, so characteristic of the immigration following the Revolution of 1848, ceased after 1880. Data are available on one such group, forty-two rabbis who came from Hungary to the United States between 1880 and 1914.[22] The rabbis came from precisely the same areas of Hungary as the thousands of other Jews entering the United States at the turn of the century. Of thirty-eight known places of birth, thirty-one were located in the northern and eastern counties; only seven came from Budapest and the central area. The rabbis accepted positions all across the country. It is not possible to determine how many went to congregations of Hungarians, Germans, or Eastern Europeans.[23] Many moved several times after they came to America, though the largest concentrations, as one might expect, were in New York, New Jersey, and Pennsylvania. Next in number were the Midwestern cities and towns. A few went south and a handful reached Texas, New Mexico, and California.

The predominant role played by the northeast region of Hungary, as reflected in the sample of passengers who arrived in 1885, declined sharply in the following two decades according to the ship lists. At the same time the proportion of emigrants from Budapest and the east central region increased dramatically, though it is not known how many of these people had earlier moved from the northeast to the center of the country and specifically to Budapest. Among the people who became citizens after 1906, the northeastern part of Hungary was more heavily represented in Cleveland than in New York. Despite these variations, the main pattern of emigration—a concentration in the north and east of the country with an under-representation of Budapest—persisted.[24]

The underlying economic motivation for Jews to leave Hungary was confirmed by the United States consul in Budapest in 1886, though he also fell prey to the stereotype of the "mercantile Jew." He wrote: "The Hungarian Jews who emigrate, usually go singly and quite voluntarily, not at all by any pressure in the shape of policy of state or public opinion. As a mercantile people they go simply because their home does not seem to offer them the necessary field for their commercial enterprize."[25]

While the search for a better economic situation set the overall climate in which most emigrants opted to leave, decisions by individuals and families were often influenced or even determined by more immediate pressures and opportunities. The desire to avoid military service was mentioned as a reason for leaving by some immigrants. Traditionally among Jews in Europe, service in the army was something to avoid at all costs, especially in Russia, where young boys could be drafted for twenty-five years. In part this aversion was because Jews could not follow their religious practices in the military forces and they were often the butt of anti-Semitism. Hungarian Jews, many of whose parents and grandparents had come from other countries, may have carried this attitude with them into Hungary. On the other hand, some wanted to serve in the army and to this day their descendants have pictures of young men proudly dressed in Hungarian uniforms.

Avoidance of army service frequently led to illegal flight to America. The memoirs of the Horowitz-Margareten family describe what happened when Osher Horowitz reached the age of twenty and became eligible for the draft in 1882.[26] Osher's father was ready to follow "the regular practice" of bribing a government official, but the particular bureaucrat responsible for registering Osher turned out to be scrupulously honest and scorned the bribe. The father then wrote out a document for the sale of a cow. The young man showed this to an illiterate border guard "and he walked forever out of the land of Hungary."

Flight was also the solution for people fleeing because of a criminal or civil offense. There were instances of people running from the law in America and returning to Hungary one jump ahead of the sheriff.[27] There was of course the whole gamut of personal misfortunes and great opportunities that always stimulate people to move to another country or continent. Sickness and death, family strife, the financial success of an uncle in New York—all these and more played a part. The dispatches of the United States consular staff in 1880 mentioned the fear of "famine by reason of the failure of the potato crop" and a "serious small pox epidemic" in Zemplén County.[28]

One of the most powerful enticements or prods to get up and leave was the sheer fact that one's relatives, friends, or neighbors were leaving or had left, especially when glowing reports came back from the emigrants. From time to time an emigrant returned for a visit and regaled relatives and friends with first-hand accounts of life in America. This type of "chain migration" accounted not only for much of the emigration, but also for concentrations of people in the United States according to their area of origin in Hungary.

This mechanism of informal social networks was confirmed by a researcher who studied emigration from Hungary through Protestant and Catholic church records. József Gellén traced Hungarian immigrants in certain American cities to their origins and found that they came from well-defined clusters of villages. One map, for example, shows the connections between New Brunswick, New Jersey, and communities in the Zemplén-Ung-Szatmár area of Hungary. Another shows the tie between Toledo, Ohio, and Abaúj-Torna County. Gellén, who studied only Gentile immigrants, points out, however, that the effect of informal networks must be seen in the context of broader economic, demographic, and political forces.[29]

There were also clusters of towns and villages which tended to send groups of Jews to America, sometimes to settle with their Gentile neighbors from the same place. For instance we will find in a later chapter that a group of Jewish and Gentile immigrants from Certizne settled in Wharton, Texas. This tendency is also apparent in ships' passenger lists that record a number of Jews from the same small town or hamlet. This movement as a bloc was reinforced by the agents of shipping lines and of American corporations recruiting immigrants in the Hungarian countryside, sometimes offering a ticket to America for as little as $25.

The small size of the Hungarian-Jewish communities from which most of the immigrants came favored these informal networks for promoting emigration. Of the 116 cities and towns we identified in the 1905 sample of ship passengers, almost half had a Jewish community of fewer than one hundred Jewish inhabitants, as shown below.[30]

Jewish Population	Number of Towns in 1905 Sample
Up to 25	22
25–100	31
101–500	31
501–1,000	15
Over 1,000	17

The tendency to emigrate with familiar people who could provide support for the long journey and the uncertainties of America carried over to the decision as to where to settle. These ties to a "landsman" from the same town helped to shape the organized life of the Hungarian Jews in America, as they banded together to organize synagogues, *landsmanschaften*, schools for their children, and other institutions, thus in rough form re-creating the kehillah of their Hungarian communities.

How many Jews left Hungary in the years between 1871 and 1914? Numbers pose a knotty problem, because the vagaries of both Hungarian and American record keeping make it impossible to give a precise figure. A reasonable estimate would place the number at 100,000.[31] The emigration was almost entirely to the United States, but some went to Canada, England, Palestine, and South America. From 1896 to 1907, on average, more than 98 percent of all Hungarian emigrants from German ports went to the United States.[32]

But we must emphasize that there was no mass exodus of Jews from Hungary. According to our estimates, between 10 and 15 percent of the Jewish population of Hungary emigrated from 1880 to 1910. The rest remained for many reasons. Some were well positioned or at least comfortably situated in Hungary's economy and its cultural life. Others feared the hazards of living in a "trefe" land (an unkosher place) where the observance of Jewish laws and traditions might turn out to be extremely difficult. As will be seen in Chapter 13, the message sent back to the Old Country by some strictly Orthodox people was blunt: Don't come to America. Stay in Hungary.

The rate of Jewish emigration from Hungary is comparable with that of Galicia and Russia, but well below Germany and Rumania. Statistics on the

Austro-Hungarian monarchy are not useful in estimating Jewish emigration from Hungary, since they do not distinguish between the Jews of Galicia and those of the Kingdom of Hungary.[33] Between 1881 and 1900, the Jewish emigration rate from Galicia was estimated at 12 percent by Raphael Mahler, but was said by Lloyd Gartner to be the highest in Eastern Europe.[34] Russia's rate was 15 percent on the average for the period 1898 to 1914.[35]

By contrast a substantially higher proportion of Jews left Germany and Rumania. The Jewish community in Germany lost at least a quarter of the population it would have had if no emigration had occurred.[36] Nearly 30 percent of the entire Jewish population of Rumania migrated to America before 1914; the number was estimated at 75,000.[37]

When Jewish emigration is compared with Gentile emigration from Hungary, it would appear that Jews left at more than twice the rate of Gentiles for the period 1899–1913. Puskás's data for immigration from Hungary to the United States from 1899 to 1913 show the rate to be 4.5 percent of total population.[38] Clearly this figure overwhelmingly represents Gentile emigrants. Comparatively, the rate of Jewish emigration was even higher in the early stages of the migration. Before 1890 even in absolute numbers it appears likely that more Jews than non-Jews left Hungary. Among the Slovaks and Ruthenians, for example, often "some enterprising Jew first became aware of the land of promise across the Atlantic, explored and reported on it, and thus set the stream of immigration flowing."[39] That the Jews were well-represented among the early immigrants from Hungary is supported by a head count we made of passengers on ships docking at New York. Jews predominated in the 1885 sample but declined steadily in the succeeding twenty years. By 1905 the Gentiles outnumbered the Jews on these ships better than two to one.[40]

The large-scale immigration from Hungary peaked in the years between 1902 and 1906 and rapidly tapered off as the First World War came closer. The war cut off all movement between the United States and Hungary, but the decline in migration between the two countries was already under way. Ideological positions and governmental policies on international migrations shift with changes in economic and social conditions. This is true of both sending and receiving countries. And so it was with Hungary and the United States. Between 1880 and 1914 certain sections of Hungary, primarily in the non-Magyar areas, experienced a loss of population. This was seen in the decrease in the numbers of young people, males particularly. It was the result not only of migration overseas but shifts of population within the country itself, a movement that also involved Jews. There had been seasonal movements of agricultural workers within Hungary for some time, but now people were moving from the rural areas to the cities, from which a portion again moved, this time to America.

The general emigration from Hungary raised wages and also brought in American dollars in the form of remittances from hard-working immigrants in the United States.[41] But there were complaints from landowners that the rural labor supply was being depleted. Further, it was said that the returning émigrés, having experienced open political debate and exposure to leftist organizations in America, were no longer respectful toward established authority when they resettled in Hungary.

The Dillingham Commission, established in Washington to investigate the immigrant situation, has been widely criticized for its biases, especially those directed toward the immigrants from Central and Southern Europe. Still it is interesting to see what the commission wrote in its 1911 report:

> The Commission was informed that there had come to be a serious danger of the depopulation of certain parts of northern Hungary because so many of the lower classes were emigrating to America. It was stated that there were villages with so few able-bodied men among the inhabitants that there was nobody to harvest the crops. The small gentry and landed proprietors were in great trouble, as they had nobody to work their estates for them.[42]

The report goes on to say that the exodus appears to have led to higher land values, increased wages for farm workers, and improvements in farming methods and machinery.

The Hungarian government, pressured by landowners who lacked workers, went through the motions of passing anti-emigration laws before 1900, although in reality it favored free emigration. All this happened at a time when American policy was encouraging Europe's "huddled masses" to enter. But the pressure for restricting emigration was building up in Hungary as in other parts of Europe where "the 'surplus' populations were already safely overseas, and imperialism, the growth of nationalism, and war preparations were all very much in the air."[43] Hungary and the United States were both making a 180 degree turn in their attitudes and actions toward the movement of people to America. The government in Budapest began in earnest to clamp down on emigration as war approached. In America industrial conflict, depressions, and social tensions with the immigrants were being expressed in strident demands for a stop to immigration.

United States policies toward aliens were tightened at the turn of the century, in part because of opposition to the entry of unskilled workers willing to work for extremely low wages, partly because of corruption in voting by noncitizens, and partly because of panic over the assassination of President William McKinley in 1901 by an anarchist. In addition, there was concern that the new immigrants from southern and eastern Europe were not making serious efforts to become citizens. In fact "the proportion of aliens among all foreign-born adult males grew from 43 percent in 1900 to 55 percent in 1919."[44]

Nativist sentiment—nurtured by certain intellectuals, most segments of organized labor, and some conservative groups—was on the rise in the United States. From 1907 to 1911 the ostensibly "scientific" Dillingham study of immigration, undertaken by a national commission, found ample "evidence" for its opinion that the immigrants from Central and Southern Europe were inferior to those of Northern and Western Europe. The Congress responded in 1921 and 1924 and in effect slammed the door shut on those immigrants the commission had found to be "undesirable." But before that, the outbreak of war in 1914 made the issue moot: the movement of people from Hungary to America simply stopped for four years and barely picked up after the war.

Before we inquire into the experiences of the immigrants in America, it will be of interest to see how they got here and what arrival meant to the "greenhorns." The journey to America could begin on a train, a wagon, or on foot. People living away from the main routes might have to take a wagon or coach or walk to the nearest railroad station. Most rail lines converged in Budapest, though some ran directly to the German ports or to Fiume on the Adriatic, which the Hungarian authorities were trying, quite unsuccessfully, to promote as their own port of embarkation.

The sale of steamship tickets was by all accounts steeped in corruption and fraud in Central Europe. Even in Hungary, with its stricter regulations and licenses governing agents, exploitation of migrants persisted.[45] Most Hungarians departed from Hamburg prior to 1890. After that Hamburg's share of the immigrant trade declined and Bremen as well as LeHavre, Antwerp, Rotterdam, and other ports were used more extensively. From Hamburg and Bremen the fare was about $34.[46] Some people saved $9 by going to England and taking a ship from Liverpool. A number of Hungarian Jews stayed for a time in England en route and some remained there.[47]

Edward Steiner, who left Hungary as a youth, has left sharp recollections of his travels. By the time he wrote his books, he had made more than thirty trips to Europe to study the problems of immigrants and had become an expert on immigration and an advocate for improving conditions. From Steiner's hometown, Szenica, in western Slovakia, it took one day by "omnibus," four days by railroad, and two weeks by sea to reach the United States. He left when he was nineteen, soon after his graduation from the University of Heidelberg, starting the journey without proper documentation. On his way to Bremen he stayed at lodging houses which charged much and gave little and where sharpies preyed on the emigrants.[48] He was told the police would arrest him and was offered protection for money.

On the outskirts of Hamburg the Hamburg-American Line maintained for steerage passengers a migrant "station" which was a walled and guarded village. Here the new arrivals were examined, ticketed, washed, fumigated, and fed. A brass band played the tunes of various fatherlands every afternoon. A hotel offered a higher level of facilities for the better-paying passengers. The passage itself, however, was for most a confinement in the worst of conditions:

> The day of embarkation finds an excited crowd with heavy packs and heavier hearts. An uncivil crew directs the bewildered passengers to their quarters . . . The 900 steerage passengers crowded into the hold of so elegant and roomy a steamer as the Kaiser Wilhelm II . . . are packed like cattle. The stench becomes unbearable, and many of the emigrants prefer the bitterness and danger of the storm to the pestilential air below.[49]

> One can always locate the steerage without a chart . . . The odor of strong disinfectants, mingling with that of various vegetables, the smell of sheepskin coats and of booted and unbooted feet, the cries of many children, the rough answers of sailors and stewards, and the babel of guttural languages are all waymarks, if any are needed.[50]

Steiner explains that tin utensils and a thin, gray cotton blanket were given to each steerage passenger. When the bell rang for food, the crowd pushed forward with their tin pails. However, despite storms and seasickness, there was both fellowship and hope among the people. Bohemians sang and a clown with an accordion kept up the spirits of the steerage passengers.

The First World War interrupted the flow of families. One woman recalled that her husband who arrived here in 1914 did not like America and wanted to return, but the war cut him off from his wife and four children for six years.[51] In 1920 his wife learned that she could rejoin him. Worried about nonkosher food on the ship, she took along a large pot of jelly and bread she had baked. Of the food served on the ship, she and the children ate only the herring. She also brought eighty-five pounds of bedding and feather quilts; bedding seems to have been a standard item that the immigrants brought with them.

Such conditions sometimes brought about changes in the travelers even before they arrived in the New World. A woman who sailed as part of a group of Orthodox Jews, very observant of religious requirements, related that at night she would remove her *sheitl*, the wig that covered the short hair of married women to make them less attractive to other men. One night the young man who was traveling with her family became seasick and vomited in her *sheitl*. From that time on, she never wore a wig and thus accidentally became less observant of the Orthodox ways.[52]

Few immigrants were not involved in bringing over relatives. Peddlers on this side of the ocean served as middlemen, selling a "shiff's carte" on time payments to any immigrant they could persuade.[53] One-way tickets for $30 were sold for $40, to be paid off one dollar a week. Surely this would today be called scalping, but buying on time meant that a father working in a garment factory did not have to wait for a year to bring over his family.

Descending from a ship after two weeks at sea and putting a foot on the soil of America was a time of turbulent feelings—excitement, hope, apprehension, confusion. One immigrant, invited by cousins to come to Pittsburg, Kansas, ended up in Pittsburgh, Pennsylvania. He found other relatives there and stayed two years before getting to Kansas.[54] Some separations were longer. Sigmund Singer came to America in 1896 from that part of Hungary that is today Rumania, leaving his brother Victor at home. It took thirty-five years for them to discover each other through a newspaper story about Sigmund's prowess as a walker. One was in Memphis and the other in New York. Sigmund did not even know that his younger brother had come to America.[55]

Once ashore, the new arrival faced a phalanx of officials, most of whom spoke only English. One can easily imagine the scene as immigrants knowing not a word of English tried to convey to officials of Yankee or Irish background the spelling of their names and the places from which they came. The officials must have had considerable difficulty tuning into the pronunciation and the spelling of Hungarian towns and names. For instance, an O'Connor or a Cartwright working on the docks could see "sz" in writing but he would hear "s". He would see "s" but hear "sh". For "cz" he would hear "ch" as in "much" and for "zs" he would hear the sound that begins the name of Zsa Zsa Gabor.

Most frightening was the medical examination. "Mechanically and with quick movements we were examined for general physical defects and for the dreaded trachoma, an eye disease, the prevalence of which is greater in the imagination of some statisticians than it is on board immigrant vessels," writes Steiner. "Already a sifting process has taken place; and children who clung to their mother's skirts have disappeared, families have been divided, and those remaining intact, cling to each other in a really tragic fear that they may share the fate of those previously examined."[56] Most of those rejected for trachoma, for some unexplained reason, were Jews.[57]

The Inspectors had to fill out a "Record of Aliens Held for Special Inquiry" and on the list for the *Princess Alice* arriving in New York on May 20, 1905, can be found an entry about the Platzner family from Hungary. Jacob, age fifty-five, had come with his wife and four children, ranging in age from one year to ten years old. He was to meet a brother-in-law in New York. The notation reads: "Dr. cert. varicose veins of leg, hernia." The family was marked for deportation.

Steiner and a group concerned about immigration visited the disembarkation of the *Wilhelm II* one day. Contrary to the expectations of the delegation, the immigrants appeared to be decent, clean, ordinary people, not the dregs of society—"evil-smelling, criminal elements"—several of them had expected to find. Steiner goes on to praise two commissioners of immigration appointed by President Theodore Roosevelt who made substantial improvements in policies and procedures at the docks.[58]

By no means were all arrivals confusing or disheartening. There must have been tremendous joy when family members, some separated for years, were reunited. On one occasion a man and his wife were met by relatives who had saved up enough money to take them out on the town. After a night of extravagant dining, drinking, and the Yiddish theater, the "greenhorn" said to his brother-in-law, "So, this is America! How about doing this tomorrow?"[59] In the same source we learn that two young men were on their way from Hungary to Texas. As soon as they reached New York, they took the first step in modernization and Americanization: changing their names, as doubtless their families had years before under pressure from the Germans or the Magyars. Yosef Schwindler became Joe Schwartz and Shmuel Josefavitz became Sam Joseph.

If immigrants were heading west out of New York, they went to a hall with money-changers and travel agents—or to a detention room to see whether they might become public charges. In these situations $10 to $20 might make the difference between deportation and entering the country, unless a relative were meeting the immigrant. The marginal notes the inspectors made on their lists include such jottings as: "Moritz Cohen. Brother to meet him. $6 on hand" or "Lorincz Schwarcz. $24. To be met by brother-in-law" or that concerning Julia Kohn, 39, arriving with seven children who was "meeting husband."

Coping with life in America began immediately for the new arrivals. The story of one immigrant's first days in New York begins when he stepped ashore, a young man of about eighteen with only a few coins in his pocket. Having had nothing fresh on the ship, according to the account that has come down through the family, he spent his money on an apple. He had a slip of paper with the name of a woman who was a distant relative. Without carfare he walked uptown to her boarding house. His new landlady advanced him the money to buy a kit of pins, ribbons, and "notions." Off he went to a supply house to buy his first peddler's pack. He left there just behind an experienced peddler. The narrative continues in his own words recorded when he was ninety:

> We started out right in front of the store where we bought the goods. A car was running and he wanted to go across 42nd Street. I didn't ask questions but I jumped on the car—he was bewildered—a horse car. Well, he had no choice, he had to pay. As we came there near the ferry he says, "Well, you can start right here." I says "No, I wouldn't start right here. I will go with you." He says "I am going way out in the country." I said "Never mind, I'll go with you."
>
> So he had no choice and I went with him on the ferry and he had to pay another fare. We came to the other side . . . Wechauken on the other side . . . and he said, "Here you can start." My whole goods was needles and pins and, in the olden times, wicks, which they used for lamps. Well, my whole stock amounted to, I judge, about $2, maybe less. I started out and he went away with another car and to my luck the first house I came to—I couldn't talk a word of English—so I approached them in German.
>
> "Wollen Sie mir etwas abkaufen? Ich habe das sehr gute Ware. Ab Sie sprechen doch Deutsch?" (Would you like to buy something? I have very good things. Do you speak German?) I was lucky and she was lucky, so the first thing she asked me was how long I am here in this country. I answered her I'm here already—that was the 5th of July—I came on the 3rd, so I'm here already the third day.
>
> "Ach, du lieber Himmel, wie kommt dass das Sie soll dem dritten tag araus gehen und verkaufen!" (My heavens, how is that on your third day you are already out selling!) So she took a few things for herself and she didn't ask me the

price but she handed me a half-dollar and a quarter. Whatever it was—I didn't know the money—but I saw it was kind of big coins.

Well, I surely finished the day and came back to my own place . . . I was so proud and I came in and said to that misses of mine where I stopped, "Geben Sie mir etwas zu essen. Ich will nicht schlaffen heit abend, aber will ich essen." (Give me something to eat. I won't sleep tonight but I will eat.) I took the money that I had and I showed her that I've got money to pay her . . . Well, surely from that minute on, she was treating me royally.[60]

Not all arrivals went smoothly. Steiner writes with passion about the experiences that awaited some immigrants at the port. "Roughness, cursing, intimidation and a mild form of blackmail prevailed to such a degree as to be common." Money changers were crooked; inspectors sought bribes and sexual favors. But however trying the passage, however intimidating the immigration procedures, however apprehensive and strange the first days, the immigrants came with great hopes. And they kept coming.

We have seen that these immigrants were essentially the "little people" from the towns and villages of Hungary. Their primary reason for emigrating was to better their economic situation, which was deteriorating in the late 1800s. They were working-class and lower middle-class people, neither as well educated nor as skilled as the '48ers who preceded them. They were more Orthodox in religion and less at home in the intellectual world that the Enlightenment had ushered in.

In common with the '48ers, the newcomers in the Big Migration were needed in the fast-growing economy of the United States. But there the similarity ended, for the '48ers started half-way up the occupational ladder. For the most part the Hungarian Jews who came just before and after the turn of the century entered America's economic system on the bottom rung. Whereas the first "wave" at mid-century was exceedingly small in number, the Big Migration brought almost 100,000 Hungarian Jews to the United States, a fact that made a difference in where and how they settled in their new land.

★

CHAPTER 10

Urban Colonies

The majority of Hungarians who crossed the ocean to America did not intend to remain here. But was this true for the Jews among them? Where did the Jewish immigrants who came after 1880 settle? And how did they make a living? These are the questions we consider in this chapter as we follow the immigrants into the largest Hungarian colonies and then into small-town America, which is discussed in the next chapter.

Although Jews and Christians were leaving Hungary essentially for the same economic reasons, their aims in coming here were very different. By and large the Christian emigrants were men of working ages coming with the idea of working a few years and then returning to their villages. This was the outlook of a sojourner. The Jewish emigration was a movement of people intending to settle permanently in America. This difference in orientation was an important factor in their adjustment to this country and in the relationship between the Hungarian Gentiles and Jews.

For the Jews from Hungary this was essentially a family migration, as can be seen in Table 6, which shows the proportions of family heads, wives, and children among the immigrants studied. It should be noted that 35 percent of the 942 people studied were children under fourteen years of age and 19 percent were couples. Overall, the profile of family roles and of ages did not vary substantially by the year of arrival. Although the mothers living on New York's East Side in 1880 were young, it was already apparent that they were having large families. The twenty mothers in our sample who were under thirty years of age already had thirty children among them. The thirty women who were thirty and over had 127 children.

The proportion of males is another indication of immigrants' intentions, for men coming without women suggests a temporary stay. For the period 1899 to 1913 the proportion of males in the total Hungarian immigrant population, which was overwhelmingly Christian, was 68 percent. The corresponding figure for Jewish males in our passenger samples was 50 percent. In New York, where Jews predominated among Hungarians, there were more women than men in 1910; women numbered 41,401 and men 35,224.[1]

Although this was basically a family migration, two out of five of the immigrants on the ships came alone. Some of them were in their early teens, but predominantly those who came alone were of working age, though they were somewhat younger than the farm workers and the miners from the Christian communities in Hungary. In short, the Jewish immigrants were for the most part young people coming to the United States to work, to settle, and to raise families. One sees this clearly with Bernard Popovick, a tinsmith from the Croatian town of Zupanja, who came here "because he wanted to leave the old rotten Europe where the clouds of war had already begun to gather. In America with hard work and savings he would be able to give his children security and the best life. This he achieved when seven years later his wife and children joined him."[2]

This quotation from the tinsmith of Zupanja makes a critical point about Jewish migration to America. Whatever the differences among them, there was a significant respect in which the Hungarian Jews closely resembled the Jewish immigrants from Germany and Russia. The overwhelming majority of them came here not as sojourners but as settlers. The German-Jewish influx has been described as "mainly a movement of the young, the unmarried, and the poor."[3] Compared with their Gentile countrymen, the migration of both the Hungarian and Russian Jews was decidedly more family based.[4]

While the dominant motivation was to settle here, some Jews went back to resume their lives in Europe. The rate of return of Jews to the Austro-Hungarian Empire including Galicia, Jonathan Sarna found, was 12 percent before World War I, compared with 7 percent for Russian Jews.[5] This should be compared with the much higher rate of 32 percent for non-Jews from Hungary. Sarna, who argues against the "myth of no return" has this to add: "Revealingly, Jews overall were almost twice as likely to return to Austria-Hungary, where they were treated comparatively well, than to Russia, where they faced persecutions and privation. In 1912, a recession year, the return migration rate among Austro-Hungary's Jews hit 19.7% (10,757 immigrants; 2,121 returnees)." He notes that the Jews from Austria-Hungary "journeyed to and from America many times." As far as Hungarian Jews are concerned, the numbers call for further research since Sarna's data include Jews from Galicia. In addition, they do not measure how many "returnees" to Europe ultimately settled in America. A most poignant account of this last possibility, in a letter written by Handa Stark, arrived in the mail one day while this book was in preparation:

My grandfather Getzel Fried was a farmer. He had five children. When the children got married they all lived on the farm. The farm was not big enough to support them all. So my grandfather, grandmother, my mother (who was 16 years old), and her youngest brother came to America.

They arrived at Donora, Pennsylvania, where some of the family lived. They were mostly peddlers. The year was 1914. My mother did not like Donora because it was a small town and she thought that in a big town they would have better opportunities. They had very little money but they were very proud and wanted no help from anybody. They moved to Detroit, Mich.

My grandfather bought a little pushcart and sold fruits and vegetables. My grandmother was a good balabuste [homemaker]. She took in a boarder; in the basement she kept some geese and force-fed them [this was customary in Europe] until the neighbors complained about it and she had to stop.

My mother could do very fancy stitchery but when she saw how she was being exploited she tried her luck someplace else. She applied for a job at Ford Motor Co. She spoke German well and this helped her with her interview. She got the job and she earned $6 a day. This was big money because in those days the wages were $6 for a whole week. She was very diligent and they soon called her the best worker in her department. Soon she got a job for her father. He was working on the construction of a ship. . . . My mother soon wrote to her relatives in Donora about the possibilities in Detroit. They all resettled except one cousin.

When my mother used to travel on the streetcar she met a lot of other Jews from Russia. They were surprised that she was reading Hungarian books. They supplied her with Jewish literature and the classics written in Yiddish. They had a much stronger Jewish identity.

The years were going by and my grandfather started to get lonesome after his married children and grandchildren. When they did not want to come to the U.S. the family packed up and sailed for Europe. By now everybody spoke English and they saved up over 5000 Czech korona. When they arrived at their home town, there was a big change. The first world war ended, it was 1921 and the town Szőllős where they lived was called Vclky Sevlus and it belonged to the Czechoslovak Republic.

Life was good but unfortunately did not last too long. My mother got married in 1922. She always talked about going back to America. I grew up on wonderful tales that she told me about the wonderful country on the other side of the ocean called America. To a small child that I was it was especially impressive when I heard that in America they buy ice cream in buckets or tubs. At that time meat was 14 cents a pound and bread was 7 cents a loaf.

Well it took another war and a lot of praying and dreaming and we made it back to America, this time (with my mother, my father, my brother and myself). I was 20 years old. After a short stop in New York where my father's sister lived, we arrived in Detroit. The family still lived there. They were all well off; some worked all their lives for the Ford Motor Company. They all were honest, religious people. They belonged to Bne Moshe synagogue. We live in California.

Even if the price of meat is not 14 cents and a loaf of bread is much more today than 7 cents I still think that it is a wonderful country to live in where we experience such freedom—religious freedom that is unheard of anyplace else in the world except Israel.

About my mother, she was a poet. She was an artist (at 60 she started to paint beautifully). She was a marvelous person. When she was 16 she wanted to enroll in a teachers college. She was rejected but told that if she converted, she would be accepted, all expenses paid. She refused and came to America.

But there were also people who simply did not like the Promised Land once they saw it firsthand. Some Orthodox Jews were shocked and repelled by the state of Judaism in America. On this subject there was a man who spoke out loud and clear. Moses Weinberger (1854–1940), a staunchly Orthodox rabbi, left Hungary for reasons that are not known.[6] In 1887 Weinberger published a book in Hebrew—in itself a clear sign that he was addressing the learned and the pious—inveighing against the conditions he found here. The immigrants' infatuation with democracy led to an egalitarianism that placed men without piety, learning, or wealth in leadership positions in Jewish life. Their synagogues were becoming "show palaces." Separation of church and state meant that, unlike Hungary, the government here could not require the payment of taxes to the Jewish community. Long hours of work and low pay disrupted not only religious observance but family life as well. The commercialization and corruption of such requirements as kosher slaughtering were rampant. Women who only recently "ate salty fish and stinking lentils in Jaszmigrad" were bustling about on the Sabbath and on holidays buying only the best and the newest things. In part Weinberger's book was directed toward young rabbis considering emigration to America. His advice was unequivocal: "stay home."

Every indication we have suggests that the post-1880 immigrants were religious Jews, most of them Orthodox in their belief and observance, though there may have been followers of the Neolog and the Status Quo Ante movements. Judging by replies to questionnaires to the families of immigrants, some were thoroughly secular Jews. Adherents of the Hasidic movement came as individuals or families in the Big Migration, but did not bring their rebbes or zaddikim with their "courts" and family dynasties. Consequently, they were not so successful, as they were later, in transmitting the Hasidic way of life to the next generation.[7] Hasidim began coming as organized communities after World War II.[8]

Where did the newcomers settle after 1880? Most Hungarian immigrants went from the northeast of their country to the northeast of the United

States. Both their points of departure and their destinations were largely determined by economic forces—over there depressed conditions and over here the quickening growth of manufacturing, mining, and commerce. This burst of economic activity was concentrated in cities that stretched from New York to Illinois.

Table 11 shows the cities with the largest numbers of Hungarian immigrants in 1910 and the number of Hungarian organizations in each city. Clearly ethnicity played a part in this process, drawing the new-comers toward certain localities rather than others. Once a few of them had made a "beachhead" in a town or an urban neighborhood, others were attracted by the magnetism of language, family, religion, and place of birth.

This broad description applied to both Jews and Christians, but the specifics were different. Catholic and Protestant peasants, miners, and skilled workers were looking for a few years of work at good pay in order to send money home and then to rejoin their families in Hungary. These opportunities were to be found in the factories and especially the mines of Pennsylvania, New York, Ohio, and New Jersey.[9]

"Skilled workers, artisans, shopkeepers, the small number of intellectuals, and the déclassé elements all headed for New York City, Chicago, and the western half of Cleveland," Puskás writes.[10] This description fits many but by no means all of the Hungarian Jews who immigrated and who were attracted toward already existing centers of Jewish population. Their two main points of concentration were New York and Cleveland. But this is an oversimplification, for a significant proportion of the Jews settled in other large cities and in small localities often in the same mining and manufacturing towns as the Gentile Hungarians. The Jews scattered more widely across the country than the Christians, some moving to the Far West and the South, whereas the Christians lived and worked almost exclusively in the factory and mining towns of the Northeast.

It is important to understand not only where the Hungarian Jews lived but also with whom they lived. The first settlers had come at the same time as their Gentile compatriots and together these '48ers had established in New York City the first Little Hungary. The Jews who arrived in the 1860s and 1870s found already established settlements of German Jews and had little difficulty in integrating with them. In the first phase of the Big Migration about 1880, the Jewish and Gentile Hungarians lived close to each other in many places and retained their "Magyar" connection. But the Hungarian Jews were also in close contact with Jews from Germany, Russia, and Poland and their institutions and lifestyles. They were, in short, pulled in different directions.

A number of large cities, in addition to New York and Cleveland, had recognizable Hungarian "colonies." Here we touch briefly on Chicago, Philadelphia, and Boston, relying primarily on the limited information that is available concerning the establishment of synagogues and secular organizations. The following chapter describes the settlement of Hungarian Jews in smaller cities and towns.

Chicago.[11] The German-Jewish synagogue Rodef Sholom, founded in 1871, soon had Hungarians in its congregation.[12] In the same year the latter formed the Hungarian Charity Society. Before the end of the decade the Oesterreich-Ungarischer Kranken Unterstitzung Verein (Austrian-Hungarian Sick Benefit Society) was organized by Hungarian Jews. By 1884 ten men were able to meet on Maxwell Street in the home of one of their *landsleit* to organize Congregation Agudath Achim, the first Hungarian congregation. Within a few years they bought a Baptist church for their synagogue.

In the mid-1880s two small Hungarian societies—Osah Chesed ve-Emes and Sheveth Achim—merged to form Congregation B'nai David Ohave Zedek. In the early years of the new century four Hungarian organizations named for Theodor Herzl, the Zionist leader, "built their own meeting hall and conducted High Holiday services." One synagogue occupied the third floor of a funeral establishment and was used by both the Czechoslovakian and the Hungarian Jews. Within the Hungarian community were a press, a public schvitz (steam bath), a private schvitz, and many restaurants. The center of these activities at the turn of the century until the 1920s was on Division Street.[13]

A women's society organized in 1905—the Woman's Auxiliary of the Hungarian Charity Society—offers an interesting example of the concerns and the welfare philosophy of immigrants and their children at that time:

> Immediate aid is given worthy persons and families in distress, who are assisted until they can gather up the thread of existence once more. The directors personally attend to investigations.
>
> The business education of girls of dependent families has been paid for, in order that they might become self-supporting. This money has been supplied as a loan, and the girl assisted allowed to return this amount advanced without feeling that she has received charity, but that the hand of a friend has grasped hers and she has received encouragement to go on.[14]

Other organizations were set up (see Table 12), and by the first decade of the new century there was a Hungarian-Jewish presence in Chicago.

Philadelphia. A parallel development took place in Philadelphia, where the first arrivals from Hungary came in the 1870s.[15] The first Hungarian shul, Emunath Israel, was organized in 1880 and was followed three years later by Oheb Sholom. Both congregations were located in South Philadelphia near 5th and South streets. The two synagogues merged in 1888 and soon bought a theater, which was renovated to hold six hundred men and five hundred women. In 1892 Moses Weinberger, the sharp critic of the state of American Judaism, became the rabbi. This Orthodox Hungarian shul lasted until the 1960s.

Before the century ended, Philadelphia had a number of Hungarian-Jewish organizations. The Austro-Hungarian Charity Society was established in 1890 with a membership of "several hundreds."[16] There was a Volkfest Verein and at least three "beneficial societies," named for the poet and revolutionary Petőfi, for the Emperor Francis Joseph, and one called simply Anshe Hungaria (Men of Hungary). Interestingly, Russian Jews formed a Michael Heilprin Lodge of Bene Berith to honor "an ardent worker and savant."

Boston. Although there is a report of "many Hungarian Jews" in Boston, only a scant record is left.[17] The First Hungarian Society was holding meetings in 1892 at 24 Hayward Place, but its origins are not known.[18]

Under the headline "Austro-Hungarian Ball A Brilliant Success," a colorful account of a costume ball in 1903 states that the sponsoring organization had been holding these gala events for twelve years.[19] Thus we can assume that the First Austro-Hungarian Benevolent Association was in existence in 1891 if not before. In any case, over a thousand members and friends—attired as Little Bo Peep, Uncle Sam, cowboys, and Carmen—danced in a carnival atmosphere in a hall decorated with the red, white, and green colors of Hungary. Not all the dancers, however, were Jewish, or Hungarian for that matter; the prizes for best costumes were won by a Miss Schwartz, a Mr. Hartman—and John Murphy.

Thus, there was a Hungarian-Jewish presence in these three cities of the East and Midwest—as well as in other places such as St. Louis—beginning in the 1870s and gathering momentum after 1880. But it was limited in comparison with New York City and Cleveland.

NEW YORK

New York City, the main port of entry and the largest settlement, had only 510 Hungarians in 1870. Ten years later the number had risen to 4,101 and it is reasonable to think that half or more of them were Jews. Thereafter the growth was rapid. Ira Rosenwaike estimated that in 1900, 70 percent of the 31,516 Hungarian-born immigrants were Jewish; 20 percent were Catholic; and 10 percent Protestant.[20]

The mixed ethnic flavor of Manhattan's Lower East Side just after the turn of the century has been described in this way: "It contains from 50,000 to 60,000 Magyars and Hungarian Jews, besides large numbers of Germans, a colony of Polish Catholics, the shattered remnant of a once vigorous Bohemian quarter, a determined line of Irish who are making their last stand along the waterfront, and many Russian Jews."[21] As for the Jews from Hungary living in this neighborhood, we have this description: "Walk West on East Houston Street . . . and you can see how the Jewish newcomers are absorbing the shock of moving into a crowded and ugly urban environment. Look right, beyond Hamilton Fish Park—there, in an area of twenty or more blocks behind the docks and warehouses of the East River, live tens of thousands of Hungarian Jews."[22] They lived close to, but somewhat apart from the concentrations of Russian, Galician, and Rumanian Jews in the heart of the East Side.

An intimate glimpse into the lives and occupations of Hungarian Jews in this area is afforded by a sample of 327 people drawn from the United States Census of 1880. This was a young population living doubled up in crowded tenement flats, many of them working in the burgeoning garment industry. Seemingly every family took in boarders to make ends meet. At least one-third of the families in this sample (and it might have been more) had immigrated between 1859 and 1879.[23]

Let us look in on the tenement at 52 Pitt Street as it was in 1880. We have time to visit three of the "dumbell" flats, which got their name from the fact that two flats were at each end of a long corridor, each flat consisting of three or four rooms. The small amount of living space in two apartments can be estimated from the fact that the buildings were made to fit the standard city lot of twenty-five by one hundred feet. It is no wonder that so many families "took in boarders" since few could afford the $10 to $20 a month rent out of their own incomes.[24]

In the first flat we find Simon Green, a twenty-eight-year-old "huckster" or peddler, and his wife Antonia. Their two children were born in the United States. The Greens have two boarders. Hasel Goldberg, a nineteen-year-old woman, is a tailor, and John Chambro, thirty, and probably not Jewish, is also a huckster.

One of the largest households is headed by a forty-eight-year-old widow, Sarah Klein, who—with help from her sister Rachel—takes care of four children and three boarders. Sarah's twins Lena and Mary, age seventeen, live at home. Mary is a coat finisher and Lena, like many unmarried women at this time, works as a servant for another family. Their younger brother Samuel is a tailor and their older sister Rosa is also a servant. The boarders are three young men, all about twenty—one a store clerk, one a machine operator, and one a huckster.

John Greenbaum, a tailor, and his wife, Mary, have, comparatively speaking, a small household. They have two babies, also named John and Mary. Honie Schwartz, twenty, works for them as a servant and their boarder Moritz Weinberger, at age seventeen, is out peddling.

For their religious services these people probably walk four blocks west to the First Hungarian Congregation Ohab Zedek on Norfolk Street. This will remain for many years the major Hungarian synagogue in New York. It opened its doors in 1872 or 1873 and soon had three hundred members.[25] Or they can go to East 7th Street to Beth Hamidrash Hagadol Anshe Hungary (The Great House of Study of the People of Hungary) or to Oestreich-Ungarn Anshe Sefard (The Sephardic People of Austria-Hungary) on Cannon Street.

In the same tenements on Pitt Street lived twelve Hungarian Christians. John and Mary Schwater in their mid-thirties had as their boarder Barbara Hudock, whose work was washing. John was a marble cutter. Another family consisted of Stephen and Anna Kovacs, both in their forties, and their two children, born in the United States. All the single Christian men boarded with Jewish families. Joseph Tarkoki and Rodick Meshka, both tailors, stayed with Joseph and Anna Brown and their five children. John Veckest, another huckster, boarded with another family. It would seem that the Christian Hungarians lived and worked much the same as the Hungarian Jews in 1880 on the Lower East Side.

It was apparently not all a matter of long hours of work and overcrowded apartments. One writer saw it this way, though he was apparently talking more about the emerging middle class than the factory and sweatshop workers: "The life of the [Hungarian] quarter is one continuous whirl of excitement. Pleasure seems the chief end and dancing, music, cards, and lounging at the cafe are the means of attaining it . . . Almost every block in the Hungarian quarter has its cafe and some blocks have four or five. Each cafe has its special clientele. One is patronized by artists and musicians, another by shop-keepers, another by professional men."[26] Dancing and lounging at cafes were not the lot of everyone.

No sooner had the Hungarian Jews established their colony on the Lower East Side of Manhattan than they were again on the move, leap-frogging up the east side of the island. Their first stop was Yorkville, another ethnically mixed neighborhood, around 80th Street. In 1910 there were twenty-two thousand Hungarian-born immigrants on the Lower East Side and seventeen thousand in Yorkville.[27] As the century turned, the original Hungarian colony, now beginning to disperse, continued to be predominantly Jewish. Marcus Braun, journalist and immigration official, was reported to have said that while on the upper East Side the Gentiles "are in the majority, seventy-five per cent" of the Lower East Side colony were Jewish.[28] There are a number of explanations for the migration uptown.

Howard M. Sachar offers one reason, although he may well have been indulging in deliberate hyperbole when he wrote that as the Tenth Ward in 1890 became a packed settlement of one-third of a million Jews, "the German or Hungarian Jews who had inhabited this area now fled uptown in terror."[29] Certainly as the Hungarians' incomes and aspirations rose, they sought out a less crowded and noisy area and gravitated to more middle class Yorkville. Here they again found a mélange of German, Irish, Czech, and other immigrant groups.

There were also practical pressures at work pushing the immigrants out of the Lower East Side. The construction of new housing, schools, and parks as well as the demolition attendant on building the approaches to the bridges to Brooklyn must have forced some families out of their flats.[30] Moreover, as early as 1879 the 3rd Avenue elevated train facilitated the movement north as far as 125th Street. The arrival of the subways in 1904–1908 further accelerated the migration.[31] For all these reasons, the Hungarians—Jewish and Christian—began filtering into the yellow and beige brick buildings of Yorkville, some of which still stand. They had been built as model dwellings, with financing from the Astors and the Rockefellers. Their courtyards, fresh air, indoor plumbing, and other amenities were seen as an answer to the old tenements.[32]

An appreciation of Hungarian-Jewish life in Yorkville appears in Sylvia Golden's novel *Neighbors Needn't Know,* which depicts some families living in insecurity and poverty; some in lower middle-class sufficiency through dint of long hours of work; still others prospering in business ventures.[33]

Most of them encouraged and pushed their American-born children to study hard and to go on to high school and, if possible, to college for professional training. The Benton parents in the novel did not dwell on their lives in Hungary in talking with their children: "The Old Country, what does it mean to you? Nothing. It is better that way. It is hard to have two countries," Mrs. Benton told her daughter. But Hungary was very much with the parents, who spoke Magyar and German to each other, and if the children began to catch on, they would shift to a Slavic dialect. Their food was distinctly Hungarian rather than Eastern European.

The family went to the annual picnics of the Petőfi Society, originally "a literary group to honor the great Hungarian poet Sándor Petőfi, but these high aims tended to get lost at the picnic and instead the day was used to bring back nostalgic memories of the Old Country," with gypsy music and much wild dancing of the *csárdás*. (In point of fact, there was a Petőfi Society formed in 1882 with its office on East 58th Street.) Mr. Benton loved the cafe down the street with its heavy smell of pipe tobacco, strong coffee, and spices, and its never-ending card games. If a family had enough money, they went "to take the waters" at Saratoga for a few weeks in the summer and came back to spend the winter disputing whether the No. 4 water was superior to the No. 2 water. The children showed little interest in the old customs. Piano lessons and school work and a great deal of visiting of other families were their activities. The boys battled the Czech gangs from a few blocks away. As the children got older, they might be taken to social clubs or to a Socialist meeting to hear a speaker like Eugene V. Debs.

We move now from the Golden novel to reality, from the Bentons to their real-life relatives, Morris and Lena Spiegel.[34] Morris's family owned a farm and sold cattle in Hungary. His mother had died and his father had remarried a woman the children did not like. An older sister left first for America and then sent for Morris and a younger sister. Morris and Lena met when they worked in a garment factory, and within a few years they opened a tailoring shop in Yorkville. The hours were long and Morris brought the work home to their apartment many nights. He put some mice in a cage to keep himself awake as he worked on custom-made suits for men. After many years he saved enough to buy a building nearby, which had a bakery in its basement. The city soon thereafter adopted new health regulations which outlawed bakeries below the street level and Morris lost his investment.

The Spiegel family belonged to the Park Avenue synagogue, but were not very religious. Social activity centered on the Friedliche Schwester Kranken Unterstitzung Verein, which provided a doctor who made house calls. The Verein maintained a "club house" where the families met on Sundays and young people found husbands and wives. This family, supported by a small tailoring shop, stayed on in Yorkville and, with their limited income, was not able to move to one of the "better neighborhoods."

Their cousins, the Golds, made quite a contrast.[35] Like so many other couples, Max and Chana met in New York as "greenhorns." After they were married, they lived for a time in Pennsylvania, but Chana found it too isolated from people she knew and, besides, they had to have kosher meat sent from New York. Max began as a peddler of supplies to sailors on the West Side waterfront and soon opened a store. Before long the Golds moved from the Lower East Side to Yorkville and some of their children went to college. As his sons began to "do well" in their paper products business and his daughters went into white collar jobs, the combined income lifted the family to a level of comfortable living. They were able to move to a prestigious part of Harlem and later to a good neighborhood in Washington Heights.

Two more vignettes suggest the various paths that the Jewish immigrants took. One was an intellectual who got his start in the garment trade. Edward Steiner's experience is recorded in one of his books about immigrants.[36] Granted that he was not a workman when he arrived since he had a degree in philosophy from Europe, he was nonetheless typical of many immigrants in the sense that he had no cash in his pockets when he reached the Lower East Side. Through other immigrants Steiner got a job as a presser in the clothing trade. His boss was an Austrian Jew and his forelady was Irish and "a tyrant." He worked on coats with a hot iron weighing ten to fifteen pounds and his first week's wages were $3.50. Although he was picking up English on the job, his friends soon took him off to night school to learn the language properly. It was not long before he was studying at Oberlin College. Later he became a Protestant minister, a sociologist, and an advocate for the improvement of conditions for immigrants.

A somewhat different route was taken by Adolph Deutsch, who came here with his three sisters from their farm in Hungary. He knew only farm work but in the Houston Street lodging house where he landed "there was talk of only one trade open at once to Hungarian 'greenhorns'—cigarmaking." He entered that trade and, as was the custom, worked for no pay as an apprentice for two weeks. Deutsch quit cigar making after a while and found a job as a farmhand in Pennsylvania. When the foreman there left suddenly, young Adolph elected himself to that position and held it successfully for almost two years. There followed a stint as a clothing salesman and then, having brought over his older brother from Hungary, they launched a carpet and furniture business that grew into an enterprise of one thousand employees that made Deutsch a millionaire.[37]

As these sketches indicate, the Jewish immigrants from Hungary were on the move in New York, economically and geographically. They moved not only into Yorkville but into Harlem, the Bronx, and Brooklyn and were fanning out beyond the city limits as the new century began. Table 7 presents the population figures for Hungarian-born residents of four sections of New York City from 1870 to 1920. While the data do not distinguish between Jews and Gentiles, they indicate the spatial distribution of the Jews who formed the majority throughout. None of this information suggests that the Hungarian Jews had abandoned their original place of settlement at the lower tip of Manhattan. On the contrary, the original colony continued to hold the largest number of them, but the Lower East Side population had begun to shift to other parts of the city, bringing with them their synagogues, their cafes, and their organizations.

The addresses of 124 citizenship applicants in New York City showed this geographic distribution, which did not change materially over the years from 1906 to 1929:

Lower East Side	53
Yorkville	21
Upper East Side	20
Bronx	14
Other	16

As of 1904 there were three major centers: the Lower East Side, Yorkville, and an enclave on the upper East Side at 117th–118th Streets.[38] There were also smaller settlements on the West Side and in such nearby cities as Yonkers.

The decades between 1880 and the First World War were devoted to intensive community activity and organization building as thousands of newcomers settled in the Hungarian-Jewish neighborhoods of New York and other cities. Synagogues were established; sick benefit societies proliferated; cultural and social organizations flourished in New York especially, as will be seen in detail in Chapter 13. Some of this organizational growth stemmed from a developing middle class, many of whom were the children of the '48ers, now doctors, lawyers, and businessmen. These were also the people who were serving as community leaders and spokesmen for Hungarians regardless of their religion.

CLEVELAND

Cleveland was a much smaller city than New York, but Hungarians formed a larger, more prominent part of the scene. And the Jews among them were a more visible part of Cleveland Jewry at the turn of the century than was the case in New York. Table 8 compares the Hungarian, Jewish, and Hungarian-Jewish populations of New York and Cleveland.

There is little doubt that before 1900 Jews constituted the majority of Hungarians in Cleveland, as is clear from the lists of members of Hungarian societies and the fact that the first Hungarian church was not established until 1891.[39] It is difficult to know what proportion Jews constituted of the 31,503 Hungarian-born residents of Cleveland in 1910, but one-third seems a reasonable estimate. As in New York, the Hungarian Jews bunched together in certain parts of the city and set up their own organizations.

In the sixty years from 1840 to 1900 Cleveland had grown from a frontier town of 6,000 into a city of almost 800,000 people and a center of "mighty, smoke-belching industries."[40] In this amazing explosion of population and industry, the city seems to have sucked hundreds of thousands of people of peasant stock from Central and Southern Europe into its steel mills, oil refineries, and machine shops lining the banks of the city's "befouled Cuyahoga River."

Cleveland could well have been called the City of Immigrants, for by 1900 foreign-born people and their children accounted for three-quarters of its inhabitants, probably more than in any other American city. By 1920 almost one in five immigrants was a Hungarian. The Hungarian-born population of the city rose from 9,558 to 42,134 between 1900 and 1920 and its proportion of the foreign-born increased from 8 to 18 percent.[41] It was said that the largest Hungarian enclave in the city was the most densely settled Magyar area outside of Hungary.[42] Indeed, they nicknamed Cleveland "The American Debrecen" after the city in Hungary considered most intensely Magyar. This was related in part to the close-knit and somewhat insular character of the community. One writer concluded that the Hungarians did not interact with the larger Cleveland society and, as a result, their cultural traditions, values, and behavioral norms persisted for many years.[43]

Immigrants arriving in New York had the problem of paying $10 or $15 for a railroad ticket to places in the Midwest such as Cleveland. This was mitigated by a drastic price cut in 1885 which enabled immigrants to take the train for a "nominal one dollar" ticket.[44] At the Cleveland depot a member of the police force was on hand to help the weary travelers through the anxieties of arrival, as well as assisting those changing trains to go on to other destinations.

On the west side of the city Hungarians lived in an area of mixed ethnic groups from Europe who worked in the factories. There are some persuasive hints that the early Hungarian settlers there were predominantly Jewish. One account says that the majority of them spoke German and were able to deal with the well-established German community.[45] A Hungarian clergyman recalled that the West Siders spoke not only Hungarian but German or Rumanian or Slavic. This knowledge of several languages was a hallmark of the Jews in Hungary. These pioneers on the West Side, he said, considered themselves "of higher culture" and had a feeling of "exclusiveness" related to the fact that they had "been tradesmen and . . . skilled labor" in Hungary.[46]

In contrast, a colorful portrait of the Magyar East Side of Cleveland in the early 1900s was drawn by a contemporary writer who felt it was "really pure Hungarian":

> One can hardly hear anything else but Hungarian there; there are hardly any non-Hungarian shops. The Hungarian institutions, churches, schools, clubs are all together. It is here that the Hungarian customs are most strictly maintained. Women do not hesitate to walk in the street with kerchiefs on their heads or barefoot in summer; men keep their "green" look longer. The houses are owned by Hungarians. There one hears Hungarian songs on the streets and Hungarian paper-boys hawk the Hungarian papers.[47]

A somewhat less favorable picture of the Magyar working class was provided by the official Americanization Committee in Cleveland: "Owing to low wages or unfavorable social conditions, the Magyars frequently must live in menial circumstances and small quarters. Such evils as the coffee houses have a bad effect on the lives of the people." The only reason for this in the opinion of the pamphleteer is that the Hungarian "squanders his money" in the coffee houses. The pamphlet goes on to say that the Magyars make heroic efforts to keep their homes clean despite the smoke and grime from the factories and that 71.3 percent of the wives earned wages or kept boarders for income. A very high percentage of the Magyars are literate, but they are slow in learning English primarily because they live in a Hungarian enclave.[48]

In a "History of the Cleveland Hungarians" written by Rabbi H. A. Liebovitz and a colleague about 1917, we learn that the East Side "Hungarian ghetto" had three sections. Around East 79th Street were found most of the Hungarian stores—groceries, butchers, and saloons, also real estate and foreign exchange businesses and the "Hungarian Pharmacies" most of whose owners—if we can believe the writers—"were rich."[49] A second area was from Woodhill Road to 125th Street.

One of the largest sections of Little Hungary was Buckeye Road "down until East 72nd street," where most of the Hungarian doctors were to be found, as well as Hungarian-owned stores, Magyar newspapers, and American shops with "Hungarian Departments" and Magyar employees. There were Jews in the Buckeye Road area, as noted in this observation: "Because Hungarian Jews were assimilated to a much greater degree into Hungarian society than those living in other eastern European countries, some Hungarian Jews migrating to Cleveland chose to reside in the Buckeye area."[50] In another part of the city could be found the downtown Hungarian area with doctors and lawyers, "amongst which it should be interesting to mention the first Hungarian woman lawyer—Miss Emma Gross." The West Side section near downtown and neighborhoods farther out on the West Side continued to have Hungarian residents.

Most Jews lived elsewhere and were employed, as in New York, in the garment industry, cigar making, and skilled trades as well as in shop-keeping, peddling, and office work. Liebovitz places this Hungarian-Jewish section on Woodland Avenue between East 38 and 65 streets. There "Hungarian Jews have assimilated with Americans far sooner than the rest of the Hungarians, not only in costums [undoubtedly Rabbi Liebovitz meant customs], but in language, nevertheless taking always great part in every Hungarian movement, social and business life and charity."[51]

The Liebovitz book continually stresses the Jews' quick pace of Americanization though "they never denied their Hungarian birth or extraction."[52] Thus it points out that the first Magyar organization in Cleveland, the Hungarian Aid Society, founded in 1863 by Jews, "had a definitely Hungarian character but later its members became more Americanized (these Hungarian Jews became businessmen sooner than the other Hungarians and in the interest of their business they lost their Hungarianness)."

In 1866 the Hungarian Jews began meeting in each other's homes for religious services and soon developed a synagogue, B'nai Jeshurun, which exists today as the Temple on the Heights. This congregation and others organized by the Hungarians are described in Chapter 13.

Anti-Semitic developments in Europe generated both protest and philanthropy among Cleveland's Hungarian Jews. The blood libel trial in Hungary, taking place in Tiszaeszlár in the heart of the region from which most of the Jews came, brought a strong response. Simultaneously the pogroms in Russia were sending a flood of refugees to this country. Jews in Cleveland, despite tensions and disagreements between the old-timers who had come from Germany and the newcomers from Central and Eastern Europe, managed to join their efforts to help the refugees coming to Cleveland.

The community leaders at the end of the nineteenth century served all the Hungarians in Cleveland and many of the leaders were Jewish. Families such as the Blacks, who had been among the '48ers, were moving up in Cleveland's economy and polity. More will be said about the Black family in a later chapter.

As the years went by the main movement of Cleveland's Hungarian Jews was eastward along the lakefront toward and into the suburbs. Those few who remained on the West Side also moved farther out, away from the downtown area. Most Cleveland streets are numbered and the movements of the immigrants and their children can easily be traced by watching the numbers of the streets. To illustrate, the addresses of citizenship applicants were divided between those who came to Cleveland before 1910 and those who arrived after that date. The homes of the first group were grouped around East 51st Street; the later arrivals lived in the area of East 67th Street.

But whether the movement was uptown in New York or eastward in Cleveland, the Hungarian Jews were again migrating and, again, it was essentially a search for more promising economic and social circumstances in an urban and suburban environment. But this took time. Their beginnings in the American economy were far more modest in their first years here.

OCCUPATIONS

The 1880 census sample from the Hungarian-Jewish neighborhood in New York's Lower East Side presents a snapshot of the immigrants' occupations near the beginning of the Big Migration. The biggest source of employment was the garment industry, which was just getting off the ground, with German Jews as entrepreneurs and employers. Another major industry was cigar making. Hungarian Jews were involved in the beginnings of the trade union movement in these two industries in the 1870s; this will be described in a subsequent chapter.

Well over half the workers in our census sample were in the apparel and related trades. Most of the others were divided among skilled crafts, selling and peddling, and working as servants. The main occupational groups were as follows:

Garment workers	74
Skilled	18
Selling	16
Service	15
Unskilled	9
Professional	1
Total	133

It is interesting to look behind these classifications to the people and the actual jobs, but we must first take note of the situation of the women and of the children who worked.

Almost all the single women worked as servants or in the needle trades, though there was one "book-folder." Women like the widow Sarah Klein, with four children and three boarders to look after, obviously worked hard within their own homes to keep the family going. This must also have been true of many women whose husbands were alive and who also cooked and cleaned and laundered for boarders. In all the records examined in this study we found no married Hungarian-Jewish woman working in a job outside the home, except for helping in the family business. Many did piece work at home. Pride and a sense of what was appropriate for women probably accounted for this taboo.

One family, badly in need of money, would not let their daughter become a factory worker. Because back in Hungary their people had been physicians and businessmen, factory work for their daughter was unthinkable. She would bring home braid and printed designs and sew the braid on the outline and then use heavy silk thread to make flower designs. As a graduate of a convent school where she had picked up some French and Latin, this young woman was eager to be a governess in a "refined home," but her parents also objected to this. The consequences of these restrictions were described by a reporter writing in the early 1920s: "Ever so many poor Hungarian young women who were not familiar with our language made neck-ties at home rather than work in factories. I knew quite a number of well-born, refined and educated women who made ties or embroidery at home from seven in the morning until very late at night, only pausing about ten or fifteen minutes at noon and in the evening to eat. These young women usually came to this country with beautiful rosy cheeks and stunning figures and much courage and hope, and after two or three years of monotonous work and worry would change beyond recognition."[53]

The year 1880 was well before the days of child labor legislation. Four of the girls in our sample who were fifteen or younger were servants; three were coat finishers and one was a tailor. Among the boys under sixteen two were hucksters. One "works at feathers," possibly for women's hats. Another boy was an apprentice "segar-maker"; two worked at garments, and one was a grocery clerk.

The men were heavily concentrated in the apparel trades. In addition to tailors and pressers, there were cap makers and shoemakers. Eleven were peddlers or dealers and four were clerks. The more skilled workers were engaged in carpentry, in making picture frames and furniture, tinsmithing, printing and the like. At opposite ends of the spectrum of skills were a teacher and a laborer.

Moving ahead some thirty years, we are able to learn from citizenship papers the occupations of Hungarian Jews in New York and in Cleveland after 1906.[54] As Table 9 shows, there were similarities in the occupational structure of Hungarian Jews in the two cities. The immigrants were essentially a working-class and lower middle-class group. About a third of the employed workers were in skilled trades. The proportion was slightly higher in Cleveland, where machinists, for example, had good jobs in heavy industry. Just under one-fifth of those employed were in commerce and sales. About 15 percent were unskilled workers. In New York one-fifth of the employed immigrants were in the needle trades, a sharp drop from what we found in 1880 when almost 60 percent were in that industry. In Cleveland only one-tenth of the Jewish workers were in the garment industry. Overall, the number of skilled craftsmen and artisans more than doubled between 1880 and the period after 1906.

The shape of things to come can be seen in information from Nashville, where the occupational profile of Hungarian Jews was extracted from the

1900 census.[55] As Table 9 indicates, the immigrants in Nashville were heavily concentrated in retail and selling activities. Almost two-thirds of the working people were merchants, peddlers, grocers, and salesmen.

In New York and Cleveland there were the beginnings of a parallel trend. With each passing year Hungarian Jews were moving out of the garment factories and into service jobs and the professions, shifts that signified, for the most part, higher incomes and a rising standard of living and the path into the middle class. Taking into account both their living arrangements and their work, it can be said that in the opening decades of the twentieth century the Hungarian Jews in Cleveland and New York were moving, geographically and socially, into new territory. As the immigrants—and especially their children—entered more skilled and professional occupations, they increasingly found housing in middle class neighborhoods. Usually it took not one but two moves to make the shift from the old, original sites of immigrant settlement to the more affluent and suburban neighborhoods.

Things were not quite the same in the small towns in which a large number of the immigrants made their permanent homes.

CHAPTER I I

Small Town Diaspora

A good number of the immigrants moved from small-town Hungary to small-town America. There was in fact a diaspora of Hungarians—Jews and Gentiles alike—stretching across this country. Of the half-million Hungarian immigrants in the United States in 1910, three-quarters lived outside of New York and Cleveland. Our focus in this chapter is on the experiences of these immigrants in the smaller cities and towns where conditions, especially in terms of earning a living, appear to have differed from the large urban centers.

On the eve of the Big Migration the Jewish population was spread out across this land. The surprising census figures in 1880 showed that Jews constituted a higher proportion in the West (1.6 percent) than in the Northeast (0.6 percent).[1] The Hungarian immigrants, however, were concentrated in the Northeast. One-fourth were in Pennsylvania, 10 percent in New Jersey, and there were substantial settlements in Illinois, Missouri, Michigan, Indiana, and Connecticut.[2] The numbers in the South and West were smaller.

It is not possible to state with any precision how many Hungarian Jews settled in small towns, but this was the choice of about one-quarter of the Eastern European Jews as a whole.[3] Lacking any firm figures on the distribution of Hungarian Jews, we must settle for an indirect impression based on the establishment of synagogues and benevolent associations, for their presence indicates a nucleus of the immigrants.

The following listing is intended only to give an impression of the spread of Hungarian Jews in the United States. It is far from complete, since it represents only what has been learned in the course of this investigation. The data are taken from Table 12. The organizations have been divided here into seventy-seven synagogues and societies established before 1900 and fifty-eight that were founded after 1900. They stretch from Connecticut to Colorado.

Location of 135 Hungarian-Jewish Organizations

Est. before 1900		Est. 1900 and Later	
New York	53	New York	37
Chicago	5	Chicago	6
Cleveland	5	Cleveland	6
Philadelphia	7	Yonkers	1
Boston	2	St. Louis	1
Nashville	1	Nashville	1
Atlanta	1	Atlanta	1
Poughkeepsie, N.Y.	1	Poughkeepsie	1
Pittsburgh	1	Fairfield, Conn.	1
McKeesport, Pa.	1	Highland Park, N.J.	1
		Wharton, Texas	1
		West Denver, Colo.	1

This listing reveals a dispersion of Hungarian Jews in twelve states, though it also confirms the heavy concentrations in a few large cities. The tempo of organization increased with each decade. More of the smaller communities appear as time passes, though some of the immigrants made their way to frontier towns long before 1880. The Denver area is a case in point. Sigmund Schlesinger was a scout with the white settlers fighting the Indians there. "There were also a number of young Hungarian Jews who had come, unburdened by families, to seek their fortunes in the West. These foot-loose young men were to be found throughout the state."[4] One of these was Sam Butler, a railroad worker and miner, known for killing a bear in a cave with his knife and for being the only person to come out alive after an Indian attack.

We now turn our attention to three small communities where some historical work has been done on the Hungarian Jews. In Nashville we have perhaps the only study of all the Hungarian Jews in a locality, based on the 1900 census reports. In Franklin, New Jersey, a Magyar wrote about his community and the role of the Jews in it. Finally, a rounded social history of Jews in McKeesport, Pennsylvania, affords a rare picture of the process of settlement unfolding over time. These examples are not necessarily typical; we simply found no alternative descriptions of Hungarian Jewish communities outside the big cities.

In Nashville, Fedora Frank studied U.S. Census reports for her book on that city's Jewry and noted the country of origin of its Jewish population.

She found that in 1870 8 percent of the 384 foreign-born Jews came from Hungary, while 43.4 percent were from Germany.[5] In 1900 Hungarians made up 26 percent of the foreign-born Jews, slightly more than those from Germany and somewhat fewer than those from Russia. Actually Hungarian Jews comprised 9.8 percent of the total Jewish community as the new century began. The total population of Nashville at that time was 80,965.

Frank copied detailed information on each foreign-born Jewish family in Nashville from the 1900 census and I was fortunate in gaining access to her hand-written work sheets.[6] Sixty percent of the Hungarians had come to Nashville in the years of the Big Migration from 1881 to 1890; the rest were equally divided between the decade before and the decade after. There were in Nashville in 1900 fifty-eight men, fifty women, and thirty-four children born in Hungary.[7] In a Jewish community of 1,650 the Hungarians were a significant element—almost one in ten. The figures given above do not include 144 children born in the United States to these Hungarian families, an indication of the extent to which they were settled Americans rather than sojourners. Only seven adults were single.

In other words, as in New York and Cleveland, this was a family migration to Nashville. The tendency of Hungarian Jews of this period to marry Hungarian Jews is evident in the census data. This was true of twenty of the thirty-two couples where both husband and wife were present. Apropos of this tendency in her book on Nashville, Frank adds this observation: "One of the largest blood and marriage ties stemmed from the early Hungarian immigrants." Intermarriage among them "provided their children with an endless chain of kinfolks and an insatiable desire for family gatherings."[8]

In Nashville "Hungarian Jews functioned well with the non-Jewish population . . . Actually Hungarian Jews were right at home in the small town rural Southern environment. After all, most of the Hungarians were from farms and small towns in Hungary where Jews were a minority. Hungarian Jews in Nashville were neighbors, classmates, and business partners of the non-Jewish population."[9] By way of contrast with the concentration of workers in New York and Cleveland in apparel and cigar making, in Nashville most of the working adults were engaged in retail shops, peddling, and sales. There were fourteen grocers, fourteen merchants, a scattering of tailors, skilled workers, and clerks, and only three unskilled workers.

One reason for moving to small towns was the presence of Eastern European peasants, now factory workers and miners, with whom the Jews shared common languages and with whom they continued the economic relationship they had in the Old Country. Another reason was a desire to be self-employed and not a worker in a sweatshop. An illustration of this comes from Franklin, New Jersey, site of a zinc mine employing hundreds of Hungarians in the first decades of the twentieth century.[10] The miners and their families had in effect re-created a Hungarian village in Franklin. "Ducks and chickens [were] in the yards and in the street. Well kept vegetable gardens were to be found beside the houses and the Hungarian geraniums bloomed in the windows. Pigs were fattened and many cows were kept." Families living in the four-room houses built by the Zinc Company were required to take in unmarried boarders in three rooms. The family lived in the remaining room. The miners' houses were overcrowded and "there often were times when the beds never got cold."

"For the completeness of the story," the writer continues, "I have to mention the Hungarians of Jewish faith also." His account is as interesting for its explicit and implicit attitudes towards the Jews as it is for its description of their role in the community.

> They arrived just as poor as the rest of the people, but their exceptional talent for business brought for them its well-deserved fruits. The growth of their wealth did not bring with it any snobbishness. They remained friendly and ready to help as humanitarians.
> If anybody needed employment, they got work for them. If money was needed, they gave them money. If they had no clothes or food they gave credit to the newly-arrived Hungarians. For those who did not know how to write, they were ready to help with filling out papers; if ship-tickets were required, they saw to it that tickets were available; if need be, they sent money to the old country and always transmitted as a very clear transaction. Many old American-Hungarians told me here that in a foreign country outside of God it was always the Jew who helped them.

Whether these rosy views were held by all the Magyars in Franklin it is impossible to know, but it is clear that the Jews' old middleman role had been transported from Hungary to New Jersey.

Not all Hungarian Jews in the American diaspora were in the middleman position, however. A small number did go into factory work—not in the garment trades and not in cigars, but in heavier industry. Westinghouse Electric opened a plant in Pittsburgh in 1886 near the Jewish neighborhood in the Hill District. Primarily Hungarian Jews but also some from Galicia took jobs there.[11] There was an unconfirmed rumor at the time that George Westinghouse, wanting to avoid dependence on the Mellons and other Pittsburgh bankers, turned to Jacob Schiff at Kuhn, Loeb in New York and that Schiff in granting credit asked the firm to be fair to Jewish job applicants.

Just fourteen miles from Pittsburgh lies McKeesport, and it was there that a substantial Hungarian-Jewish community developed. An account of that community by Sarah Landesman begins with the note that "here, on the banks of the Monongahela for a time, at least, the East European shtetl with its folk ways and its religious overtones" was reproduced.[12]

McKeesport grew slowly until rich coal deposits were discovered there in the middle of the nineteenth century. By 1858 the first German Jews arrived and they soon set up retail shops to sell clothes, groceries, and the like. They mixed easily with the Germans already there, joined their vereins for singing and socials, and even attended the Sunday sermons in church. "The liberal, mild doctrines expounded there," Landesman notes somewhat wryly, "did not seem contrary to the equally mild, dogmaless Judaism of the post-Mendelssohnian era of which the German Jews were the product."

As the city became a center for steel production its mills reached out to Central Europe to fill their jobs, even advertising "in the little provincial newspapers of north east Hungary." The National Tube Works opened in 1871 and gave McKeesport "its mill-town character." A trek of Slovaks, Croats, Ruthenians, and chiefly Hungarians made its way to the town. "Along with the peasantry of the hamlets of north east Hungary came its Jews," mostly poor people whose passage to America was eased financially by a price war among the shipping lines. Their meager savings sometimes were exhausted by the time they reached New York and "many a man walked all the way" to McKeesport, a four-hundred-mile journey that took three weeks. Practically all the Hungarian Jews began life there by working at National Tube.

By the 1880s Hungarian and Russian Jews had come to McKeesport but "there was no social fraternization between the newcomers and the 'Deutche Yehudim' [the German Jews] . . . The difference in outlook, in social status, in religious practice, manners, and mode of life erected a barrier which 3,000 years of common suffering and shared history could not scale." By 1890 there were about two hundred Hungarian-Jewish families living in a place filled with the sounds, sights, and smells of steel making and the burning of soft coal—and the news of workers maimed and killed in the course of their twelve-hour days in the mill.

The men sent for their families or if they were single they arranged for brides from Hungary, New York, or Pittsburgh. One family described its beginnings thus: "They had six rooms, six children, six boarders and the couple itself slept on the table-bed in the kitchen." Life was hard: health conditions were "appalling," disease rampant, and poverty a steady companion. And yet a young man could somehow make it to medical school, but "when his red pants had to be patched my mother had only a piece of purple patch to go with it," one person recalled, so "he developed the technique of walking sideways along the wall." The ambition of young women and their families was for them to become teachers.

Gradually the Hungarian Jews began to leave the mill and open butcher stores, groceries, and bakeries. In 1886 they established Gemilas Chesed Anshe Ungarn, which had 225 members four years later. But the inclusion of the phrase "Men of Hungary" in the congregation's name "did not go down well" with the Russians and the few Germans who joined and they subsequently seceded and set up their own congregation. The Hungarian women formed a Beneficial Society for charitable purposes, but it also served to demarcate social distinctions. These were the "bessere leit" (the better people) who could read and write and had certain manners. Landesman points out that the Lithuanians "shuddered at the Hungarian Jew's 'uncouth' Hebrew pronunciation; the latter watched with a raised eyebrow the Litvaks 'cold' religion; and together they frowned on the informality and impetuosity of the Galicianers."

Despite these divisions the immigrant Jews of McKeesport attained a "certain sense of unity and solidarity." They made efforts to cut across ethnic lines to provide Jewish education for the children. Weddings and circumcisions were the main occasions for celebrations, at which Hungarian songs added to the enjoyment. The Hungarian Jews loved "the language and music of their homeland . . . They used 'Gusti's gypsy band' as much as the Gentile Hungarians did." In an earlier chapter we noted that a favorite tune on these occasions was that of the Hasidic Rabbi Eizik Taub, the Kalever—the allegory of the bird walking alone in the meadow and representing the messianic yearnings of the Jews.

The Jews were fully accepted into the general community of McKeesport. The local newspaper was sympathetic and interested in their affairs and the Jews entered local politics, but it was the public schools that "achieved magical speed" in the Americanizing of the "children and through them of the parents." It was not long before there was a harvest of graduates of teacher training schools and universities—doctors, lawyers, pharmacists, and in time a Rhodes Scholar and a Fulbright Scholar.

By this time the Jewish community had lost its "shtetl" look and people were moving to another part of town. The lodges were drawing more people than the synagogues. B'nai B'rith became a strong influence in 1904 with its social and charitable activities. Sons of David, a fraternal organization, was organized to provide insurance, loans, and social help to the immigrants and it spread to surrounding towns. Reform Judaism reached McKeesport, though the new congregation had to moderate its "extreme stand"; it invited a graduate of the new Conservative Jewish Theological Seminary to occupy its pulpit. Zionism gained adherents and funds flowed to Jerusalem and to the Denver Hospital. As the decades passed the immigrant character of this heavily Hungarian Jewish community faded.

From another source we know something about Pepi and Meyer Lebowitz who lived in McKeesport, among other places on their nomadic route in America.[13] It is appropriate to list Pepi first since this represents roughly the division of labor between wife and husband: 90 percent to 10 percent. This pattern—a practical, energetic woman and a man who leaves the responsibility for the family primarily in her hands—is not unique among Jewish families. In Europe this arrangement of sex roles was prevalent among certain Orthodox families where religious study was the full-time activity of the man and the household, including the earning of income, was the wife's role. In the Lebowitz household a major substitution had been made in the old pattern: card playing replaced Talmudic study.

The Lebowitzes had met and married in McKeesport in 1891 and raised a family of seven sons and four daughters. "Pepi was a dynamo who seemed to have boundless energy," writes a relative of theirs. She used to get up at 4 A.M. to do her family's laundry and then would work with her husband in their business for most of the day. (This does not contradict the general finding that Hungarian Jewish women did not work away from their families; Pepi would not have been found in the National Tube mill.) "Pepi was the moving force in the family. It was Pepi who saw to it that all the children finished school, had music lessons, and even made certain that the son who wanted to be a physician accomplished his goal." "Meyer was a handsome aristocrat who preferred playing cards with his cronies to working. But in spite of everything, Pepi adored him . . . Because Meyer was a poor provider, the family moved about a good deal." (He was a mill worker and a baker in McKeesport, ran a hotel-saloon near Pittsburgh, another bakery in Lyndora, and eventually a butcher shop in Canonsburg.)

In quite a few places, unlike McKeesport, there was only a handful of

Hungarian-Jewish families. They came either on their own or as part of an organized program to resettle Jews. This movement, initiated primarily by the established German Jews, was motivated in part by their distress at the accumulation in New York City of hundreds of thousands of Eastern European Jews, with their "strange" ways. But the German Jews' embarrassment and their fear that the newcomers would undermine their social status and acceptance in American society was balanced by a contradictory motivation. They wanted to help the newcomers make a good start in America. They believed the immigrants would find better opportunities in the hinterland than in the big East Coast and Midwestern cities. So they offered them financial aid and sought to mobilize Jewish communities "in the interior" to accept and settle the immigrants. They tried to bring the immigrants in through Galveston, Texas, and other ports of entry in preference to New York, the great funnel through which hundreds of thousands were then pouring each year and where many of them stayed.

The scheme was not blessed with success. Some communities in the interior returned the "settlers" to New York. Some settlers refused to stay put and chose their own place to live, which frequently turned out to be New York. Rischin concludes that "even the United Hebrew Charities, the Baron de Hirsch Fund, and the Jewish Agricultural and Industrial Aid Society showed unimpressive results. The more effective Industrial Removal Office, founded in 1901, specifically for the purpose of distributing immigrants, helped over 60,000 East European Jews to find a place outside of New York City in the following decade."[14] In the end, only a very small percentage of the two million Jewish immigrants were helped by these endeavors.

But others like Joe Schwartz—whom we met in an earlier chapter as the "greenhorn" Yosef Schwindler—made it on their own.[15] Certizne in the foothills of the Carpathian Mountains and Wharton, Texas, near Houston are like the ends of a long string which guided Schwartz as he made the journey. Early in the 1890s people from Certizne in the Slovak area of Hungary were settling in Wharton and other towns in the rural parts of central and south Texas.[16] When Schwartz reached Texas he found Slovaks, Czechs, and Poles as well as German Jews. Joe began as a peddler walking through the Texas countryside before he acquired a horse and wagon. Later he set up a dry goods store.

The Hungarian Jews of Wharton brought their relatives over and by 1913 there were enough people to organize a synagogue. In the almost half-century that he lived there, Joe Schwartz was active in both general community affairs and in the small Jewish community. He served for thirty-five years on the local school board and joined the Masons. For years Schwartz was a member of the Slavonic Benevolent Order of the State of Texas, a fraternal insurance society of Slovak and Czech immigrants. A member of the lodge wrote many years later that "like all businessmen" at that time (did he mean Jews?) Joe Schwartz "helped with things when asked to do so" but in general was inactive when it came to social and fraternal organizations. The comment suggests that Schwartz's relationships with Gentiles from Austria-Hungary were cordial, but were based essentially on commercial and organizational roles.

This part of Texas was an area in which the Ku Klux Klan operated, concentrating its efforts more on Blacks than on Jews. One night when most of the townspeople had locked themselves in their houses, "unidentified" hooded klansmen marched through town brandishing their torches. To Joe Schwartz they were not "unidentified." Peering from his window he could figure out who they were by the shoes they had bought in his store.

When Schwartz died in 1939 his family received expressions of condolence from many individuals and organizations in Wharton. He seems to have been generally successful as a businessman, but this was not the case with a number of Jewish immigrants in small towns. In her study of Eastern European immigrants in Johnstown, Pennsylvania, Morawska learned that for many of the Jews, mostly shopkeepers, this was a fragile economic situation, one that she called "insecure prosperity." The experience of Louis Holitser is a case in point.[17]

Holitser had left Kassa and was living in Albany, Georgia, in 1870. Within a few years he was a partner in a store that sold men's clothing and luggage. The partners moved their enterprise to Eastport, Maine, the site of several sardine canning factories. The business prospered and the Holitser family grew. They had both Jewish and non-Jewish friends. Since there was no synagogue in Eastport, they joined the Unitarian church. But in 1898 the Holitsers' problems began with the loss of investments Louis had made; the business failed, as did their marriage. He left his family and became what was not uncommon among immigrants—a "family deserter." Louis was next heard from using his language skills to sell real estate to Slovaks in Emporia, Virginia, where he died in 1925. For Louis Holitser, the streets were not paved with gold.

The Schwartz family of Syracuse, New York, illustrates what happened to many Hungarian-Jewish immigrants in small localities: their gradual absorption into the general Jewish community. The family reached America in 1890 and moved to this upstate New York community after five years in Ohio. Syracuse had its own shtetl, a collection of small houses surrounding a courtyard known as Steinberg's Alley. Most of the people were from Russia and a few from Germany; the Schwartzes were the only family from Hungary. "All were poor, all were friends," one of the Schwartz daughters recalled years later.[18]

The Schwartz family, which spoke Hungarian but also luckily Yiddish, entered fully into the life of the small Jewish community and its Orthodox synagogue. As elsewhere, disagreements about how the congregation should function were frequent and people left it in anger but then returned. After the First World War the women reorganized their "auxiliary" and soon a new synagogue was built. An organization was set up, similar to the urban *landsmanschaften*, to assist the poorer families; to visit the sick; to provide fees for doctors' visits and medicines and coal for heating and cooking; to prepare the dead for proper burial; and to ensure a minyan for prayer in a house of mourning.

As one reads the reminiscences about the Schwartzes, no mention is found of their origins in Hungary or of any associations with Magyars in Syracuse, which by 1910 had 212 people born in Hungary. Perhaps if they had stayed in Youngstown or Akron, these connections might have been a more prominent part of their lives. As it was, they took their place, an active one, as part of an Eastern European Jewish community in upstate New York.

There were only a few Hungarian Jews in Johnstown, Pennsylvania, where Morawska conducted her study of Eastern European immigrants. Their experiences were in most respects similar to those of the Polish and Russian Jews, who lived somewhat precariously, neither in poverty nor affluence. These small town Jews were, perhaps by a self-selection process, less upwardly mobile and ambitious than those who settled in the large cities. Their children, for example, did not attend college to the same extent as the urban Jews.

Morawska found the Hungarian Jews different in certain ways from the other Jews.[19] While most Jewish-Gentile social contacts were at the margin of business relations,

> the only group with which they developed into a greater closeness was the Hungarian one—one more carry-over from the old country, where the cultural

integration of Hungarian Jews and Gentiles had been more pronounced than in the surrounding Slavic-populated areas. Business collaboration between a Hungarian Jew and his Gentile counterpart in a soft-drink venture in one of the "foreign colonies" of Johnstown was the single recorded case of such intergroup partnership, and some members of a Jewish Hungarian *landsmanschaft* in the city participated in the local Gentile Hungarian cultural and national celebrations.

Uniquely, too, in comparison with immigrant groups of Slavic origin, the Hungarian Gentile community counted as "theirs" the town's Jewish Hungarian businessmen and professionals . . . This identification was not reciprocated.

What can be said in general about life in small towns as distinct from the big cities? First, some people must have seen positive similarities between living in South Sharon, Ohio, and living in Stropkov, Zemplén County. Indeed it may have been a dislike of large cities—especially the bursting Lower East Side of New York—that provided some of the motivation for the folks from Hungary's rural northeastern countryside to settle in places like Franklin and Nashville.[20]

Second, the absolute number of Jews of all backgrounds was limited in these places and this threw them into closer contact with each other. The number of Hungarian Jews was even smaller. The forces at work could be either centripetal or centrifugal, depending partly on how many families settled in a particular locality. One outcome, as we saw in Syracuse, where there was only one Hungarian-Jewish family, was integration into the Jewish community and the erosion of any Hungarian distinctiveness. Where there were no other Jews at all, the Holitsers became Unitarians, though other families would have chosen another alternative. Where the number of Hungarian Jews reached some critical mass, as in McKeesport, they were able to form their own synagogues and associations.

Third, in many small towns the Hungarian Jews were in direct contact with Gentile Hungarians. These contacts were probably closer and more frequent than in urban neighborhoods with their greater impersonality and autonomy. This circumstance re-created some of the conditions in which the two groups had lived together in Hungarian towns and villages. This was particularly true of the high proportion of Jews who became retail storekeepers in the diaspora. The Jewish shopkeepers and the white collar service workers, such as insurance or real estate agents, were repeating the middleman economic role they had performed with Hungarian and Slovak peasants in the Old Country.

Fourth—and this again replicated their background in Hungary—life tended to be slower and more isolated from the currents of urban living, both secular and Jewish. Closely related to this was the fact, drawing on Morawska's research findings, that the small town Jews were less upwardly mobile and somewhat slower to follow the path of urban families striving to enter the middle class.

Looking back over the descriptions of life in New York, Cleveland, and small town America, it seems clear that where one lived was important in the adjustment of the Hungarian Jews in their new land. This set limits or opened opportunities for contacts with people of differing backgrounds. And, in combination with other factors, influenced one's social and economic mobility. Cutting across these differences in locale and even in social class were the principal adjustments that Hungarian Jews had to make in their new country. This brings us back to the central issue raised in the opening chapter.

Three Worlds

★

C H A P T E R   1 2

The Magyar Connection

We come now to the question of how the immigrants managed their three-way identification as Hungarians, as Jews, as Americans. Did they retain both their Hungarian culture and their Jewish heritage in the process of Americanization? The generally favorable status of Jews in nincteenth-century Hungary would suggest an affirmative answer to this question, but once in the United States, the immigrants were pulled in different directions by strong forces that made this tripartite identity problematic.

The culture that the immigrants brought with them was a powerful force, but it was not monolithic. Whereas certain elements of culture which the Jews shared with Gentile Magyars tended to strengthen that connection, religion and a long history bound them to Jews. Language, which proved to be an important determinant of the Jewish immigrants' social and organizational affiliations, had the effect of diluting the Magyar connection since they spoke various combinations of Hungarian, German, Yiddish, and other tongues.

In a fundamental way work and the economic roles the newcomers performed had much to do with the people they met and the ideas to which they were exposed; their income set their standard of living and largely determined their social mobility. Finally, the political and organizational structures that the immigrants found here—or created—influenced how they defined themselves. In part it was through these organizations that they sought to satisfy their needs for individual and group welfare and for self-expression.

As is so often the case in setting forth categories such as these for purposes of discussion and analysis, these influences overlapped and criss-crossed in a way that confounds "cause and effect." Obviously they are not independent and objective factors, but simply various aspects of the dynamics that shaped the immigrants' lives in this land. It will also become clear that particular influences waxed and waned over time. This chapter first considers those things that connected the Jews with the Christian Magyars and then the factors that divided them.

It has been said about Hungarian Jewish immigrants that they were "still intoxicated with Budapest and regarded themselves as Magyar Jews."[1] In a literal sense the observation exaggerates. The bulk of them came from small towns and may never have seen Budapest. They were more attuned to the daily demands of making a living than to the glitter of the capital. But there is little doubt that the Hungarian Jews "shared the culture and interests of their non-Jewish compatriots."[2] Many did think of themselves as Magyar Jews.

There is ample evidence that the Jewish immigrants were not to be outdone in patriotic devotion to their Hungarian fatherland. They were, for instance, active in 1896 in the events surrounding the celebration of the arrival of the Magyar tribesmen in Central Europe in 896. On that occasion a delegation of Hungarian Americans went to Budapest; the wreath-laying committee consisted of six people from various American cities, all Jews.[3] In 1883 and again in 1888 when the Danube overflowed its banks, the Hungarian-Jewish community in Cleveland raised money to aid the flood victims.

In expressing their patriotism and their attachment to Hungarian culture, the Jews took an active part in programs and organizations that they had in common with Hungarian Gentiles. Probably the best example of this consisted of the colorful festivals and parades that were held in the 1880s and 1890s in many American cities and towns, often on March 15 to honor Kossuth and his revolution. The Cleveland Festival of September 1887 illustrates this outpouring of patriotic sentiment, as reported in full in the *Plain Dealer* over a period of weeks.[4] Preliminary plans called for a wedding procession with people in typical Hungarian costumes, including "Hussars on horseback" and "the Csikos, the daredevil bareback riders of the Puszta whose method of riding a horse is not unlike that of the American cowboy." There would be three bands for the procession and a gypsy band for dancing. Hungarian societies were invited from Columbus, Cincinnati, and other cities. The Hungarians along the line of march would be asked to decorate their houses. "A mass meeting of Hungarians, irrespective of their membership of any society, will be held."

It is difficult to identify a non-Jewish name on the planning committee, which represented five organizations. On the other hand it is clear that the wedding procession was designed to simulate a Christian marriage. Wagons would carry the bride, the groom, the maid of honor, a priest, a country judge, landowners, and a Hungarian nobleman and lady. The retinue would include gypsies, shepherds, and peasants, as well as veterans of the revolutionary war of 1848. In preparation, Adolph Deutsch and several other Jews organized a choral society.

After the event the newspaper reported that "the rain yesterday played havoc with the Hungarian festival . . . [but] the ardor of Magyar enthusiasm could not be dampened by rain. . . . Hussars, Honveds [soldiers] and Csikos in their national costumes on horseback were galloping along the downtown streets, while the picturesque wedding procession was forming." No word but *resplendent* could describe the Hussars in their "tight scarlet knee breeches, enameled top boots, a sky-blue dress coat ornamented across the breast with gold lace frogs." Each man wore a white coat trimmed with fur and on his head a *kalpec* ornamented with heron feathers.

Speeches were made in Hungarian, German, and English. It appears that half the parade marshals were Jewish, half Christians. Joseph Black, a leader in the Jewish community, took the occasion at the reception the following day to issue a call for a convention to form a national federation of all Hungarian societies in the country. It was in short a happening in which Jewish and Gentile Hungarians shared, apparently without distinction.

For another illustration of devotion to Magyarism, consider the case of the patriotic statues.[5] In 1902 the Hungarians of Cleveland put up a statue of Louis Kossuth in a public park. There were four officers of the committee to make the arrangements—three of them were Jews. Three years later Hungarians in a number of American cities raised funds for a statue of George Washington to be erected in Budapest. The Hungarian-American newspaper editor Tihamér Kohányi, a leading Catholic in Cleveland, led the delegation. A list of the several organizing committees shows fifty-one Gentiles and fifteen Jews.

On a political issue, following the dismemberment of Hungary after World War I, the Jews living here were vociferous in demanding the restoration of pre-Trianon Hungary. Their newspaper appealed to world Jewry to protest this "grave injustice" and proclaimed—with a dash of hyperbole—that "for a thousand years we have had a peaceful blessed home at the feet of the Carpathian mountains . . . We found protection and refuge . . . and enjoyed religious freedom."[6] Earlier they had joined with Gentile Hungarians in public calls for reversing the decisions taken at Trianon.

But in these same years when Jews were cooperating with Gentiles in demonstrations of patriotism and nationalism, they were asserting a separate Jewish identity with regard to Hungary. Three years before the big festival in 1887, the Jews condemned the Hungarian government for its handling of outbreaks of anti-Semitism. Four Hungarian-Jewish organizations in Cleveland joined in protesting "the barbarous excesses" that were then being carried out against Jews in the Magyar homeland. "We invite them to come to America, the harbor of refuge of all nations," the protest said, "since the Hungarian government is unable to defend them." The Hungarian Jews of Cleveland stood "ready to aid them not only with advice but also materially to the extent of our means."[7] They shared concern with the Jews of Hungary, especially during "menacing times such as the Tiszae-szlár blood libel in 1883."[8] Overall, however, a strong feeling of patriotism brought Jewish and Christian Hungarians together in America in demonstrations of national loyalty and ethnic solidarity.

On the cultural level, Gentiles and Jews shared tastes in food and music. In the American novel by Sylvia Golden about Hungarian immigrants, there are many references to *palacsinta* or thin pancakes; *pogasca*, rectangular cookies made from pie crust, and *goulash*. The Bentons enjoyed dancing the *csárdás* and Mr. Benton his card game of *calabrias*. From other sources it seems that these tastes cut across Jewish-Gentile lines.

Undoubtedly of greater importance was the matter of language. Both Jews and Gentiles had studied the Magyar language in school, along with the country's history, its poetry, and the lives of such national heroes as Kossuth and the poet Petőfi. Both groups, incidentally, had a very high literacy rate. It must be emphasized that the uniqueness of the Magyar language set them apart from other ethnic groups. Despite the widespread and erroneous practice of calling them Slavs, the immigrants from Hungary did not have much in common with the large Slavic population in this country, a population incidentally which was becoming more nationalistic and at times anti-Hungarian. The Magyar language fostered the use of the same reading matter by Jewish and Gentile Hungarians and encouraged their participation in common cultural activities and organizations.

The most obvious result of the exclusive nature of the Magyar tongue was the newcomers' need for news and information in their own language.[9] Many newspapers for Hungarians were launched—the estimates range from 67 to 113—representing different political orientations and constituencies, including several in German and English, and possibly one in

Yiddish. Some of the very early journals were highly literary and addressed to intellectuals among the '48ers; generally these lasted only a short time. The later efforts to establish newspapers were beset by problems of financing and finding professionally adequate journalists. The Magyar press and its difficulties were typical of the foreign language press in general.[10] Three periodicals became national daily papers: *Szabadság* (Liberty); *Amerikai Magyar Népszava* (American Hungarian Voice of the People); and *Előre* (Forward), a socialist paper.[11]

Szabadság was established in 1891 in Cleveland, but had a national circulation.[12] Its principal financial backers were Theodore Kundtz, a Catholic, and Joseph Black, a Jewish leader in Cleveland. Its editor was the forceful Tihamér Kohányi, a prominent figure in the Gentile Hungarian community. Judging by excerpts from its first two years of publication, *Szabadság* was ardently devoted to Magyar nationalism, strongly prolabor, and Democratic in its politics.[13] The paper was vehemently opposed to pan-Slavism among the emigrants from Hungary. Chafing at the subordinate place that Hungary occupied in the Austro-Hungarian Empire, the paper objected to the way the Hapsburgs' embassies in this country treated the Magyar immigrants. A few quotations will illustrate the paper's concerns and its orientation.

A number of articles reflected the dangerous occupations of the Hungarian workers: "Many of our countrymen work in the plough factory at South Bend, Indiana. The whetstone has already killed two of them. We warn our countrymen in time . . . The dust created by the grinding of the plough steel on the whetstone settles in the lungs of the workmen and causes consumption in a few years." Repeatedly the editors railed against pan-Slavic ideas: "Dr. Francisci has been expelled from all Hungarian societies in Cleveland for his pan-Slavic feelings. Now, however, he would like to sneak back into the Kossuth society as official physician." But there was also occasional compassion for the non-Magyar. The following quotation did not apply to Dr. Francisci: "Despite the fact that he is a Slovak, he is still our countryman."

The paper helped people locate each other in a very mobile work force: "József Viszlai of Etna, Pennsylvania seeks the whereabouts of Jószef Gunya." The village back home was never far away. In the August 25 issue of *Szabadság*, József Uhlar of Freeland, Pennsylvania, asked those who emigrated to America from Tállya, Hungary, to contribute to the sum needed to repair the cracked bell of the Roman Catholic church there. Mr.

Uhlar regrets that the contributions have not come up to his expectations so far.

Obviously, much of this material did not reflect the concerns of the Jewish immigrants. With the possible exception of the small minority engaged in heavy industry, most of them would not have been so interested in the things that worried the miners and steel workers. This difference in interests of course applied to the news about church affairs. Nevertheless Jews were very active as editors, publishers, and journalists in the Hungarian press. Among them were Martin Himler and Ernest I. Mandel, who worked on labor and leftist newspapers, as did Vilmos Loew on the staff of the socialist paper in Cleveland in 1895. Others were Marcus Schnitzer, Marcus Braun, and Géza Berkó.

Berkó edited the *Amerikai Magyar Népszava*, which began publication in Cleveland in 1895 as a socialist organ, failed, and reopened in New York two years later under his direction. A look at its edition of June 1, 1907 suggests the kind of material Berkó judged would interest his Hungarian readers.[14] The front page carried news of Emperor Franz Joseph's political problems and a notice of the appointment of a Polish bishop as a Greek Catholic cardinal; an editorial weighed in on the Polish-Hungarian struggle within the church. There was news of a visit by an Austro-Hungarian warship and the normal New York crime and city hall news. Inside the paper was much coverage of churches, funerals, and appeals for both Hungarian patriotism and Americanization.

There were notices which told of a hundred men needed by an iron mine, of apartments for rent (with or without food and washing), English lessons, and men trying to find their wives. Sickness insurance was advertised as available regardless of the applicant's religion. Many of the ads carried Jewish names for dentists, lawyers, and doctors; for "banks" that sold cheap tickets to Europe or sent money there; and for real estate brokers. Two Jewish midwives trained in Budapest were looking for work.

What was the role of the Hungarian press in "the Magyar connection" between Jews and Gentiles? It is a fair assumption, even though there is no way of measuring it, that Jews by the thousands were readers of the Hungarian newspapers and in this way were exposed to much of the same information and editorial opinion. The newspapers also published the work of Hungarian poets and novelists, some of whom were working newspapermen in this country. All this the Jews read along with their non-Jewish countrymen. But, as we saw with the quotations from *Szabadság*, much of the newspaper content did not fit the needs and interests of the Jewish immigrants. In this connection the twentieth anniversary edition of *Szabadság* furnishes us with an example of this and of what we earlier called the "invisible Hungarian Jew." This lavish issue of the paper on December 21, 1911, had sixteen full pages on the religious history of the Hungarian churches, but not a word on Hungarian synagogues. Table 12 shows at least forty-five Jewish congregations in existence at that time.

The Jews from Hungary typically knew more than the Magyar language and thousands were therefore able to read the Yiddish press and the German press. It is known that Hungarian Jews provided editors and journalists for both. Rabbi Morris Wechsler, for one, edited the German-language *New Yorker Judische Zeitung*, apparently addressed to Orthodox Jews.[15]

The Hungarian Jews had few journals of their own, perhaps evidence that they were satisfied reading the Magyar, German, Yiddish, and English press. A weekly paper called *Béke* (Peace) was published for Cleveland's Hungarian-Jewish community in 1916, but it was of short duration.[16] Only scattered copies can still be found of the *American Hungarian Jewish Review*, which had published five editions by 1922 and boasted, with little fear of being contradicted, that it was "the only periodical in the U.S. defending the interests of the Hungarian Jews." In 1922 it appeared in English and, as with many other periodicals, was essentially the house organ of an organization, the Federation of Hungarian Jews in America, but more about that enterprise later.

There is also a trace left of *The Hungarian Jew*, the second edition of which appeared in 1932 also in English. At that late date it was still valiantly, though erroneously, claiming a close Jewish-Magyar relationship in the thousand-year history of the Hungarian kingdom. "Hungarian Jewish publications," one observer concluded, "emphasized less religious issues than their emancipation and the struggle against Antisemitism. Some short-lived papers fought for this purpose. They, however, did not affect Hungarians outside their own circle."[17] There was a paper in Yiddish directed primarily to Hungarian Jews. Rabbi Wechsler and David Apotheker published the *Idishe Weibershe Zeitung* (Jewish Women's Newspaper) in 1888 for Hungarian readers.

In general, while the ties of language may have helped to some extent to maintain the connection between Hungarian Jews and Gentiles, language signified a divergence of interests as well, since Jews were also reading the Yiddish and German press and increasingly the periodicals in English.

The Hungarian immigrants needed more than newspapers to confront their problems and to meet their everyday needs as aliens in a strange land. They needed religious institutions as well as organized ways to provide them with economic security, social contacts, recreational activities, and cultural nourishment. For these purposes they formed organizations of all kinds. One estimate puts the number of Hungarian organizations above two thousand in 1920. (See Appendix 4 for information on the numbers and types of these organizations.) Foremost in number and evidently in importance among these organizations were the sick benefit lodges, but let us first consider the cultural and social associations, a few of which brought Jewish and non-Jewish Hungarians together on the basis of common language and shared interests.

The Hungarians' love of music, theater, and dancing colored the activities of many societies, including hundreds of local fraternal and insurance lodges.[18] They sponsored choruses and brass bands, amateur drama groups, orchestras, and dances. Athletic associations, literary societies, and political clubs sprang up.

Amateur Hungarian theater, consisting mostly of operettas, folk plays, and church plays, began in New York in the 1860s and a permanent non-professional company was established there in 1887.[19] One of the actors was the Jewish journalist Géza Berkó, and he and another Jew by the name of Gyula Roth joined with other Hungarians in 1906 to organize a professional theater, though it did not last long. Nevertheless, fifty-three adaptations and productions of Hungarian plays in both English and Magyar appeared on the New York stage between 1908 and 1940.[20]

By far the largest number of Hungarian organizations consisted entirely of Gentile members. Those with all-Jewish membership will be discussed in the next chapter. A few included both Jews and Gentiles. Some of these were found in the incorporation papers filed in New York, as described in Appendix 4. A "verein" was set up in 1881 to assist indigent immigrants to find jobs. Shortly thereafter the New York Hungarian Art Amateur Association was launched for social, literary, and musical purposes and "to cultivate and spread the Hungarian language" through lectures, drama, and vocal performances. Learning English was the stated goal of another club. The most unusual of the mixed membership groups was the First Hungarian Janitor's Instruction Association of New York, established in 1912 "to instruct the members how to properly and carefully perform the duties of Janitors," as well as to provide fellowship.

Most prominent of the Jewish and Gentile organizations was the *Magyar*

Társulat (Hungarian Association), formed in New York in 1885. Its original intent was to aid and protect Hungarian immigrants and it was launched with money raised at the first Magyar folk festival in the city. The association was headed by the energetic Dr. Árpád Gerster, who became a famous surgeon, a leader in medical circles, and a founder of a Catholic Hungarian church in New York.[21] Dr. Gerster had had many Jewish acquaintances throughout his life and practically all the members of his incorporating group for the Hungarian Association were Jews. Rabbi Aaron Wise, father of the famous Stephen Wise, was among the founding members. The society offered legal advice and gave clothing to poor immigrants and sometimes tickets back to Hungary. It opened a bank so immigrants could send money home. But *Magyar Társulat* fell on hard times. "It could not operate as a cultural association, so it continued as a travel bureau. It could not operate as a travel bureau, so it became an exchange office. It could not operate even as such, and finally had to close its doors."[22] Its final undoing was an unsuccessful plan to send a thousand Hungarians to Budapest to celebrate the one thousandth anniversary of the Magyars' arrival in Hungary.

The demise of the association was not unlike the fate of many other immigrant organizations. They were ephemeral. They set high goals but had trouble attracting and holding people. These organizations came and went and new ones arose to satisfy the newcomers' need for comfort and enjoyment in a Hungarian atmosphere where they knew the language and the culture. In some places, such as Pennsylvania, there was a good deal of interaction in organizations between Gentile and Jewish Hungarians. "The Jews," Joseph Balogh found, "have played significant roles in Hungarian cultural circles. Their financial contributions have aided many a floundering Hungarian institution."[23]

Attempts to establish federations of Hungarian organizations, both at the local level and nationally, were undertaken in the late 1880s. A reference was made earlier to an event at which "the first steps were taken to call a national Hungarian convention" in connection with the 1887 festival in Cleveland. This was "for the purpose of uniting the Hungarian societies throughout the country, the principal object of the union being to receive Hungarian emigrants at New York and distribute them through the country in places where they can do the most good for themselves and others."[24] Joseph Black, Mór Weinberger, and other Jews were among the leaders in the move to form the united organization.

A strong motivation for such a national federation was the desire to buttress the shaky financial base of the many scattered sick benefit societies and thus to develop, in effect, national insurance programs. Some of the societies were as small as the group of men living in one boarding house. Still another objective of the proposed organization was to have a protective association that would be a channel for communication with the Old Country and would raise the status of Hungarians vis-à-vis native Americans. Hungarians, who were called "Hunkies," were often the butt of ridicule and discrimination.

Tihamér Kohányi, the editor of *Szabadság,* was an ardent promoter of the new federation in the columns of that newspaper. However, the new confederation fell victim to rivalry between Hungarian communities in New York and Cleveland and other stresses, and it soon expired. In 1897 the United Hungarian Societies of Cleveland was launched to coordinate cultural, charitable, and welfare activities in that city and seems to have lasted much longer. When a renewal of anti-Hapsburg agitation in Hungary in 1906 brought strong reactions among Hungarians in America, the leadership again held a convention and called for a national organization, the American Hungarian Federation.[25] This attempt, supported mainly by intellectuals and middle class leadership including Jews, did not strike deep roots and it had also collapsed before the First World War.

We complete this survey of the factors that tended to hold the Jewish and Gentile Hungarians together with an examination of the reciprocal roles they occupied in everyday living in urban neighborhoods and small towns. For this we recall Morawska's study in Johnstown and the surrounding towns of western Pennsylvania, where Slavic and Hungarian immigrants were principally employed as laborers in the mills and coal mines. The Jewish immigrants were mostly shopkeepers, artisans, and peddlers who served the eastern European laborers. In these small localities the two groups were in effect recapitulating the interlocking roles they had had before coming to America.

It is not known for certain to what extent Jewish shopkeepers and lawyers and carpenters in the big cities were serving Gentile Hungarians. One gets the impression in reading about areas such as Yorkville in New York and the Buckeye Road neighborhood of Cleveland that a good number of Jewish merchants, artisans, and professionals were living side by side with their Gentile compatriots and were providing them with goods and services. One observer wrote: "On the basis of Hungarian-American newspapers and anniversary publications, we can conclude that Hungarian-

Jewish immigrants who had already been engaged in commerce in Hungary made up a significant portion of Hungarian shopkeepers."[26] Another said that the Jews had "begun to learn the English language and American political ways and to invest in small businesses, for which the Hungarian sojourners soon furnished a natural clientele."[27] A third researcher found with respect to the early Jewish settlers in Cleveland, many of whom were Hungarian, that "their urban background and aptitudes proved to be of great service to the larger number of immigrants from rural villages who shortly settled in the Buckeye community."[28]

On the national level, there is a useful source of information about the professional and business leadership of the American Hungarian community at the turn of the century. In May 1896 *The Hungarian American* published its Millennial Festival Edition to commemorate the one thousandth anniversary of the Magyar entrance into Hungary. It was an occasion to parade the leading Magyars in America, and a count of those mentioned by name shows this division between those with clearly Jewish names and others:

	Jewish	Others
Lawyers	11	2
Businessmen	10	2
Physicians★	10	1
Clergy	1	3
Architects	1	2
Other	7	7
Total	40	17

★Includes one pharmacist

It is clear from this listing that on the eve of the twentieth century Jews occupied a central position in the middle-class and professional ranks of Hungarians in the United States. In commercial pursuits and in the service roles of lawyer and doctor, they were predominant in the Who's Who list. Among all these high-achieving men one woman appears. Rosalie Loew was, according to the editors, one of a few women then practicing law in New York City and the only "Hungarian-American girl lawyer." She was the granddaughter of Rabbi Leopold Loew of Szeged, a famous intellectual, theologian, and historian, and a leader in the Enlightenment movement. Her family had emigrated and she had been born in New York in 1873.

We can now summarize the factors that bolstered the Jews' Magyar connection. These were the ties of patriotism and of culture, of reading the same newspapers, of participating even to a limited degree in the same cultural activities and organizations, and finally of daily dealings with each other in commercial and service relationships. These influences had the effect of holding the two groups together as "Hungarian immigrants all" in their first days as newcomers to America. An observer of the scene, writing in the 1920s admittedly with sweeping rhetorical flourishes, supports this conclusion. Géza Kende, in his book on Hungarians in America, rejects the notion

> that the Jewish Hungarians are not good Hungarians. The history of the American Hungarians proves the contrary, that is, the American Hungarian Jews participated and played prominent roles in the patriotic, social, and cultural movements of the American Hungarians. If there was a need to contribute for Hungarian charity, the American Hungarian Jews were among the first with their exemplary generosity, not as Jews but as Hungarians.[29]

That there was close contact between the two groups can be seen in interviews with Jewish immigrants and from their relatives' recollections.[30] Mrs. F. says she went to Hungarian parties and was "very involved in everything Hungarian." She had come from a very religious family and was active in a Hungarian synagogue. Mr. O. read Magyar newspapers, vacationed at Budapest Rest in Big India, New York, but was "not very involved in Jewish affairs and did not speak Yiddish." By contrast, Mr. F. said he read the Yiddish press and joined a Jewish lodge, but he also enjoyed a Hungarian club where people could drink and gamble. A true Magyar patriot, he said his friends talked him out of going back to Hungary to fight for his fatherland in World War I. "His whole working life, Hungarians had helped him to get jobs." Mr. N. was active in Hungarian Jewish affairs. He bought and loved Hungarian records, dancing the csárdás, and enjoyed Hungarian art, clothes, and excellent Hungarian cooking and baking. "This family's preference for Hungarian ethnicity definitely took precedence above Judaism and Hebrew culture, education and values."

There were, in short, strong attachments to Hungary and Magyar ways. There were also strong divisions and even antipathies between the Jews and Gentiles from Hungary.

Religion was of course a sharp divider in several respects. In the realm of ideas and theology, there was a vast chasm between the two groups. And the institutions of religion—the synagogue and the church—sharply divided the two groups. They had been focal points of spiritual and social life in Europe and continued to be very important to the immigrants here, pushing the Christians and the Jews down different paths. From the moment the Jews arrived in numbers in the 1870s they began to set up small, loosely structured groups for worship and for communal activities. It took only ten men to form a minyan, or prayer group. They did this in their apartments and homes on the Lower East Side of New York, in downtown Cleveland, and wherever they settled.

The churches began to develop in the 1890s along denominational lines, some of them growing out of the sick benefit societies. There were problems in financing the churches, which in Hungary had been supported by the government. It was difficult in the beginning to obtain Hungarian pastors and there were problems in relating to the various American denominations.[31] The complexities and obstacles facing the churches lie beyond the scope of this inquiry. What is important to recognize here is that the considerable energy and resources that went into organizing for religious purposes tended to pull Christians and Jews farther along down diverging routes.

Much the same can be said about the sick benefit organizations, which for the most part were established along religious lines by both Jews and Gentiles. These "became the cornerstone of community life" among the Gentile Hungarians.[32] Day laborers needed "a small pool of money they could draw on to pay their room, board, and medical bills in case they were sick or injured." By 1910 there were more than one thousand of these.[33] Some of them took on a religious function for the Christians (as they did for the Jews) since they provided spiritual comfort as well as a small measure of economic security. In a later stage of development some emerged as churches and synagogues.

Although Jews were much involved in the attempts to consolidate the sick benefit societies into national federations, at the local level the societies were almost invariably either Gentile or Jewish, thus becoming another factor that separated the two constituencies. A case in point was the First Hungarian Aid Society, organized by a group of German-speaking Hungarian Jews in Cleveland in the 1860s. The same Hungarian writer who insisted that the Jews were in fact "good Hungarians" said of this society that it "did very little in maintaining Hungarian life."[34]

Work was a source of difference between Jews and non-Jews from Hungary. The former were concentrated in the garment and cigar-making trades and petty commerce; the latter were in heavy industry, especially in the mines and steel mills. Not only were their work places separate and very different in nature, but their working-class politics diverged considerably. It appears from Puskás's study that the Gentile miners and factory workers were in general militant in their political orientation.[35] Some were attracted to the Socialist Labor Party (SLP) and others favored either the more moderate Socialist Party or the more revolutionary Industrial Workers of the World.

Overall the Jews chose less radical, "bread and butter" unions, middle-of-the-road socialist organizations, and even the mainstream politics of the Republican and Democratic parties, as we shall see in Chapter 14. In the main, the Christian and Jewish Hungarians belonged to different trade unions and political organizations, which became still another divisive force in their relationship.

Anti-Semitism, Hungarian style, had managed to make the trans-Atlantic trip without difficulty. It took several forms. A few Hungarian organizations explicitly excluded Jews. The First Magyar Conversational and Sickness Aid Association was the first to do this in New York.[36] The Slovak associations, particularly, by defining their fraternal associations in Christian terms, barred Jews from membership—and even paid a living Jew the full death benefit in order to get him out of the organization.[37] An analysis of the by-laws of sick benefit associations found that seven out of thirty-six barred Jews.[38]

One of the largest insurance programs took its name, Verhovay, from a member of the Hungarian parliament known as an anti-Semite. When the founders were challenged on this, they said they had not known his reputation, but it turned out they had earlier considered naming the association after an even more "rabidly anti-Semitic" member of parliament.[39] Jews responded to these expressions of anti-Semitism by falling back on their old mechanism of disdain and contempt for the people who did these things. They called this "rishus," a word that connotes both evil and anti-Semitism.

Jews were frequently looked upon as intellectuals, a category of people heartily disliked by certain Hungarians of peasant background. The target of their antagonism was the Jewish intellectual of the educated middle class.[40] This anti-intellectualism was built into the constitutions of some organizations which barred anyone from holding office who had not been a physical worker in Hungary.

Earlier we pointed to the leadership positions of Jews in the Hungarian community in 1896; we must now call attention to the reverse side of that coin. Their leadership, together with their rapid steps toward Americanization, were bitterly resented in some Magyar circles. This is evident in this bitter, sarcastic dispatch written by Baron Lajos Ambrózy, a consul of the Austro-Hungarian monarchy, to the ambassador in Washington, Ladislaus Hengelmüller von Hengervár, who represented the governments of both Austria and Hungary in the United States. Ambrózy was reporting on his interviews with Hungarian clergymen in New York:

> We came finally to speak of a matter which inflammed the rhetoric of the clergy to a passionate pitch, namely the role of the Jews in the Hungarian colony in New York. Reverend Kovács asserts that the Jews—of all immigrants from all lands—are by far the quickest to become naturalized. By means of an ostentatious patriotism toward Hungary and America/Marcus Braun/and by becoming close-knit, the Hungarian Jews have pushed to the top of the Hungarian colony of New York and there is no dislodging them.

The reference to Marcus Braun, a Hungarian Jewish journalist and political figure, probably stems from the fact that, a few years before the baron wrote this dispatch, Braun had published a report, commissioned by the United States government, entitled "Immigration Abuses: Glimpses of Hungary and Hungarians." This could hardly have endeared him to the Hungarian authorities. The baron's dispatch continues with its description of Hungarian Jews in New York City:

> The large majority are Catilinarian types—deserters, embezzlers, counterfeiters, and every kind of evader of justice. Nevertheless, there is in New York no Hungarian lawyer, not one Hungarian doctor, and not one banker who is not Jewish.
>   They dominate the well-run home for Hungarian immigrants and all important Hungarian associations. This keeps the Hungarian Christian intellectuals of New York from participating in any communal activities. Any decent person withdraws and the only element that can be relied on in Hungarian church and school affairs is the poor working class.[41]

The consul was reporting the views of Hungarian clergymen, who must be reckoned among the leaders of the Magyar community.

The Hungarian government treated the Jewish émigrés quite differently from the "true" Magyars. The government was eager to retain the loyalty of its people in the United States, primarily with a view to having them return. This was their attitude toward the departing Magyars; they were not displeased to see the Slovaks and other minorities leave the country permanently. To reinforce their ties to the Magyars, the Hungarian government undertook an ambitious program known as "American Action." Among its strategies was the provision of funds to Hungarian churches and newspapers in this country in order to enlist them in the effort to promote loyalty to the government in Budapest.

The Jews were omitted from American Action.[42] Interesting evidence of this comes again from a report by Baron Ambrózy to his ambassador in Washington. He wrote concerning the Hungarian press: "About the above-mentioned paper of Jewish-socialist tendencies edited by G. Berkó (originally Berkovics), I need hardly say another word with a view to a possible subsidy."[43] The parenthetical phrase concerning "Berkovics" appears in the original Ambrózy dispatch.

Although the prime minister's office in Budapest was sending and receiving thousands of documents concerning emigration in the years from 1902 to 1918, only two documents deal with the Jews and these were "highly critical and hostile to Jews and Jewish leaders in Hungarian-American societies," Yeshayahu Jelinek found.[44] He notes that reports in the files accused the Jews of "overzealous patriotism and activities harmful to Hungary. The documents pointed out the republican tendencies of these Jews, which were displayed in a show-off fashion." Apparently they felt that too much Jewish patriotism was not a good thing for Hungary.

Immediately after the First World War much was done by the churches and other Magyar organizations to protest the "dismemberment" of Hungary in the peace treaty. Jews took the same stance, but it is noteworthy that the two groups were acting more and more independently of each other through different organizations. Moreover, the Magyars in this country were engaged in a burst of intense ethnic activity after the war. Probably because many of them had now decided to remain in this country, they built new churches and clubs in Cleveland and the immigrants enjoyed a flowering of festivals, picnics, plays, and lectures.[45] "Grand committees" in several cities "raised money for Hungarian prisoners of war, and observed Hungarian national holidays" and again attempted to form a national federation.[46]

But Jews were no longer prominent in these activities. Their efforts were being channeled through organizations they were developing. A disengagement was occurring between the two groups year by year. This can be seen by taking a glance at what happened to the Hungarian colonies in Cleveland and New York. Fifteen years after World War I the central coordinating body in Cleveland, the United Hungarian Societies, listed forty-four affiliates, none of which can be identified as a Jewish organization.[47] Only four or five names among the scores of officers appear to be Jewish. The list is heavily oriented toward the churches and their auxiliary societies. The information from New York yields the same result. One can scan a list of fifty-four Hungarian lodges and societies as of 1940 and not find a single Jewish organization.[48] A number of churches are included and many branches of the national insurance organizations, but none of the Hungarian Jewish fraternal orders or *landsmanschaften* in existence at that time are listed.

The Gentiles were finding it difficult to pass along to their children knowledge of the Magyar language even in such Hungarian strongholds as Cleveland. More and more people in these families spoke English, though the churches were trying valiantly to teach Hungarian to the children.[49] That language was fading out even more quickly among the American-born children and grandchildren of Jewish immigrants from Hungary. For them Hungarian culture was becoming a thing of the past. There were fewer and fewer Jewish weddings at which the csárdás was danced.

In the interwar years, the Hungarian miners and factory workers were moving to the larger cities and within the cities were improving their living conditions by shifting to better residential areas. Their movements were very similar to the changes the Jews were making, but overall they did not move to the same places—geographically, occupationally, or economically.

There is ample testimony about the outcome of the disengagement that was occurring.[50] "By the end of the Depression, the majority of Jewish Hungarian organizational and religious leaders withdrew from active participation in Hungarian-American affairs," Susan M. Papp wrote.[51] Hungarian diplomats and writers "frequently complained," Jelinek found, "that the Jews were among the first to assimilate in America and lose their Magyarhood."[52] Paula Benkart puts the situation succinctly: "In the long run Protestant and Catholic Hungarians proved to have much more in common with each other than with their Jewish countrymen."[53] The converse was of course just as true. James MacGregor Burns concluded with respect to the situation in the Lower East Side as far back as the turn of the century that most of the Jews "act far more like Jews with a common culture, however, than Hungarians or Russians or Romanians with separate national identities."[54] In short, the Jews' Magyar connection had been stretched thin and was disintegrating well before the approach of the Second World War.

★

C H A P T E R 1 3

The Jewish Bond

One of the "three worlds" the immigrants faced was the American Jewish community and this posed a number of questions for them. Would the Hungarian Jews form their own separate organizations or would they quickly blend into an emerging American Jewry? If the newcomers stayed together, how would they organize themselves? Would they, for example, establish religious or secular organizations? How long would their organizations last? Finally, how would the immigrants relate to the tensions in American Judaism between traditionalists and reformers?

A useful point of departure is the assertion that at first the Hungarian-Jewish immigrants had more in common with each other than they had with Jews from other lands. This was much more the case with those who came after 1880 than it had been with the more secular and assimilated '48ers. The earlier arrivals mixed easily with other Hungarians and with German Jews as well as with the established German community, but the people who arrived in the Big Migration were more tightly connected to each other by Orthodoxy, by small-town ties, and by custom and tradition. The same human needs and shared experiences that caused them to cluster together as they left the Old Country bound them to each other when they stepped ashore in a new land far from—and very different from—Eperjes and Sárospatak. These centripetal forces had the result, in the short run, of separating the Hungarian Jews from the much larger body of Polish and Russian Jews who were arriving with them after 1880.

This observation recalls the quotations in our introductory chapter to the effect that the Jews from Hungary were perceived as different. "Different" in the eyes of many Russian and Polish Jews often meant worse. There were several strands in this attitude. The Hungarians were seen to be aloof, snobbish, clannish. They lacked the warmth and earthiness of Yiddishkeit. After all, they spoke German or at best a kind of Germanic Yiddish. Their Judaism was watery; they had succumbed to the Reform spilling over from

Germany. They put on airs of middle-class gentility and were more eager to be considered Magyars than Jews. Back in Hungary the Jews had stayed out of the great movements of modern Jewry: Zionism, Jewish labor organization, socialism. It was, to put the best face on it, a diluted kind of Jewishness.

The sentiments of the Hungarian Jews toward those from farther east in Europe were just as pejorative. The people from Russia and Poland were, in the view of some of the Magyarized Jews, uncouth anachronisms, throwbacks to an earlier time. Their "jargon" was just that—a deteriorated form of German. Decent people, probably, but not very cultured. When Howard Morley Sachar characterized the way "Western" Jews perceived those from Eastern Europe, he used much the same imagery: "backward, poverty-stricken, unhygienic, frequently quite ignorant of the world's most cherished secular values."[1] Marriage to a non-Hungarian Jew was most unusual among the Hungarian immigrants.

Possibly this overstates the case, both ways. How many people actually held these opinions is hard to say. But vestiges have hung on in the half-jokes about Hungarian Jews and in their half-forgotten gibes at Galizianers and Litvaks. Nonetheless, to the extent that Hungarian Jews were whole-hearted participants in the Magyar-cum-German culture of the Austro-Hungarian monarchy, they really did differ from the people of the Pale of Settlement in some of the ways suggested by the stereotypic views. This is despite the fact that many immigrants came from the northeastern part of Hungary, where Jewish life was not utterly different from that in Galicia only a stone's throw away. In fact, many of them were only a generation or two away from Galicia, from which their parents and grandparents had migrated to Hungary.

For the majority of Hungarian Jews there were language and cultural differences that set them apart from Eastern European Jews.[2] One evidence of this is that Hungarian Jews did not participate to any real extent in the rich, throbbing Yiddish life of the Lower East Side in New York.[3] On the contrary, they showed a preference for an atmosphere where Magyar or German was spoken, where people could relax and talk about things they had in common "on the other side." Consequently the Hungarian "greenhorns" went through an initial period of what might be called separatism before they and their children entered fully into the Jewish community in America.[4] This first stage of self-separation was very likely seen from the Russian and Polish side as aloofness and snobbishness. From the perspective of the Hungarian Jews, the ambience they sought and created was more comfortable than the unfamiliar world around them. The same dynamics of course were at work with the other ethnic groupings among the Jews. In St. Louis, for instance, besides the "Hungarische Shul" there were the "Roumanische Schul," the "Polische Shul," a "Bavarian Shul," and a "Bohemian Shul."[5]

Responding to this need for the security that comes with familiarity, the immigrants lost no time in setting up Hungarian Jewish organizations. The religious people among them got together in groups of ten or more to pray. As workers concerned about a loss of income through sickness, they organized "sick benefit societies." They wanted cemeteries of their own. These needs were joined with the desire for companionship, recreation, and cultural activities. The result was the outcropping of many small, independent organizations. Hungarian Jews established so many of these societies "that they were able to support a weekly newspaper of their own" in 1922.[6]

The word *landsmanschaften* indicates that these societies brought together people from the same place or "land."[7] Not many of the Hungarian societies carried the name of a particular city or town, a practice which seems to have been more prevalent among Polish and Russian Jews.[8] Perhaps because the Jewish communities in Hungary from which the immigrants came were so small, there were not enough people from the same place to form an organization. But there were some: the First Bereg Munkacser Sick and Benefit Society and those which traced their origin to Huszt, Kőrösmező, and Ungvár.[9] Most often the associations were called "Hungarian" or "Austro-Hungarian" rather than being identified with a specific city, town, or county. Among them there was, naturally, a Kossuth society; one was named for the Magyar poet Petőfi and one for a Hungarian count.

Most *landsmanschaften* were not explicitly undertaken as "Jewish activities," but the immigrants' participation in these secular organizations of their own making had the effect of strengthening their ties to other Hungarian Jews. At the same time this participation on the part of workers with little free time drew them away from contacts with non-Jewish Hungarians.

In the course of this study, as shown in Table 10, we identified 156 Hungarian Jewish organizations which we classified as follows: seventy-two sick benefit societies, some of which took on philanthropic functions; thirty-one social, cultural, and recreational (and occasionally political) associations; fifty-three congregations and synagogues.[10] The largest concentration of records on these organizations was a collection of incorporation papers filed in New York City between 1850 and 1920.[11] Consequently New York is probably disproportionately represented in the findings. On the other hand, the characteristics of these societies—both religious and secular—did not seem to differ much by locality.

Few of these organizations were established before 1880. Half were formed after 1900, which suggests that there was a need for them as new immigrants arrived right up to the First World War. Our discussion will consider first the sick benefit societies, then the social clubs, and finally the religious organizations. These distinctions, however, are inherently artificial. Frequently small knots of Hungarian Jews came together to pray in a minyan which simultaneously took on the self-protective functions of a sick benefit society. Or they began the other way round. But in time most of these groups divided the functions and evolved into separate bodies—secular and religious in nature.[12]

The societies that were developed to provide financial aid in case of sickness or death were the most prevalent, forming almost half of the total of 156 organizations. The first, which we encountered in an earlier chapter, was the Hungarian Aid Society organized in 1863 by Morris Black and his friends in Cleveland. Two years later in New York a group of women set up the Ungarischer Frauen Unterstitzungs Verein (The Hungarian Ladies Assistance Association), whose goals were to aid the sick and needy and to defray burial expenses. The vice-president and the treasurer were women; the president was a man. The third, called the Hungarische Kranken und Unterstitzungs Verein— later the Hungarian Society of New York and later still the Mutual Benefit Association for the Sick—was also set up in 1865. Within a few years it had, according to its annual report printed in German, assets of $4,687.35—a tidy sum in those days—"no liabilities," a cemetery plot, and 127 members.

These associations were typical of the many self-help organizations the immigrants founded. They soon turned their energies to helping others, including newly arrived immigrants. An association was set up in 1901, for instance, to establish a hospital that would give free treatment to Austro-Hungarians. The Hungarians' interests also extended to the Holy Land. The Lovers of Zion was set up to protect Austrian and Hungarian Jews who either lived in Jerusalem or who were American citizens planning to emigrate to Palestine.[13] The Bonai Jerusalem Association Anshe Ungarn in 1910 set about purchasing "property in the City of Jerusalem or its environs for the purpose of erecting buildings thereon in which poor and needy Talmudists shall receive free habitation with their families."

What is noteworthy is the wide range of purposes and activities of the *landsmanschaften*. True, one cannot take too literally either their names or what they wrote in their applications to be certified as an incorporated body. For most of these groups we have no information beyond their statements in the incorporation papers and so we do not know how things turned out. Nonetheless, allowing for some unrealistic aspirations, they combined their primary purpose, the provision of financial benefits, with other interests. And this brings us to the social, cultural, and recreational associations, which constituted 31 of the 156 organizations studied.

One finds here the pull between the old and the new. Some, for instance, wanted to "cultivate and spread the Hungarian language and literature," while others wanted to teach and foster English. Those who put on dramatic performances, one can only guess, stayed with the Magyar tongue and its dramatists. Other societies directly sought ways of taking an active part in the American scene. One organization hoped to achieve "political advancement, good representation in this state and the United States." Still other groups allied themselves directly with the Democratic or Republican party. Perhaps the most inventive and comprehensive in its objectives was the Ungarisches Infanterie Corps, which intended to combine "mental improvement" with aid to the sick and distressed, recreation, and military drills, stipulating that members could "wear suitable uniforms to parades." Two other societies also included military drilling in their charters, possibly a throwback to days in the Hungarian army.

In the years before World War I these organizations tended to be local in scope and small in membership. Later some grew into larger bodies that became national or joined others already in existence. Through the activities of these larger organizations, the *landsmanschaften* "introduced their members to American business practices and civic organizations."[14] A case in point is the Independent Order Brith Abraham, whose emergence in 1887 was the result of a split in an earlier organization. It was set in motion at a meeting of twenty-seven men at the Hungarian synagogue Ohab Zedek on Norfolk Street in the Lower East Side. The chairman of that meeting, Jacob Schoen, will turn up later as a prominent leader in Hungarian-Jewish trade unionism. The original purpose of Brith Abraham was to aid members in need, to provide medical services, burial, and death benefits to families, and citizenship assistance. By 1909, thousands of

Russian and Polish immigrants had joined the German-speaking founders. With 210,000 members it became for a short period the largest Jewish fraternal order in the world.

One account asserts that Hungarian and German Jews jointly established six fraternal and self-help organizations between 1843, when B'nai Brith was organized, and 1887, when the Independent Order of Brith Abraham was founded.[15] Several histories of B'nai Brith, however, do not substantiate the role of Hungarian Jews in the founding of that organization.[16]

The social and cultural societies tended to emerge after 1890. Perhaps the purely social clubs were developed only when more basic needs had been addressed and when the immigrants had more time and money for such pursuits. Judging by their names, these were organizations of young, unmarried people, in contrast to the organizations established earlier to meet the needs of families. Music, drama, and readings were popular features of their programs. One society modestly stated its aims as "social entertainments, mutual benefit, benevolent, musical, dramatic, literary, economic, patriotic and other lawful and kindred purposes."

In Cleveland, membership and record books of organizations show a tendency by Hungarian Jews to belong to several Jewish organizations that were not limited to Hungarians. This may also have been the case in New York. The records show dues payments of five or ten cents a month.[17] One man belonged to the Sons of Isaac Association, which kept its records in Yiddish, English, and German; the Franz Joseph Unterstitzung Verein; the Montefiore Lodge of B'nai Brith; the Independent Order of Odd Fellows; and the Hungarian Benevolent and Social Union (HBSU). This last organization merits more description for several reasons, not the least of which is that it is still functioning today though it has changed in many respects.

The beginnings of the HBSU go back to a masquerade ball held in 1883 by younger people among the Hungarian Jews in Cleveland. It was so successful that they decided to set up a permanent organization for social purposes and to care for themselves in case of sickness or other "unfortunate circumstances." In its early years the Hungarian Benevolent and Social Union was a workingman's organization, to judge from a list of nine applicants for membership in 1903. They were all in their twenties and included a cigar maker, a jeweler, a milk dealer, and some garment workers and clerks. The books of the Hungarian Benevolent and Social Union record the payment of $7, $9, and $14 in sick benefits in 1909 and larger amounts in 1913.[18] The society also passed resolutions expressing their condolences, couched in the florid language of the day, with references to the "unsparing hand of death" or the fact that "an overruling Providence has invaded the home of Mr. W." The organization exists today under the name HBSU and it will be taken up again in a later chapter.

Anti-Semitism could also play a part in the formation of an organization. The Knights of Pythias was a large fraternal order, presumably open to all people who believed in the "brotherhood of man." Forty Hungarian Jews, members of the HBSU and their friends, feeling that they had been black-balled simply because of their religion, decided to form their own lodge within the order.[19] They called it the Deák Lodge No. 334 in honor of a revolutionary Hungarian leader.[20] There were denials of anti-Semitism but Louis Black, by then a leader of the Hungarian-Jewish community, observed in a low-key statement that the new Deák lodge "consisted almost entirely of Jewish members and was chartered for their benefit." The lodge exists today.

We get a sense of the atmosphere of these societies from Edward Steiner's description of a meeting he attended.[21] While he does not identify the group, it appears that it was Hungarian, as was Steiner. The meeting is taking place in "the lodge room" on the top story of a rickety old building in which a Polish wedding is in progress, and the sound of the mazurkas and the dancing from the floor below make it difficult to conduct the meeting. (A synagogue occupies the first floor and a saloon the basement.) The occasion was the installation of the society's officers, and men and women were wearing their best clothes. "All the red tape of the American lodge," Steiner writes, "was observed in this society in which most of the members knew nothing of parliamentary law . . . The President used the gavel freely."

The eighty members of the organization come "almost entirely from one district in the old country. Except for three or four men, they are all engaged in manual labour." The retiring president is a graduate of a gymnasium who "speaks four languages poorly and English very well." The officers include Democrats and Republicans plus a cloak presser who is "a strong Social Democrat [who] belongs to the Social Labour wing and hates the Social Democratic wing with a desperate hatred." The secretary, a dealer in plumbers' supplies, "speaks English fluently although only ten years in this country, and is on the road to Harlem—that is, to wealth."

The *landsmanschaften* served important functions for the immigrant. They have been characterized as "a setting for a shared and legitimate venting of nostalgia . . . a loosely structured link to the old country . . . an agency for partial adaptation to American ways without having to suffer exposure to native hostility or condescension."[22] For the Jewish immigrants who came "to monthly meetings to debate fine points of procedure, vote relief for friends back home, and honor one another with office, after which they might settle into a game of pinochle, the *landsmanshaft* was an equivalent to the beer hall or pool parlor of other immigrant communities."[23]

The organizations formed by the immigrants barely outlasted their generation. If one looks for the ninety *landsmanschaften* and synagogues incorporated in New York around the turn of the century in a list compiled in 1938 by a WPA Yiddish Writers' Group, it is apparent that only a handful survived.[24] Some of the sick benefit associations that continued to exist changed their functions and became purely insurance programs or social clubs.

As background for considering how the immigrants related to the Judaism they found in America, let us recall briefly the religious conditions they left behind in Hungary. The Reform movement, which originated in Germany, had made deep inroads into Hungary. At the same time there was a strong Orthodox establishment, especially in the eastern and northern counties from which most of the immigrants came. In these same areas Hasidism had gained a devoted following. These differences had severely and bitterly fractured Hungarian Jewry. Each camp had its own organizations at the community level and the national level. Some Jews, especially in the middle class, had abandoned their religion entirely.

As the immigrants stepped into the Jewish world in America, they may well have felt very much at home, in that American Jews were also vigorously debating what Judaism should be. The 1880s were a time of extraordinary ferment and controversy. Groups and leaders were struggling with the bedrock question of how Judaism could survive in a society where neither government nor rabbinical authority could dictate religious affiliation and practice. Could the Jews retain their religious identity in an essentially Christian country? One rabbi put it this way: The Jews have survived persecution, but can they survive emancipation?[25]

America offered freedom for religion but it also presented conditions that militated against the retention of traditional Judaism. There were strong pressures to work on Saturday and thereby violate the Sabbath as well as

the difficulties of maintaining the dietary laws or *kashrut*. And in an intellectual sense there were competing and alluring movements. A rabbi wrote in
1908: "There seems not to be the slightest qualm of conscience about
changing from Judaism to Christian Science, Unitarianism, Comptism,
Ethical Culture, Atheism and Christianity."[26] For Jewish congregations
there were questions of liturgy and form: should services be held in German, English, or Hebrew? Should organs and choirs be introduced and
should services be held on Sunday?

The question of how to preserve Judaism and still hold on to the younger
generation under such conditions elicited a range of ideological positions.
Until 1860 or so, American Jews had a flowering of Reform Judaism at the
hands of German-speaking rabbis from Europe. Their approach was to
slough off what they saw as outmoded rituals and beliefs and—based on
science, rationality, and ethics—to create a Judaism attuned to the circumstances of nineteenth-century America. Most of the Hungarians, both laity
and rabbis, who came following the Revolution of 1848 moved easily into
the synagogues of the Reformers.

But that was not the end of it; what followed was more complex than
Peter Wiernik's statement that at the turn of the century the Hungarians
"slowly draw nearer to the German and American element in religious
matters."[27] When the Orthodox Jews of the Hungarian towns and villages
came, beginning in the 1870s and gaining momentum after 1880, they
encountered a troubling set of circumstances. Much as in Hungary, Reform
had become the dominant force in American Judaism.[28] The immigrants,
however, could not accept Reform. On the other hand, they found an
Orthodox rabbinate struggling ceaselessly, but with little success, to continue the ways of worship, education, and daily life dictated by the Law.

For the deeply observant, Judaism in America was a scene of disaster,
articulated clearly and audibly by a Hungarian rabbi, Moses Weinberger.
In his book published in 1887 Rabbi Weinberger bitterly assailed the state
of Judaism in America.[29] He found that Jews were ignorant of their own
religion, were violating the most basic Jewish laws, and were debasing the
role of the rabbi and the teacher. He complained that wealth not piety was
the criterion for leadership in the Jewish community. The practice of
kashrut had been commercialized and corrupted.

Weinberger's book appeared at precisely the time that three movements
were organizing to confront the challenges of keeping Judaism alive in
America—and organizing to confront each other. Within the space of a few

years each group acted to formalize and strengthen its position and its institutions, a situation not unlike that in late nineteenth-century Hungary. The Reform movement issued its Pittsburgh Platform in 1885, which accepted the "God-idea" but tempered it with "science and biblical criticism." The Platform discarded ceremonial practices that were presumed not to be in harmony with modern life and placed great store on an ideology compounded of moral truth, universalism, and democracy. The following year the Orthodox rabbis met to plan an organized response to the perceived threat from the Reformers. And a year later the emerging movement of Conservatives organized the Jewish Theological Seminary to train rabbis who would combine elements of both Orthodoxy and Reform.

It is not the intent here to discuss in detail the substance of these religious divisions and developments.[30] Our purpose rather is to indicate in broad terms what the religious currents were in order to understand how the Hungarians fit into them. For this we shall rely primarily on rabbis whose ideas and experiences are recorded.

Among the first rabbis who came to America from Hungary in the years between 1859 and 1873 were a group who shared much the same background: they had studied at both rabbinical academies and universities in Central Europe. They had thus combined traditional Jewish learning with the scientific and secular knowledge of the late nineteenth century. When these men reached the United States they were much closer in their views and practices to Reform Judaism than to Orthodoxy. We speak here principally of Adolph Huebsch, Benjamin Szold, Aaron Bettlehcim, Solomon H. Sonneschein, Leopold Wintner, and Aaron Wise. A brief sketch of Huebsch will serve as an illustration.

After his student days in Prague and his experience in the revolutionary army in Hungary, Huebsch came first to a pulpit in Cincinnati, where within five years he was chosen president of the Rabbinical Council.[31] He then moved to a pulpit in New York where he drew about him a group of wealthy people who built a "moderate Reform temple" on Lexington Avenue. A scholar and author of works on Arabic and Syrian proverbs, Huebsch wrote a revised ritual and prayer book for his congregation and was engaged in the development of Reform institutions, having taken part in the formation of the Union of American Hebrew Congregations and of Hebrew Union College.

It is important to note that six years after his arrival in this country Huebsch was already being called one of the new "Conservatives."[32] This shifting of labels and definitions is quite typical of this period and of the rabbis from Hungary. Some remained strong, even radical proponents of Reform. None exemplifies this more than Solomon Sonneschein, who had grown up in an Orthodox environment in Hungary but then turned toward Reform. A charming but impetuous and erratic man, after moving to America he engaged in "excessive, intemperate polemics" against Orthodoxy, Jewish rituals, and even moderate Reform. He helped to formulate the Pittsburgh Platform of the Reform movement.[33]

Sonneschein believed fervently that Reform Judaism shared much common ground with liberal Christianity. He was part of a "broader interchange" then taking place between Reformers and Unitarians.[34] Indeed, in a series of lectures in which Rabbi Sonneschein expounded the similarities and differences between Unitarianism and Reform Judaism, he was hard pressed to spell out the differences. He was sharply criticized by other rabbis for his thinking, and his friend Leopold Wintner, another avid reformer from Hungary, came to his defense. Wintner meanwhile was drawing women into the running of his synagogue in St. Paul and he was also raising his voice publicly against efforts then under way in the Congress to adopt a constitutional amendment establishing Christianity as *the* religion of this nation.[35]

In 1886, after long and heated feuding with his congregation in St. Louis, Rabbi Sonneschein resigned and secretly traveled to Boston to sound out some leading Unitarian ministers on the possibility of affiliating with them and "being given a Unitarian pulpit." The discussions came to nothing and Sonneschein returned to his synagogue, but the story came out in the Jewish press and created a furor among American Jews. Eventually the storm blew over and Sonneschein resumed his career as a Reform rabbi.

Some historians writing about this period use political terms to indicate a person's location or movement on the spectrum of American Judaism. They place Sonneschein far on the "left." But the group who arrived with him before 1875 was in fact moving toward the center. They may have retained their formal identity as Reformers or as new Conservatives or even as Orthodox, but this group of Hungarian rabbis contributed importantly to the development of the middle range of American Jewish belief and behavior. Three men will be mentioned here to illustrate this tendency: Aaron (Albert Siegried) Bettelheim, Aaron Wise, and Benjamin Szold.

Bettelheim studied at the Orthodox seminary at Pressburg and then at the university in Prague. He was later a journalist in London, returned to

Hungary to direct Hebrew schools, and married Henrietta Weinstraub, the first Jewish woman to become a public school teacher in Hungary.[36] He attended the fractious Jewish Congress in Hungary in 1868 and was criticized for his writings on "progressive principles . . . prejudicial to Judaism." Together with a young rabbi by the name of Alexander Kohut, who was a friend of Kossuth, Bettelheim was secretary of the Congress.[37] Later in America, Kohut became Bettelheim's son-in-law.

Saddened by the conflict within the Hungarian-Jewish community, Rabbi Bettelheim took his family to America "to enjoy respite from fanaticism." He went first to a synagogue in Richmond and while there obtained a degree in medicine; he also edited a weekly journal and wrote for daily newspapers.[38] The Bettelheims then moved to San Francisco, on a train that was twice attacked by Indians. There he organized a Society for the Study of Hebrew expressly for Christian clergymen, which was not uncommon among Hungarian rabbis in this country. Following a visit to a Jewish prisoner in San Quentin, Bettelheim undertook a public campaign to improve prison conditions. Concerned more with social issues than with observance of the dietary laws, he is quoted by his daughter as having said, "It is more important to guard that which comes out of the mouth than that which goes in."[39] Despite such sentiments, Bettelheim put the brakes on efforts to eliminate a number of traditional practices and, when the new Conservatives organized the Jewish Theological Seminary, he affiliated with that institution.

Aaron Wise's background reads much like those already described. He had been a "staunch leader of Orthodoxy" but in New York he took a position with a Reform congregation.[40] He tried to bring his congregation "back to the traditional fold, while yet retaining some of the Reform innovations." He too joined in the creation of the Jewish Theological Seminary.

Aaron's son, Stephen S. Wise, became perhaps the most prominent of all American Reform leaders (and of Hungarian-born rabbis) in the early twentieth century.[41] After the family reached America, young Stephen attended the public schools, was graduated from Columbia University, and went to Vienna for rabbinical ordination and to Oxford for graduate study. On his return Wise served as rabbi in Portland, Oregon, and in New York, where he founded the Free Synagogue. As a mover and initiator he went on to establish the Jewish Institute of Religion and the American Jewish Congress.

Probably most active and prominent in what might be called "the movement toward the center" was Benjamin Szold. He came from a family that had been landowners in Hungary since 1700.[42] He was nineteen when he fought on the barricades of Vienna in 1848 and was banished from the city when the revolution was suppressed. His studies left him as familiar with Homer and Horace, Schiller and Goethe as he was with "the sea of Talmud."

When Rabbi Szold moved his family to Baltimore in 1859, they had no difficulty fitting into the large German community there and integrating with the German Jews. The rabbi brought with him strong political convictions which, in those pre–Civil War years, placed him on the side of the abolition of slavery and the preservation of the Union, views not calculated to make him popular in a city that favored the Southern cause. He was a leader in Baltimore in "civic, humanitarian, as well as Jewish communal, relief and scholarly affairs."[43]

In religious terms Szold has been called "a man of peace and moderation," for which he was attacked by a Radical Reformer, Rabbi David Einhorn.[44] Szold was equally opposed to extreme Reform and rigid Orthodoxy. For example, he fought to preserve the Sabbath, but traveled on that day when he felt it was necessary. Like the others, he tried to lead his congregation "away from Reform to a moderate middle-of-the-way Judaism which allowed for changes and innovations in ritual practice but not in basic tenets."[45] His new prayer book was widely used.

When the Reform movement at Pittsburgh articulated its position on the main issues facing Judaism, Szold—in common with Bettelheim and others—veered away. He was incensed when one of their rabbis denied the idea of a personal God and when the Pittsburgh Platform used the phrase "God idea." He determined to counter Reform and found it congenial to his convictions to join with those who were cultivating the new Conservative movement. In short, while he challenged established Jewish orthodoxy he and others like him showed a tendency to be "moderate or centrist."[46]

Some years after these moderate reformers and "leftish" traditionalists came to America, there arrived in 1885 at the peak of the controversies a man of unusual vision, capacity, and leadership, Alexander Kohut. Respected in Hungary and throughout Europe as an Orthodox rabbi, author, scholar, and educator, he arrived along with the sudden onrush of hundreds of thousands of eastern European Jews. Kohut was born the son of a peddler in a tiny village near Pest.[47] A brilliant student in both Hebrew and secular studies, at age thirteen he got the idea for the major written work of his life, the *Arukh Completum*, an exhaustive lexicon of Talmudic materials. Ordained as a rabbi, he served in several communities and while still in Hungary published the first four volumes of his work. The prime minister was so impressed by Kohut that he had him elected to the Hungarian parliament to represent the Jews, but he never took his seat because he was called to America.

In his own words Alexander Kohut arrived on these shores in a "period of white heat" in the conflict between traditionalists and Reform. He also tried to turn his New York congregation "back to more traditional practices which it had given up under the guidance of his predecessor, Adolph Huebsch." The pattern of transmitting a pulpit from one Hungarian rabbi to another occurred with some frequency. The anti-Reform forces hailed Kohut's arrival and he immediately was asked to assume the ideological leadership of their movement.

In a series of exchanges with Rabbi Kaufmann Kohler, a leader in Reform, Kohut set forth his position. Without invective he entered the fray, but argued both against radical Reform and "narrow or fanatic Orthodoxy." He argued for a Judaism based on "the ideas of the Sabbath, *kashrut*, Synagogue, and Eretz Yisrael" and emphasized the importance of Hebrew as the language of the Jews, yet he was "receptive to the ideas of the present.[48] Kohut became, according to Davis, "the architect of the Historical School of the eighties," transforming their convictions into an ideology. Beyond that he gave it concrete form by establishing the Jewish Theological Seminary, modeled on Kohut's experience at the rabbinic seminary in Breslau. Kohut helped to raise money for the new training institution, designed much of its curriculum, and joined the faculty as professor of Talmud. In the end, "middle-grounders found a champion in Kohut."[49] The circumstances of Kohut's death, as recorded by his wife, show that as he lay dying he learned of the death of his friend, Lajos Kossuth.[50] Despite his own condition, Kohut insisted on going to the synagogue and delivering a sermon on the Hungarian revolutionary leader. He collapsed and died not long after that.

There is perhaps no better way to summarize the moderating or bridging role of these Hungarian rabbis than to note that when the Orthodox rabbis called their conference in 1886 to counter the advance of Reform, they were joined by Alexander Kohut, Aaron Wise, Aaron Bettelheim, and others.[51]

Before leaving this group of rabbis, we must take note of the social relations among the Szolds, the Bettelheims, and the Kohuts and of the activities of the women in their families. The social connections are nicely illustrated by a book written by Rebekah Kohut, the daughter of Aaron Bettelheim.[52] The Bettelheims had welcomed Kohut in their Baltimore home when he came to America. Rebekah married the widowed Kohut not long afterwards and brought up his eight children. The introduction to Rebekah's book was written by her friend, Henrietta Szold, who pointed out that it was unique on the American literary landscape, since it was the biography of a Jew, an immigrant, and a woman. The full story of Henrietta Szold lies beyond the confines of this book, but it deserves brief mention. Rabbi Benjamin Szold eagerly shared his intellectual life with Henrietta and as a young woman she became a teacher, then secretary of the Jewish Publication Society, and ultimately a national leader in educational, philanthropic, and welfare endeavors. Probably her greatest impact was as a Zionist organizer and founder of Hadassah, which became a women's voice in the Zionist movement.

Rebekah Kohut's life, her ardent work to set up playgrounds in New York, her leadership in the National Council of Jewish Women, and her social service and philanthropic interests constitute a valuable picture of middle-class Hungarian-Jewish life. In New York, the Kohuts had a steady stream of intellectuals as visitors, among them the ubiquitous Michael Heilprin, by then a well-known writer.

Data on some sixty Hungarian-born rabbis who emigrated to the United States show that a clear majority conformed to the pattern of combining rabbinical training with a degree from a university.[53] Those who had not attended universities in Vienna, Prague, or Breslau were now going to Ohio State University, the City College of New York, and the University of Cincinnati, and to rabbinical seminaries in the latter two cities. In addition to their religious duties, many of these rabbis took part in writing, scholarship, education, and social and political action. These rabbis were divided along the religious spectrum. Fifteen could be classified as Orthodox, ten as Conservative, and eighteen as Reform; it was not possible to determine this for the remaining seventeen. The experiences of a few of these rabbis have been chronicled.[54]

It would be misleading to leave the impression that no Orthodox leaders were prepared to seek an accommodation between the old ways and the demands of life in urban America in the late 1800s. Orthodox rabbis among the Hungarian immigrants included some who had also graduated from

European universities where they had incorporated elements of the Enlightenment in their learning. Philip Klein was one of these.

Rabbi Klein occupied "a unique position in the Jewry of New York and the country, being recognized as a Talmudic authority, and at the same time possessing the secular learning obtained by studying at the University of Berlin," though his doctoral degree was from the University of Jena.[55] Klein had been a rabbi in Kiev and Latvia and very active in Zionist circles before he emigrated to the United States. In 1891 he became the rabbi of the First Hungarian Congregation Ohab Zedek in New York, established in 1872 and "a growing, prestigious immigrant congregation."[56] Rabbi Klein's sermons were delivered in such classical High German that a committee of his congregants had to call on him repeatedly to speak so he could be understood.[57] Ultimately as fewer of them spoke German, Klein took on Rabbi Bernard Drachman as his colleague and they alternated weeks preaching in German and English.[58] For thirty-six years Klein remained at the head of Ohab Zedek as it made its way uptown in several moves from the Lower East Side. By 1908 the synagogue had reached West 116th Street and had a seating capacity of 1,400. "Rabbi Dr. Ph. Philip Klein," as the *American Jewish Year Book* listed him, was described years later by one of his congregants as "a very dignified Hungarian gentleman."

Though Klein held office in the Orthodox council, Agudat-ha-Rabbonim (Union of Rabbis), he was also looking for ways to make traditional Judaism and Americanization compatible.[59] There was in fact some tension between the German-speaking rabbis and their Polish and Russian colleagues who dominated the Union of Rabbis.[60] Klein involved himself in activities and organizations that were essentially the work of Reform-minded German Jews. In 1911 he was a member of the New York City district organization of the newly formed American Jewish Committee, an effort initiated by German Jews to forge a central organization representing all Jews in America.[61] A few years later the New York Kehillah was established under similar auspices to achieve the same objective, and Philip Klein served on its first executive committee. After hesitating about associating with such an enterprise, the Orthodox Union of Rabbis agreed to cooperate if they were given control of the management of *kashrut*. It was a "tenuous marriage of interests" and a short union.[62]

Disappointed by the results of this attempt at cooperation, Klein and a colleague resigned from the executive committee of the Kehillah and withdrew Orthodox involvement in its work. He returned to his interests in

Jewish education, charity, Zionism, and the concerns of the Orthodox community. One of those concerns was the establishment of a rabbinical seminar. Like Kohut among the Conservatives, Klein based his ideas on the Central European model—the Orthodox-cum-secular program of Azriel Hildesheimer's Rabbiner Seminar in Berlin, which Klein had attended. And yet despite this retreat from active engagement with the Reformers, Klein, like Szold and Kohut before him, tried to harmonize disparate elements in the Jewish spectrum. Like them, he sought to serve as a moderator both in terms of ideology and organizational structure. A staunch proponent of Orthodoxy, Klein nevertheless wrote: "The Torah is not poured into rigid forms and formulae which it must preserve in their entirety lest it lose its inner essence . . . They who will not permit Jewish institutions to be developed in accordance with the demands of modern times" have, Klein insisted, narrow minds.[63]

It was surely a time of realignments and attempts at conciliation. Rabbis like Benjamin Szold, Aaron Wise, and Alexander Kohut had "found common cause" early on with the leaders of the Reform movement.[64] But such alliances began to fray in the 1880s. The Pittsburgh Platform of the Reform movement pushed these "moderates" away from radical departures from tradition. The Szolds and Kohuts were drawn toward the center. What distinguished them and others like them from most of the Orthodox rabbis arriving from Russia was their education. Despite doctrinal differences among people like Philip Klein and Aaron Wise, their "common educational training provided an immediate basis for cooperation. They had been trained at Western European theological seminaries."[65] And, one might add, at secular universities.

There were also rabbis who had traditional training, but no university degrees. One of these was Shraga Mendlowitz, who arrived in 1913.[66] Born in Zemplén County, he was studying with Hasidic rabbis when he was twelve. He married and opened a confectionary store in Hommona and continued to study on his own. Mendlowitz left for America and settled in Scranton as teacher-principal of a Talmud Torah. After the war he brought his family from Hungary and moved to Williamsburg in Brooklyn, where he found his calling and became a well-known Jewish educator. He is credited with being the founder of the Jewish day school movement in America and he developed a new type of high school for Orthodox students and a yeshivah camp for them in the summers.

Rabbis like Kohut and Szold and Klein and undoubtedly most of the others were men of integrity, principle, and unselfish service. But not all were. Edward Benjamin Morris Browne was a man of many failings. Born in Kassa, Browne came here and within a few years had obtained degrees as a rabbi, a physician, and a lawyer. There followed four short, disastrous rabbinical appointments in five years, a private scolding from his mentor Isaac Meyer Wise, numerous public controversies, and accusations of embezzlement. His most "striking characteristic," the *Atlanta Constitution* remarked, was "his capacity for getting into trouble."[67]

We have been discussing the struggle to define an American Judaism through the thinking and actions of a group of rabbis, but these developments can also be appreciated by following the story of one congregation. This began in Cleveland in 1866 with a small Orthodox minyan of working people.[68] These Hungarian immigrants began meeting in their homes and then in Gallagher's Hall to pray together.[69] Some could not afford the membership fees in the two established German-Jewish synagogues; others preferred Yiddish or Hungarian to the German they heard there. The congregation soon developed a religious school for the children and by 1875 had hired a man as preacher, cantor, and teacher. These were the beginnings of what emerged as B'nai Jeshurun and, after many changes, as today's Temple on the Heights.

When the Cleveland congregation announced plans to expand, this received a chilly reception from the well-established German Jews, who said through one of their journals: "Some Hungarian Jews sustain a congregation of their own and lately purchased a church, to which they want pious people to contribute their mites. Is there any particular need for a Hungarian synagogue in Cleveland?"[70] The Hungarian Jews clearly felt that there was a need, for they not only proceeded to buy and renovate the church, but to set up at least five more congregations in the years between 1880 and 1925. Some of the new congregations were offshoots of B'nai Jeshurun.[71]

The clash of ideas as to the practices of Judaism broke out in connection with the dedication of B'nai Jeshurun's new building in 1887, when one Reform rabbi refused to wear a hat at the ceremonies. The leading Cleveland newspaper proclaimed in a headline: "Dr. Hahn and the Hat, The Excitement in Jewish Circles Increasing. Members of the Hungarian Congregation Take a Hand and Threaten to Make It Warm for Dr. Hahn if He Undertakes to Speak With Uncovered Head at Their Dedication Ceremonies."[72] Another Reform rabbi, issuing a resounding call to join the "new Judaism," said on this same occasion that "the customs of the dead and buried must be obliterated whenever they conflict with the demands of the present age of refinement, education and culture."[73]

A week later the rabbi of B'nai Jeshurun spoke out against the Reformers, expressing the hope that his congregation would "remain faithful to the traditions of ancient Judaism."[74] By the end of 1888 the rabbi found himself in a battle over holding Sabbath services on Sunday instead of Saturday. He pointed out that this change had been tried in Budapest in 1849 and within a few months it had collapsed.[75] Saturday remained the day for Sabbath services.

The struggles continued. Should men and women sit together in "family pews"? Should organ music be played in the synagogue? Disagreements over matters such as these resulted in periodic defections from B'nai Jeshurun and the formation of new Hungarian synagogues, some more Orthodox and others more Reform in orientation.[76] Only a few survived. Gradually Jews who were not Hungarian were joining the congregation. Its membership and its form of worship were changing and ultimately B'nai Jeshurun opted for the middle position being developed by the Conservative movement. When the First World War began, B'nai Jeshurun had over seven hundred members. Less and less did it stress its Hungarian origins.[77]

By World War I immigrant congregations tended to imitate the existing Reform "temples." B'nai Jeshurun had a Sunday School and a "confirmation class," which would likely have been considered alien trappings by its founders.[78] These changes were expressions of what Naomi Cohen calls the immigrants' search for the way to become "proper American Jews."[79]

Through conflict and compromise over the years, B'nai Jeshurun changed from being a little Orthodox shul for Hungarian-Jewish working-class people to a middle-class Conservative synagogue. Thus symbolically it came to stand midway between the small, informal East European prayer houses and "the august Reform temples of the German Jews, just as Hungary itself lay between Russia and Poland and the West."[80] As Hungarian synagogues became more affluent their buildings reflected their middle-class status, often resembling those they had left behind in Hungary. Like the huge edifice on Dohányi Street in Budapest, some were designed in the Moorish Revival style.[81]

Thus B'nai Jeshurun wended its way through decades of debates and decisions that echoed those of the rabbis described earlier in this chapter. But one must wonder how much these things interested the masses of working-class Jews from Central and Eastern Europe who were flooding into the country after 1880, almost 100,000 Hungarians among them. How much were they concerned with intellectual redefinitions of Judaism and how much effect did the ringing manifestos at the conferences have on them? The immigrants were, as some historians and sociologists have put it, "the little people, the common people," the garment workers and peddlers who were for the most part not touched by the winds of the Haskalah, of Reform, and of the new Conservatism. On the other hand, in the eyes of men like Rabbi Weinberger and other critics of American Judaism, the immigrants were in jeopardy of neglecting, diluting, or utterly abandoning their Orthodox heritage.

Regardless of what others were writing or doing, a significant number of the Hungarian immigrants immediately set about creating what they wanted and needed. They established scores of small, intimate *chevras* or minyans cast in the traditional, Orthodox mold. These close-knit groups served their need for prayer, performance of rituals, and observance of the holy days. As we pointed out earlier, these "shuls" as they called them, often overlapped in function with the *landsmanschaften*. All these organizations were in effect attempts to re-create the Jewish community or kehillah in Hungary, which was described in Chapter 5.

Table 10 contains information on fifty-three of these congregations. Except for one in St. Louis that called itself Conservative, all seem to have been Orthodox. Generally they had fifty to one hundred members, who in addition to the standard Hebrew liturgy used mostly German and later English in their services. They usually met in an apartment or a small room or hall and had many of the characteristics of what today are described as "storefront churches." This was a highly decentralized and flexible system of organization since it took only ten men to initiate and maintain a chevra or "shul." The usual pattern was for a few families to form a small congregation, which grew and then often merged with another or split into two. The fissions occurred because some members moved out of the neighborhood to a more affluent one or because of differences in their attitudes toward change in the ritual. There were also frequent mergers in the larger cities and an opening up to Jews from other countries. For example, the Atlanta congregation was formed by several dozen Orthodox Hungarian families "to which Russians and Galicians were also admitted."[82]

A few of these organizations persist to this day, but most suffered the same decline as Chevra Emunas Israel Ohev Sholom in Philadelphia. At its peak the congregation had 1,200 people at High Holiday services. By the 1960s, according to its written history, "it became very difficult to get a minyan together. Mr. J. the Shammus would stay outside and beg people to come in to make a minyan." The synagogue disbanded in 1968.

Rabbis and teachers in these traditional shuls sought to give the immigrants' children the kind of Jewish education that had been carried out for centuries in Europe. But they were contending, not really effectively, with the pull of the public school, the settlement house, and other institutions that were helping the immigrants with their task of Americanization. Many of these worship groups did not have a trained or certified rabbi or any rabbi at all, but some did. Indeed, Rabbi Moses Weinberger was for a time the leader of Beth Hamidrash Hagadol Anshei Hungary (The Great House of Study of the Hungarian People) in New York and of a congregation in Philadelphia.[83]

The spirit of full devotion that members brought to these Orthodox congregations is evident in the written history of a congregation formed in Fairfield, Connecticut, in 1904: "Sixty years ago, a number of Sons of Israel, residing in the West End of Bridgeport, joined hands and hearts to establish the foundation for a Torah-True Synagogue. A Congregation was organized and the inspired men, with prophetic insight, prayerfully and hopefully, accepted the beautiful name, "Ahavath Achim"—Brotherly Love![84] From its beginnings in the homes of its members, the congregation grew, moved to permanent quarters, and bought cemetery land.

When the congregation celebrated its seventy-fifth anniversary, it paid tribute to its members who were over eighty. Twenty of the twenty-five whose place of birth was given were Hungarian immigrants who arrived between 1904 and 1921. As they settled into the community, they became storekeepers and skilled workers. One woman was a teacher; one man was known as "Josi Bácsi" (Uncle Joe) because of his "terrific goulash." As they prospered and the congregation expanded, they made plans for a synagogue which "would reflect the earnestness, the zest and the loyalty of the rising generation. The Congregation would build a magnificent structure [using] the most modern techniques, glorious stained-glass windows, a beautiful Aron Ha-Kodesh, a lovely, traditional Bimah, Colonial pillars, a breath-taking landscaping development . . . a gorgeous edifice that would evoke for a blessed generation the proud statement: 'This is *my* Synagogue!'" Ahavath Achim exists today, but most of the small Hungarian "shuls" of the turn of the century have long since disappeared.

Before summing up the religious patterns of the Hungarian immigrants, we must mention another aspect of Jewish activity and identification—Zionism. The yearning for a return to the Holy Land was another topic of heated controversy among the rabbis and organizations we have been discussing. In general the forces of Reform opposed the idea, rejecting it as inconsistent with being Americans. Conversely, the moderate and fully Orthodox supported the sense of attachment and responsibility to Palestine.

Rabbi Stephen Wise was an outspoken Zionist and the founder of the Zionist Organization of America. Rabbi Philip Klein was the first president of the United Zionist Societies of the United States. There was an organization of Yiddish-speaking Austro-Hungarian Zionists in New York City; it celebrated its tenth anniversary in 1915, with Boris Thomashewsky (*sic*) on the program and greetings from Louis D. Brandeis. And several of the Hungarian *landsmanschaften* were devoted to Zionist purposes. Thus, just as in the Old Country, while Hungarian Jews as a whole were not strongly committed to Zionism before the 1930s, a minority of them took an active part in the movement.

Looking back over the religious experiences of the immigrants, our summary should note first that as the Hungarian rabbis moved into Orthodox, Reform, and Conservative institutions, a number of the leaders projected a moderating influence which emphasized compromise and cooperation. The questions being debated were not new to them. They had come from bitter conflicts between the Orthodox and the Neologs (not to mention the Hasidim and the Status Quo adherents), as a result of which parallel and competing Jewish organizations had sprouted in almost every town and county in Hungary. They had seen a considerable number of conversions to Christianity. Perhaps because they had been through so much controversy, some of the Hungarian rabbis felt impelled to bring a sense of balance and accommodation to the controversies in which American Judaism was then engaged.

We have no firm knowledge of how many Hungarian Jews in America drifted away from Judaism or converted to other religions. Impressions would suggest that the number was not negligible. It is probably correct to assume nevertheless that far more of them established Hungarian shuls and congregations before the turn of the century. But these distinctively Hungarian congregations constituted only an initial response which did not last.

By the mid-1920s Antal Kaufman, a Jewish newspaper editor, wrote

There are Hungarian Jewish religious communities in New York, Chicago, Cleveland, Detroit, St. Louis, Bridgeport and perhaps in some smaller cities, but these are Hungarian only because of the circumstances of their establishment, the majority of their members are from many other nationalities . . . There are no purely Hungarian religious communities any more. In these only nominally Hungarian communities, there are only a few Hungarians, even among the rabbis.[85]

The history of the *landsmanschaften* and of the congregations has shown that, like many other groups, the Hungarian newcomers to America first went through a period of self-segregation. In organizations of their own making and of "their own kind" they tried to meet their needs for security, familiarity, and companionship. As they settled in and as their children grew up, this period of separatism tapered off and they merged with other Jews in a community that could only be called "American Jewish." They had earlier turned away from their associations with the Gentile immigrants from Hungary. Now they became less and less Hungarian-Jewish "green-horns" as their eyes were fixed more steadily on their new country and as they rearranged their priorities and undertook new tasks for themselves as Americans.

★

CHAPTER 14

The American Door

The immigrants and their children traveled many routes on their way to being Americans. These were not so much distinct highways as they were intersecting paths along which the newcomers crisscrossed their way into American society. Three of these pathways are explored in this chapter. One consisted of citizenship, voting, and participation in the Democratic and Republican parties, a route favored by the rising middle class among the Hungarian Jewish immigrants. The second route, important for the working class, was trade union organization and socialist politics. Finally and probably most significant, the economy itself provided opportunities to walk through the door to America.

The "American Action" program of the Hungarian government encouraged "indifference to American politics" by stressing the goal of returning to the homeland.[1] This was indeed the purpose of most of the early Gentile arrivals. But it was not the motivation of the Jews, a fact that irritated the authorities in Budapest. A dispatch to the prime minister's office from Pittsburgh in 1902 is worth reviewing in this context.[2] The writer of the dispatch reports that Hungarian immigrants are retaining their loyalty "to the homeland." They Americanize, he wrote, only under the pressure of political and economic necessity. They are told it is important to have more voters, so they become citizens in order to raise their economic and political status. The report adds this observation: "This tendency applies only to Jews and to the less-educated people who have been in the U.S. longer."

In point of fact Hungarians were regarded as uncommonly slow to take out citizenship papers. It was estimated that before World War I only 15 percent of the Hungarian immigrants, most of whom saw themselves as sojourners, had even applied for citizenship.[3] The proportion among Hungarian Jews seems to have been markedly higher. Consider the situation in New York City in 1920: 41 percent of all Hungarian immigrants were citizens. Since at least two-thirds of these were Jews, it is reasonable to suppose that their citizenship rate was much higher than the Gentile Hungarians.

Speaking primarily of the industrial workers in Ohio and Pennsylvania who were being subjected to derision and rock throwing, Puskás says that as they formed their own organizations they reached out to political figures to convince them of "the significance of the group (often exaggerating their numbers)" and of "the importance of winning their support" in elections.[4] But their lack of citizenship status must have weakened their position in the political arena. The political forays of the Hungarians as a whole were neither very assertive nor effective, according to Steven Bela Vardy.[5] He concluded that the role of Hungarians in American politics was "more modest than their numbers would have warranted." For example, their lack of success in obtaining public office was particularly evident in Cleveland, where they had the strongest position in numbers. The points of reference in Vardy's analysis were the overwhelmingly peasant character of the Hungarian population, their sojourner stance, their limited sophistication in politics, and their lack of ethnic allies.

This political ineffectiveness seems not to have been the case with the Jews. From the early days of the '48ers, they had given their political allegiance to the Republican party, essentially because of its antislavery policies. There was an important exception to this: some were active in the socialist parties that had been formed primarily by German immigrants. As the century turned, some Jews, especially on New York's Lower East Side, were attracted to the Democratic party. Some of the middle class turned to the reform politics that sought to counter the corruption and "bossism" of the two major parties.

It was the Hungarian professionals and businessmen—by definition predominantly Jewish—who made the first attempts to enter the mainstream of American politics. This came at a time when the two major parties were going through a realignment of interest groups following the Civil War. Republicans and Democrats were jockeying for the support of labor, business, the farmers, the veterans, the blacks, and particularly the ethnic immigrants who could vote. But, a historian observes, "the result was often a sham battle. Each party stretched across such a wide spectrum of interests and attitudes that clean-cut conflict over policy, program, and ideology was impossible."[6]

Probably the maneuvers of the two parties on the national scene mattered little to the majority of the new immigrants. Nor was their attention seized by such issues as the government's treatment of American Indians or its policy toward Spain's colonies in the Americas. There was discussion of free trade versus protectionism and the Hungarian Democrats went to great lengths to prove that Kossuth, like President Cleveland, favored free trade and undoubtedly would have been a Democrat! However, in general the accounts of Hungarian support for the Republicans and the Democrats do not mention policy issues in which the Hungarians were particularly interested.

The political questions addressed by the major parties on the national level were removed from the everyday interests and problems of Hungarians who were struggling with life in America's cities, with work in its factories and mines, and with discrimination and harassment from Americans who resented the immigrants from Southern and Eastern Europe. What immigrants wanted most from the two main parties—and their leaders articulated this—was recognition of their problems and practical help.

Some Hungarians turned toward the Democrats and enlisted in the effort in 1887 to reelect President Grover Cleveland.[7] A Hungarian-American Democratic Association was organized and all eight men listed as the "most prominent in the movement" turned out to be Jewish. The defeat of Cleveland sent this organization into decline, but it revived again in 1892 and, this time with three Jews and two Gentiles as leaders, took part in that campaign.

The immigrants wanted to communicate their concerns directly to those who held political power at the turn of the century. And so Teddy Roosevelt, when he was governor of New York in 1899, was persuaded by the Hungarian Republican Club in New York, largely a Jewish organization, to come down to the Lower East Side to a dinner at Cafe Boulevard. The cafe, toastmaster Marcus Braun pointedly remarked, was a "place eminently typical of the 'East Side,' in the very heart thereof, in the tenement house district, the home of the poor, the foreigner, the cosmopolitan, the immigrant." The very fact of the governor's presence was interpreted by his hosts as a form of recognition and at least an opening for taking up the problems of the tenements, the foreigners, the poor. Roosevelt chose, however, to take a different tack: "If you bring into American life," he said, "the spirit of the heroes of Hungary, you have done your share. There is nothing this country needs more than there should be put before its men and its future men—its boys and its girls, too—the story of such lives as that of Kossuth."

Six years later Roosevelt was invited back, this time as president of the

United States, to a restaurant named Little Hungary for another banquet and more exposure to Hungarian immigrants. The arrangement and reception committees of the Hungarian Republican Club on that festive occasion in 1905 consisted of fifty men, thirty-four of whom were Jews. Again Roosevelt spoke about Americanism and the contributions of the immigrants, stressing that the men before him "show by their actions that they know no difference between Jew and Gentile, Catholic and Protestant, native-born and foreign born."[8]

However, Roosevelt had already spoken out on behalf of Jews when they were being persecuted in tsarist Russia and he had begun to attract Jewish support. Hungarian Jews were starting to make their way into the Republican party—for example, Marcus Braun, who had been the toastmaster at both banquets. Born in Hungary, he had become a journalist in New York's immigrant press, writing for the *German Herold* and the *Morning Journal*. In the 1890s he published *The Hungarian-American* and the *Oesterreichisch-Ungarisch Zeitung* (The Austrian-Hungarian newspaper).[9] Braun joined the Republicans and, as he moved ahead in the party, was appointed to investigate the problems of immigration from Hungary and to report to the federal government. His report, "Immigration Abuses: Glimpses of Hungary and Hungarians," was published in 1906 and drew angry reactions in Hungary. By that time he was president of the Hungarian Republican Club of the city of New York.

In 1904 the largely Austro-Hungarian 16th Assembly District in New York City, which had been a Tammany Hall stronghold of the Democrats, went Republican. Subsequently Samuel Koenig, a Hungarian, known as "Little McKinley" for his vigorous support of the Republican tariff, was elected secretary of state in New York and later held important offices in the state party.[10]

On the other hand, Hungarian Jews also affiliated with the Democrats. Morris Cukor reached America in 1884, became a lawyer, a spokesman for many Hungarian endeavors, and the organizer of the first Democratic club among Hungarians in New York. He represented the Hungarian embassy in the United States and provided legal counsel to Hungarian churches and banks. Later he served as chairman of the Municipal Civil Service Commission in New York City.[11] His signature appears on many of the applications of Hungarian-Jewish organizations for incorporation in New York State. In addition, he was active on behalf of Hungarians during the First World War.

The events connected with America's entry into World War I lie beyond the confines of this book, but it would be short-sighted not to take notice of the war and its effect on the Hungarian immigrants. It created a serious dilemma for them. Their homeland was on the side of Imperial Germany, but America was siding with France, England, and Russia. An "anti-Hun" hysteria was sweeping the United States and any expression of support for the Austro-Hungarian monarchy would have been unwise if not dangerous. For the sojourners, who hoped to return home and live in postwar Hungary, silence seemed the best course. The Jewish settlers, despite their attachment to Hungary, gave almost solid support to the Allies and redoubled their efforts to Americanize and become citizens. After the war, however, the Jews were vehement in their protests against the dismemberment of Hungary in the Trianon treaty.

Morris Cukor's role mirrors the dilemmas of the Hungarians during and after the war. In 1917 he organized the Citizenship League to promote naturalization and the learning of English among Hungarians. In 1918 he went to Washington and convinced President Woodrow Wilson not to intern the pastors of the Hungarian Reform churches in the United States. (Almost twenty-five years later Cukor persuaded President Franklin D. Roosevelt during World War II to name a Liberty ship for Louis Kossuth. In addition he helped to raise $2 million through the sale of war bonds among Hungarians.)

In general, immigrants were important to the major parties. They were the object of highly successful efforts by the city machines of both parties to control and manipulate the immigrants' political support. The main mechanism for this was the system of ward heelers in close touch with the newcomers. Some of these local political figures, such as "Czar" Harry Bernstein, boss of the heavily Jewish Fifteenth Ward in Cleveland, were of the same ethnic group as the immigrants whom they both helped and controlled. In other words, the real political action—from the perspective of most immigrants—was not so much at party dinners and conventions as it was in their own neighborhoods. There the political machines were exquisitely well-geared to trade practical assistance for votes.

Immigrants in Cleveland were pushed through the examinations for naturalization by the Republican ward heelers just in time to vote in the 1900 elections. They were met by the representative of the political boss at the railroad station. Because the time of arrival was uncertain, working people found it difficult to meet their incoming relatives, but political henchmen had time for this. In the process of offering such concrete, helpful services, they built obligations to the political boss. Among these services in Cleveland were

> boarding houses and hotels to which the stranger was guided, aid in getting a job, small loans, and saloon and eating houses which served as clubs. Within the community, the ward leader enhanced his influence by making donations to charity, contributions for the celebration of various local and racial holidays, bail and legal aid for the immigrant in court, acting as mediator in domestic and community disputes, and supporting all projects for church and community welfare added to his influence and power within the ward.[12]

Increasingly these political ward captains and their lieutenants spoke the languages of the immigrants because they themselves were immigrants or the children of immigrants.

This was a time of venality and corruption in most American cities and these conditions gave rise to a reform movement among middle- and upper-class people. In Chapter 8 we saw examples of political activity of this type on the part of the Black family. Louis Black was active in civic affairs and city politics; his nephew Morris was an outspoken reformer who got himself elected to the city council and challenged the political boss of Cleveland. Political reform was on the move in New York as well. In the mayoral election of 1901 the "uptown Jewish Establishment," primarily acculturated German Jews, strongly backed the candidacy of Seth Low, president of Columbia University.[13] One of the critical issues in their eyes was the growing stain of prostitution in the Jewish neighborhoods of the East Side and its links to political powers in the city. But the whole gamut of corrupt politics had aroused the German Jews to the point of overcoming their customary reluctance to enter politics on an organized basis.

The campaign was pitched to the immigrant community—understandably since 67 percent of New Yorkers in 1901 were either immigrants or their children. The "uptown" reformers backing Seth Low appealed particularly to the "downtown" Jewish voters. The Kohuts had long been friends of Low, and Rebekah "traversed alleyways and climbed flights of stairs along with women of the Young Women's Christian Association and the Women's Municipal League" to address East Side meetings to promote the reform ticket.[14] Low was elected but served only two years before Tammany Hall took back City Hall.

We should note in passing that Rebekah Kohut's foray into the Lower East Side for the Seth Low candidacy came a few years after she had been down there working among Russian and Rumanian Jews.[15] With Emma Lazarus she had also visited Castle Garden, the entry point for immigrants. These activities on her part were consistent with the work of her friends among the German Jews in aid of the newcomers.

Adolph Edlis of Pittsburgh was probably closer to the daily experiences of the immigrants than the Blacks of Cleveland or the Kohuts of New York. Born in Hungary in 1860, Edlis came from a pious and prestigious family, which also had had experience in public service.[16] His grandfather, Shlomo Zalman Spiegel, had been appointed to an important county office by the emperor. Young Adolph came to America when he was fifteen and went through the usual stint as a peddler. Among his wares were styptic pencils, and he soon learned how to make and distribute them. It was a small step from that to traveling salesman for a barber supply house. His knowledge of German came in handy in places like Milwaukee and St. Louis. He married, settled in Pittsburgh, and opened his own barber supply business. Adolph was a joiner and a leader in many lodges and in his synagogue.

"After his first few years in Pittsburgh, Edlis became aware that Jews simply did not get any recognition from local politicians. He went to Senator William Flinn (known as Boss Flinn) and asked him why, in 1896, when there were over five thousand Jews in Allegheny County, they were ignored. Flinn told him that they would get recognition if they would get out the vote."[17] Edlis went to work urging Jews to become citizens, to register, and to vote. Then he decided to run for the Common Council. He got his friend Joseph Selig Glick, the editor of the Yiddish newspaper *Der Volksfreund*, to back his campaign, to the extent that the paper stated brazenly that to vote for Edlis was a "mitzvah," or religious obligation. The Reform Jews, most of them German, were horrified by this crass ethnic and religious politicking. They believed that immigrant Jews should stay out of politics as a group. The *Jewish Criterion*, the newspaper that reflected their views, commented: "There is nothing as distasteful as this to the good Christian and the better class of Jew."

Nevertheless, Edlis was elected to the Common Council on a reform ticket. One of the fringe benefits of the election was an invitation to Mr. and Mrs. Edlis the following month to attend President McKinley's inauguration in Washington. Adolph came back, organized the Allegheny County Political Club (also known as the Hebrew Club), and took his seat on the council. A pressing problem for Orthodox Jews concerned the Sunday Blue Laws. They were fined for doing business on Sunday that they could not do on Saturday. Edlis realized that the remedy lay in the state legislature. He stood for election and on his second try became the first immigrant Jew from Eastern Europe to enter the Pennsylvania House of Representatives. His efforts to amend the Blue Laws were not successful.

An even more painful problem in the Jewish Hill District of Pittsburgh was prostitution. This time Representative Edlis was successful. He proposed a bill which focused on the pimps and patrons of "the bawdy houses," rather than on the women involved, and in 1905 it became law and was credited with bringing about a marked improvement in the situation in Pittsburgh. In the years that followed, Edlis was active in Pittsburgh city government and the Republican party and ended his career with widespread acclaim that he had been an honest and an effective politician.

One difference between the political activities of Cukor and Braun on the one hand and Edlis on the other warrants mention for it foreshadows the shift in orientation that was taking place among the Jewish immigrants from Hungary. The first two were Jewish political leaders acting for all Hungarians in their cities. Edlis was a Hungarian representing all Jews in Pittsburgh, not only those from Hungary. As time went on there were more of the latter and fewer of the former type.

The mainstream parties, however, did not fully meet the needs and frustrations of the immigrants, and they turned to other vehicles. Two movements in particular claimed the participation and loyalty of many immigrants: the socialist parties and the trade unions. There was considerable though not complete overlap between the two movements. Each had a splintered array of ideologies and organizations, but two main tendencies can be discerned. One pointed toward dismantling capitalism and replacing it with a socially owned and controlled system of production and distribution. The other accepted capitalism but wanted to achieve incremental improvements in the workers' living and working conditions.

German immigrants had brought with them ideas of socialism based on Marx and other political theorists. One outgrowth of this was the organization of the Socialist Labor Party in 1877. Hungarian and Russian Jews were attracted to the SLP clubs in New York, but by 1891 it was estimated that they numbered only 140.[18] Their impact increased somewhat when this "politically timid German party" acquired Daniel De Leon as spokesman. De Leon was an effective street corner orator; he ran repeatedly for office but was never elected.

The socialists' idealism and far-reaching proposals for change were in conflict with the pragmatic, "bread and butter" unionism of the Knights of Labor. That organization in 1871 called for "the eight-hour day, the graduated income tax, prohibition of imported contract labor, consumers' and producers' cooperatives, an end to the monopoly power of railroads and banks."[19] The Knights of Labor had a stormy and difficult fifteen-year history before it disintegrated. In the political field its counterpart was the moderate Social Democratic Party, bitterly at odds with the far more militant and radical Socialist Labor Party.

This was the atmosphere, in the 1870s, when Hungarian Jewish workers were entering two industries in New York and Cleveland: the making of clothes and the making of cigars. They organized in the garment trade— together with German, Austrian, and Galician Jews—locals of the Knights of Labor as well as groups of socialists. These unions, as Irving Howe put it, were not only bargaining agents, but social centers, political forums, and training schools for union leaders, politicians, entrepreneurs, and intellectuals.[20] Moreover, they were "preparatory schools for immigrants who had broken from orthodoxy yet needed callings such as in the past had been sustained by orthodoxy."

In the socialist groups the Jewish greenhorns were in contact with radical German immigrants.[21] At the same time a less radical group was laying the groundwork for a union of cigar makers. We can follow these labor organizations through two Hungarian Jews who were leaders in their development.

Jacob Schoen of Eperjes in Sáros County came here in 1879 and soon thereafter became a presser in a ladies garment shop. Within four years he had taken the lead in organizing the Dress and Cloak Makers Union, which affiliated with the Knights of Labor. As a radical, he also joined the Socialist Labor Party. In 1883 the union called a strike of "750 inside shop workers, almost half of them women" and most of them "native-born Gentile girls." The men were German and Austro-Hungarian Jews.[22] They demanded $2.50 for a workday that ran from 8 A.M. to 6 P.M. and a minimum of $15 a week for those doing piece-work. The New York press called this "the first emigrants' strike." The strike was won and almost all the demands were met, but the union went out of existence soon after. Other more powerful ladies garment unions followed in its path.

A few years later Schoen wrote "a manuscript in Yiddish dealing with the eight-hour day—one of the first socialist manuscripts in Yiddish." Later, as was often the case with garment workers, he became a contractor, "but his shop was always a union shop and he always sided with the workers in their struggles, often helping them in their organizational efforts." He later became Grand Secretary of the Independent Order Brith Abraham, a major fraternal order.[23] From socialist to entrepreneur to leader of a national fraternal association, Jacob Schoen had found his way in the new land and left his imprint on the trade union movement.

The number of Hungarians, primarily Jews, in the clothing industry continued to grow. In 1890 over two thousand of the men and women in the industry were Hungarians.[24] It is not known what part Hungarians formed of the foreign-born tailors in 1900, but Jews constituted 72 percent of those men and women.

By comparison with Schoen, a less aggressive role was chosen by Adolph Strasser, "a cigarmaker by trade, a Hungarian by birth, an organizer for the Social Democratic Party, a member of the Cigarmakers' Union."[25] Rumored to have come from a "well-to-do cultured Hungarian family," Strasser was "able and brainy—but not always tactful." He could be blunt in English and German. On one occasion Samuel Gompers, a Jew from London, had finished a speech and Strasser told him: "That was all right, Sam. You will yet a good speaker be."

Gompers and Strasser knit together seventeen local branches of a cigar makers' union by "recruiting women, unskilled bunchbreakers and tenement workers; organizing German, Bohemian, and Hungarian sections and establishing a cooperative store. But the dream of solidarity fast vanished. The disastrous 1877 tenement strike by ten thousand workmen broke the union's back."[26] ("Bunchbreakers" refers to the operators of a new machine in the production of cigars which required less skill than hand work required. "Tenement workers" were people who made the cigars in their own rooms and apartments.)

The cigar makers' union revived in the 1880s and Adolph Strasser became president for many years. It was a period, in Gompers's words, of "growth, financial success, and sound development" during which better wages, a shorter workday, union benefits, and use of the union label were achieved.[27] Both men were strong proponents of "business" or "bread-and-butter" unionism and fought the socialist faction within the union. Strasser gave a Senate hearing in 1883 an exposition of his moderate kind of unionism. Asked by a senator: "Do you not contemplate, in the end, the participation of all labor and all men in the benefits of trade unions?" Strasser answered: "Our organization does not consist of idealists. We do not control the production of the world. That is controlled by the employers. I look first to cigars." As for his ultimate goals, Strasser added: "We have no ultimate ends. We are going on from day to day. We are fighting only for immediate objects—objects that can be realized in a few years."[28]

The year 1886—the same in which the Statue of Liberty was dedicated—was significant in labor and "left" history and in the rise of Gompers and Strasser. Henry George was the founder of the single-tax movement designed to eliminate the vast gap between the rich and the poor in America by obtaining all government income from taxes on land. In 1886 he was almost elected mayor of New York City after a campaign in which he received strong Jewish labor support. Probably a more significant development occurred in the same year with the organization of the American Federation of Labor, a new national interunion organization. The emergence of the AFL bears directly on the history we are following, for "its origins lay in a remarkable craft union, the Cigarmakers' International" with Samuel Gompers and Adolph Strasser in the leadership.

> In part because the cigar-makers had to face new technology, such as cigar molds and bunch-breaking machines, that threatened their jobs, in part because they lived amid philosophical debate and indeed liked to make their cigars while someone read aloud from the classics, this union had to face all the urgent questions of organization, discipline, centralization, political action, craft exclusiveness that had challenged trade unionism from the start . . . The cigar-makers were lucky to have leaders able intellectually to meet this challenge.[29]

By and large the Hungarian-Jewish workers tended to follow Strasser's pragmatic philosophy of labor organization and political action rather than the ideas of the Marxists and the Socialist Labor Party.

> In contrast to the Russian-Jewish intellectuals, this group [Austro-Hungarian workers] was more closely concerned with immediate problems of the workers . . . Theoretical questions concerned them but little, although they were under the influence of the German socialists and were devoted readers of the *Volkszeitung*. They invested little energy in the soul-searching and 'clarifications' characteristic of the early East European radical groups.[30]

These comments about the pragmatic political bent of the Hungarian Jews invite comparison with an earlier observation concerning their religious orientation in Hungary. We noted in Chapter 5 that the yeshivot in Hungary were essentially concerned with practical applications of Jewish law to everyday life. This was in contrast to the more abstract and intellectual pursuits of the yeshivot in Lithuania, which emphasized the scholarly analysis of Jewish texts. Perhaps there is a parallel between the two situations despite the fact that they were so widely separated in time and substance. In both circumstances the Hungarian Jews opted for a more practical and less theoretical stance. Further evidence of this preference among Jews from Hungary can be extracted from a study of Jewish immigrant radicals. Among the 170 individuals born in Europe and active here in socialist unions and socialist politics, one looks in vain for a single person from Hungary.[31]

There were, however, a few Hungarian Jewish socialists of the less militant and radical stamp. Victor Berger, who was born in Hungary, had edited a German socialist newspaper in Milwaukee and then an English-language Social Democratic paper.[32] In 1911 he was sent to Washington as the first Socialist congressman. As a pacifist, he was indicted during the First World War for giving "aid and comfort to the enemy" but later had this conviction reversed by the Supreme Court. In 1918 and 1919 Berger was reelected and served in the Congress until 1929.

It is not known how many Hungarian Jews continued to work in the garment and cigar industries after 1900. The United States census reports counted all Hungarians without regard to religion and thereby buried the fundamental differences between Hungarian Jews and Gentiles. Thus, one analysis concluded that from 1900 to 1950 "Hungarians continue an association with heavy industry" and the second generation "shows a considerable degree of occupational continuity" with their immigrant parents.[33]

But one catches a hint of the changes that were occurring—primarily among the Jews—in this statement concerning Hungarian males: "The very small second generation had moved away from manufacturing and domestic and personal service, and had made great gains of employment in the professions and in trade and transportation."[34] It appears reasonable to think that the statement referred essentially to Hungarian Jews. The absence in the literature after 1930 of references to Hungarian-Jewish cigar makers or garment workers suggests that Hungarian Jews had left those occupations and were entering other fields, probably the sectors of the American economy where Americanized Jews were concentrating: commercial, white collar, and professional jobs. Support for this view comes from information collected for this book.

Table 9 compares the occupations of a sample of residents on the Lower East Side of New York in 1880 with the occupations of applicants for citizenship in New York and Cleveland between 1906 and 1929 and with Nashville in 1900. The table shows that over time the Jewish workers were moving out of the garment industry into skilled work, service jobs, and selling. This movement is consistent with the rapid upward mobility of the whole Jewish immigrant population. "Occupational change," Arthur Goren wrote, "was a critical component of rapid acculturation . . . Within the span of one or two generations, eastern European Jews transformed themselves from a working-class population to a middle class group in business, white-collar jobs, and the professions."[35]

Goren notes that the proportion of Jewish men in industry dropped from 60 percent in 1900 to less than 25 percent in the 1930s. The corresponding figures for Hungarian Jews cannot be quantified, but it is known that many opened small shops as tailors or dry goods merchants, both in the big cities and in small towns. Undoubtedly this included many former hucksters and peddlers. There is a rich literature about Jewish peddlers, beginning with the German Jews who fanned out across the country, but it does not specifically identify the Hungarians among them.[36]

A newspaper presentation of who's who in the Hungarian-American national community affords a picture of a number of Jewish immigrants at the very close of the nineteenth century.[37] Patently it was a time of tremendous social fluidity, for one reads of men moving quickly from journalism to banking, from teaching to the law, from service in the army to manufacturing and business. The Jews in this compilation were beginning to enter philanthropy and to raise funds for such causes as the great flood in Szeged or the Montefiore Home and the Lebanon Hospital.

As the century turned, the immigrant parents had their eyes on a different future for themselves and their children. They encouraged their children to prepare for that future on another crucial pathway. As one immigrant put it, "Just like you can't breathe without air, you can't live without an education."[38] They expected their children to get the most out of public school and then, for many, to go on to college and a profession. Another significant agent of Americanization was the settlement house and the "Y" (either Jewish or Christian), with its classes for adults and for children, its gym, and its emphasis on becoming American. Schools and settlement houses moved the immigrant families farther and faster on the routes into the American system.

The following snippets from tapes made by immigrants in Pittsburgh give a sense of what it was like to begin the journey into America.[39] Mrs. B.

was not happy with their first stop in a small town where they were the only Jews, but once they moved to McKeesport, where she and her husband ran a meat market, life improved. In Hungary she had been "very friendly with non-Jews" and this continued here. She was an active member of Jewish organizations and went into Pittsburgh for the theater and concerts. One of her goals was to see her son through medical school, which she was convinced could only be done in the United States, and which she accomplished.

Somewhat more dramatic were the experiences of Mr. K., who started as a butcher and a part-time interpreter in the courts. The meat store became a clothing store and then a department store. One year he bought a Swedish Lutheran church and remodeled it as a synagogue, for which the congregation later repaid him. In 1914 he went with his wife to see his parents in Hungary and while in Budapest he called the United States consul to offer to do intelligence work since he knew English, German, Hungarian, Slavic, Croatian, and some French. He spent more than two years delivering secret communications to the U.S. ambassador in Rome, for which he received a pension from the government.

The woman who had found the Russian Jews more idealistic than the Hungarians came from a thoroughly Magyarized family. Her father had been an army officer in Hungary; she had studied music in Vienna, and her mother had taught her English while they were still in Miskolc. Her father was one of those who did not succeed in America and after his restaurant failed, he returned to Hungary. But they ultimately came back and their daughter married an American-born pharmacist. She gave piano lessons and attended many cultural activities. One of her children is an Ivy League professor; another got a degree from Oxford.

And so it went. Many immigrants had hard times peddling and long hours in their stores, and not all of them moved up. Others did and their children consolidated the families' increasingly middle class status. Hungarian-Jewish immigrants were finding their way into the American system by many paths. One was through the contacts their leaders were making with the Republican and Democratic parties. At the same time, workers were expressing their demands for better living and working conditions through the Jewish trade union movement and the various socialist and left-wing parties.

There was a sharp differentiation between the Gentiles and the Jews from Hungary: the former were in heavy industry and the latter in light, consumer-oriented industry and in commerce. Commerce and trade offered the main route out of the working class for the Jews; the professions provided the route taken by their children. Most of the immigrants did not remain in the working class; they moved through it and through the door to America and into its middle class.

★

CHAPTER 15

Flickers and Reflections

The passing of time, and not much of it, brought profound changes. By 1914 the large influx of Hungarian Jews was over and those who had come before then were letting down roots in American soil. This final chapter will survey the changes that took place between the two world wars as the Jewish immigrants and their children became less and less connected to the Magyars, here and overseas, and to their own Hungarianness. That process was like a candle gradually going out, now and again throwing out flickers that recall its former light. The second part of the chapter will offer some reflections on the 150 years of immigration and adjustment described in this book.

World War I cut off all immigration, and in the postwar period about thirty thousand Hungarian sojourners went home as they had planned. Approximately the same number arrived in a spurt of immigration in the 1920s just before the gates to America were in effect closed to them.[1] Professionals and Jews made up a good proportion of this limited immigration, as was the case just before and after World War II.[2] But the Big Migration had already ended.

In the aftermath of World War I Hungarian Jews were striving to move beyond the parochial concerns of local *landsmanschaften* and synagogues. They were seeking a national presence and a capability of acting in a concerted manner on the problems left by the war. At the same time this marked their growing distance from the national federations of all Hungarians and a recognition that, in a period when conditions were changing for the worse for Jews in Hungary, their interests were diverging sharply from those of Hungarian Gentiles.

They organized the American Economic Council for Hungarian Jews to raise $14 million to aid Jewish refugees expelled during the Communist period under Béla Kún. When the White Terror followed in the early 1920s and poverty and anti-Semitism gripped the Jewish population in Hungary, the Hungarian Jews in America responded. In addition they cooperated with the American Joint Distribution Committee in providing aid through small loans, assistance to war widows, and support for religious institutions in Subcarpathia, part of postwar Czechoslovakia.[3]

During these years efforts were made to unite the many Hungarian-Jewish organizations then in existence in a national coordinating body of the type that Russian, Galician, and Rumanian Jews had established. The Federation of Hungarian Jews in America was set up in 1919 "for the purpose of rendering Hungarian Jews articulate in the United States of America and of assisting Hungarian Jews abroad in a social, political and charitable way."[4] In 1920 the Federation protested the *numerus clausus* law enacted in Hungary to limit the number of Jewish students in universities. From 1919 to 1938 it published the *Jewish Hungarian Chronicle* and reported in 1922 that there were 2,000 to 2,500 members working to help new immigrants and refugees who needed assistance in obtaining citizenship and jobs and in locating lost relatives.[5] The Federation was also fighting Hungarian anti-Semites who were touring the United States, cooperating with Zionist organizations to promote a homeland in Palestine, and condemning the impact of the Trianon treaty on Hungary.

The federation, which appears to have reorganized and changed its name from time to time in the interwar years, in 1941 had a membership of 107 lodges, benevolent societies, social circles, synagogues, and labor unions. At its peak it claimed 35,000 members in the mid-1920s. It is not clear whether the Association of Hungarian Jews in America, established in 1932, was the same organization or a new one, but the Association bought land in Haifa to settle Hungarian Jews there and in the late 1930s and early 1940s was representing Hungarian refugees entering this country and sponsoring cultural programs.

It is difficult to assess the effectiveness of these efforts to coordinate the resources and influence of Hungarian Jews in America. They lasted less than twenty-five years and apparently did not achieve the inclusiveness they sought. In 1932 *The Hungarian Jew—A Magyar Zsidó*—sent greetings to the central bureau of the Union of Orthodox Congregations of Hungary and added wistfully: "We are sorry that, for lack of an official organization, embracing all American Jews of Hungarian descent, we cannot yet speak in the name of all Hungarian Jews of America."[6]

In New York the virtual cut-off in immigration after 1914 did not entirely stop the formation of Hungarian-Jewish organizations. The incorporation papers cited in earlier chapters show a new congregation in Yorkville and a few sick benefit societies still being formed on the Lower East Side. Several new social circles, literary clubs, and lodges were set up, though there was no discernible new organization outside of New York. For example Pannonia Lodge No. 185 of the Independent Order of Odd Fellows was established in New York in 1916.[7] It had a relief committee and a cemetery committee; it provided loans and maintained an old age and disability fund. Until 1939 the lodge conducted its meetings in Hungarian. Pannonia Lodge furnishes one of the flickers of times past in terms of contact with Hungarian Gentiles. In 1941 when the lodge celebrated its twenty-fifth anniversary, the "eulogy" was delivered in Hungarian by the Reverend Géza Takaró of the First Hungarian Reformed Church. The lodge's records go up to 1963 and show that in its later years the organization contributed to the United Jewish Appeal, HIAS, and the Federation of Jewish Philanthropies in New York.

The secular organizations of the Hungarian Jews declined in number and activity in the decades following World War I and it was much the same with religious organizations, though some persisted. Bet Hamidrash Hagadol Anshei Ungarn, the Great House of Prayer of the People of Hungary, founded in 1877, has been mentioned before. Michael Shai, ordained a rabbi in Hungary, came here in 1925 and in the mid-1930s was its rabbi. But by that time there were few such synagogues. In 1938 one source claimed, without giving the details, that there were thirty Hungarian synagogues in New York City alone, but this was probably an overestimate.[8] A Hungarian newspaper looking around the country in 1950 was very likely closer to the truth when it wrote: "In the past Hungarian Jewry maintained several congregations but these soon became totally Americanized. Today there are only one or two congregations in the United States which can be considered Hungarian institutions."[9]

Those synagogues that were not disbanding were fast losing their Hungarian character. In 1929 Shomrei Hadath Congregation in Cleveland adopted a constitution that stated: "All business and records shall be conducted in English, however, no member shall be deprived from using the Hungarian language, or Jewish language, during meetings to express his or her opinion."[10] The following year in Highland Park, New Jersey, Ohav Emeth Anshe Ungarn could no longer afford a full-time rabbi and was in crisis. "Things finally eased when the younger generation assumed the leadership after an agreement to drop the ethnic emphasis."[11]

Nevertheless, beginning in the 1930s a new immigration of Hungarian rabbis occurred and this was augmented after World War II by those who survived the Holocaust; some are listed in a compendium of Orthodox rabbis published in 1950.[12] Moreover, a Magyar-speaking congregation was established in New York in the late 1930s.[13] But overall fewer Hungarian rabbis came and fewer congregations survived. The day of a vigorous Hungarian-Jewish presence in America did not come closer as the years passed. It receded.

By the 1940s one can see the last sputterings of truly Hungarian-Jewish life based on the Big Migration. The Munkács (or Carpathian) Society was still holding its gatherings at 87th Street on the West Side of New York City. This was a social club which, among other things, provided a meeting place where the mostly American-born daughters and sons of Hungarian Jews could meet each other and have the opportunity of marrying within that fold. Several organizations continue to function today, though under circumstances that are far removed from the intentions of their founders. There is something to be learned from following the histories of these organizations and we have chosen one in New York and another in Cleveland for this purpose.

Six nights a week people still walk up the stairs of an old building in Yorkville on Manhattan's East Side to enjoy Hungarian food and conversation, cards, and companionship at the First Hungarian Literary Society. The society has come a long way since its first meeting by candlelight in 1889 in a cigar store on Stanton Street on the Lower East Side. Its incorporation papers were prepared by the ubiquitous Morris Cukor, probably with more than usual care since his father was the moving spirit behind the new society. It was originally established to promote "debates, recitations and readings . . . to improve literary talent and to cultivate the social relations" among its members. The association was a "pioneer of Hungarian-American self-culture societies" and "self-training centers."[14]

In its early days the society, besides being "the center and champion of Hungarian culture and literature in America," offered financial aid to its members when necessary and free burial plots.[15] Over the years it encouraged Hungarian poets and musicians, fought against persecution of Hungarians and of minorities in Hungary, and patriotically celebrated the March 15 anniversary of the 1848 revolution. More recently it has raised funds for the Red Cross, the March of Dimes, Israel Bonds, and many other causes.

Several things are remarkable about the First Hungarian Literary Society. About 10 percent of its members are Gentiles and one of its four cemeteries is for Christians. Along with a Passover Seder in recent years, there is the customary Christmas party. Second, the society is still thoroughly Hungarian. Magyar is the language one still hears around the tables these days, though only a few people who came to America before the 1920s are still alive among its three hundred members. Most came here in 1956 or even more recently, including some young people who are not Jewish.

One of the old-timers in his eighties was asked how and why this organization survived into the 1980s and his reply was immediate: "We bought this building in 1925 and have had a base since then." Interestingly, the Hungarian-Jewish Sick Benefit Society Testverigseg was described as one of the longest-lasting societies in Cleveland, though the newspaper did not give the year it was established. The society boasted in 1928 of being the only such organization "which owns a large and well equipped home."[16] Probably several hundred ephemeral societies have come and gone in rented quarters and crowded apartments since the Hungarians came to New York in any numbers. The First Hungarian Literary Society, secure in its own building and today essentially a social club, was able to modify its purposes and its programs decade after decade to suit new times, including the arrival of younger Hungarians in the past thirty years. On the other hand, the grandchildren and great-grandchildren of the founders do not speak Hungarian and do not take part in the society.

Now to Cleveland, where there is an active organization, founded in 1881, whose official name is HBSU. Even in today's world of acronyms, HBSU stands out. Originally it was the Hungarian Benevolent & Social Union and it had much the same goals as the literary society in New York, minus the literary purposes.[17] By the time of the First World War there were almost eight hundred Hungarian-Jewish members in the organization; today there are about five hundred members but the Hungarian connection has long been dropped. In fact, the name was changed to HBSU in 1919 to indicate "that membership was no longer based on Jewish national origin." In other words, it long ago ceased to be a Hungarian society and became simply a Jewish organization. Its activities in the past fifty years read much like those of the society in New York. Significantly, the HBSU "never had its own meeting hall."

The literary society in New York is rare because it is one of very few that have survived as a predominantly Hungarian-Jewish body, still Hungarian in atmosphere.[18] The HBSU is more typical of those societies that are now Jewish in membership and program and devoid of anything reminiscent of their Hungarian origins. The HBSU has lasted far longer than most of its contemporaries, though some of these continue to function today as lodges or family circles.

In short, there are few organizations that today can be called Hungarian-Jewish. Surely one of the last flickers is the United Jews of Hungarian Descent in Chicago. Incorporated in 1948 by people who had come mostly in the twenties and thirties, the organization now has about one hundred members and devotes its efforts to raising funds for charitable purposes. One should note that the World Federation of Hungarian Jews maintains an office in New York.

One hundred years after the '48ers came here as a result of turbulent events in Hungary, refugees from Hitlerism and World War II began arriving. Steven Bela Vardy speaks of three waves.[19] In 1945 about sixteen thousand people, mostly displaced persons and Jews from concentration camps, entered this country. Another ten thousand political émigrés came between 1947 and 1949. Following the Hungarians' abortive attempt to oust the Russians in 1956, there was a larger wave of forty to fifty thousand immigrants—largely made up of "a new class of young and prospective technocrats" with marketable skills.[20] These waves of post-World War II newcomers did not integrate to any extent with Hungarian Americans already here. The common characteristic of the postwar immigrants was their strong nationalistic and anti-Communist political orientation.

The most recent information on people in the United States of Hungarian "ancestry"—the word itself indicates how much time has passed since the immigrants arrived—shows them living primarily in the northeastern states.[21] They are concentrated in and around the same places their grandfathers settled: New York, Cleveland, and the mining and steel towns of Pennsylvania, West Virginia, and Ohio, though there has been a "substantial shift" out of the heavy industries.

It has been next to impossible to find recent or current information on Jews of Hungarian background, except for a few scattered fragments. In 1940 a census was taken of all foreign-born Jews in New Brunswick, New Jersey, an area in which many Hungarians settled decades ago. Of the 1,002 foreign-born Jews, 18.3 percent were from Hungary. This is undoubtedly higher than the norm for the country as a whole. A study in Boston in 1985 provided data that suggest that 8 percent of the Jewish families had originally come from the Austro-Hungarian monarchy. But since on a national basis Hungarians accounted for less than half the immigrants from Austria-Hungary, the percentage was probably less than 8 percent.[22] The total number of Jews who can be identified (or identify themselves) as Hungarian in origin is impossible to measure today. There is indeed little left on the American scene to remind one of the presence of 100,000 immigrants not many decades ago.

We arrive finally at reflections about the people of this book and their experiences. Our interest is attracted first to the assumption we made at the outset that the historical experience of Jews in Hungary would somehow "make a difference" in this country. We propose to approach this by asking what were the characteristics of the Hungarian Jewish immigrants? Can a case be made for their distinctiveness? Second, a comparison with the immigrant experiences of other Jews was implied in the original assumption. Examining similarities and differences in the adjustments and acculturation of the German Jews, who were similar in some significant ways to the Hungarians, may help us to see the latter more clearly. A comparison of a totally different kind may throw light on the extent to which Hungarian Jews retained the language of the Magyars and other cultural elements. We refer to the Hasidim who came here from Hungary in the 1940s.

How does one set forth what is characteristic of Hungarian Jews? The very question suggests that it is possible to describe a "typical" Hungarian Jew, but that is a risky business. We have seen wide disparities in ideology and lifestyle among the people in this book. Those who came to America before 1880 were on the whole urban, middle-class people, well educated in Western European terms, and oriented toward the Germanic culture of Central Europe. And though culturally they had much in common with those who followed them, the latter were poorer, more religious, and in general more traditional and conservative.

It was as though the "two Jewries" described in Chapter 6 had been transported, one after the other, to America. But the "little people" of the rural areas were much greater in number, and therefore this attempt to describe Hungarian Jews relates primarily to them and to the Big Migration that picked up momentum in the 1880s. The place to begin, in any event, is with the Hungarian part of the puzzle.

In the days of the mass influx from Southern and Central Europe immigrants were frequently perceived as a threat to American-born workers and to the middle class. It was popular then to ridicule the immigrants with caricatures and stereotypes. Many used the derogatory term "Hunky" for Hungarian. Keeping this in mind as a caveat, we have a composite description of "the Hungarian" drawn from five accounts, which are remarkably consistent.[23]

The average or typical Hungarian, so goes their common interpretation, is fiercely attached to his nationality and his culture. This is not hard to believe about someone who spoke a unique language and lived as an ethnic minority in his own country. In addition to this pride of country bordering on chauvinism, he stressed his love of freedom. This was often wrapped in a florid rhetoric such as these words from a Hungarian Jew speaking in Cleveland about Hungarians in general: "The liberty which in all things he demands for himself he freely acknowledges in all others. Freedom, indeed, is the word which consecrates in itself the whole life and being of a Hungarian."[24]

The Hungarian, this composite sketch continues, is proud, emotional, and passionate and puts much store by personal honor. "Happiest when saddest" one pundit wrote; "great lovers and good haters" said another. He is intensely social, preferring conviviality to work. The Magyar is polished, graceful, and hospitable. He loves dancing, music, card playing, cafes . . . and women. One writer pointed out that Hungarian women had independence long before others achieved it. In some respects this portrait begins to resemble a high-living bon vivant and does not quite fit hardworking miners and factory workers. But there must be some grains of truth in these attempts to sketch the "average" Magyar.

Presumably, judging by the descriptions that are available, some of these traits and tastes also applied to the Jews among the Hungarians. As a result of their position in Hungarian society and their adherence to the quid pro quo arrangement, the Jews seem to have been more Magyar than the Magyars when it came to patriotism and adulation of Hungary's culture, its monarchs, and its national integrity.

In Hungary they were certainly in a more politically secure position than their brothers in the Pale of Settlement. Being less desperate, they were less given to the ideological and revolutionary movements that attracted Russian and Polish Jews. There have been suggestions in these pages of an inclination to "moderation" in these matters on the part of Hungarian Jews. They were not so interested, for example, in the more radical and militant organizations in America and in debating the fine points of socialist politics. They gravitated to the pragmatic, "bread and butter" unionism of Gompers.

In religious matters we have also seen a tendency toward the middle ground. As in Hungary so in America, the Reform rabbis were not as extreme in the pace and direction of change as were the German Reformers. On the traditionalists' side, one does not find Hungarians among the leaders of the staunchly Orthodox to the extent that one finds rabbis from Russia and Poland, except for the Hasidim. On the contrary some of the better-known Hungarian-born rabbis—from both Reform and Orthodox orientations—collaborated in strengthening the center by seeking a pragmatic, working balance between the opposites. This appears to be consistent with the characterization that was made of yeshivot in Hungary: they were more given to emphasizing the practical everyday applications of the Law than to arguing fine philosophical points.

Rabbi Bernard Drachman, who was not Hungarian, wrote a sketch of Hungarian Jews based principally on his experience in the First Hungarian Congregation Ohab Zedek in New York in the opening decade of this century.[25] He shared rabbinical duties there with Rabbi Philip Klein for many years. The congregation, which had "become largely Americanized" by 1900, nevertheless was a place where "Hungarian Jewish customs and usages were all prevalent." Drachman had also known Hungarian students at the seminary in Breslau.

The Hungarians, Rabbi Drachman found, had achieved a "synthesis of modern Occidental culture and etiquette with ancient Jewish learning and piety better than most other elements of Jewry." They were less assimilated to their non-Jewish environment than Jews in Western Europe, but they possessed Western culture which the Eastern European Jews "steeped in Jewish lore" lacked. One might conclude from this description that the Hungarian Jews were somehow less Jewish than others. Not so, Drachman decided; he was surprised "to observe how very Jewish these Hungarian Jews were in their manifestation of Judaism. Most of them had a very fair knowledge of Hebrew and the traditional Hebrew culture; a not inconsiderable number were deeply learned in Talmudic lore."

Drachman's own bias shows up in his statement that Yiddish is spoken by the "lowly and uncultured class" among those in the congregation, not by the people of "higher social and intellectual standing" who speak German and also Magyar. He goes on to say that the latter are not only cultured in the "Occidental sense" but also "refined and courteous in bearing and actuated by a strong sense of personal honor." While these qualities, he adds, are inculcated by Judaism, they have been influenced by their Magyar environment. This Drachman attributes to the favorable condition of Jews in Hungary and to the beneficial outcomes of the quid pro quo agreement. He draws this parallel: "The Magyars seem to be very similar to the Spaniards. The same feeling of *grandezza*, the same courtly manners and the same delicate sense of honor, are characteristic of both nations, and their Jewish elements have acquired them with remarkable fidelity from their Gentile co-nationals." Drachman ends his little essay on a note that recalls the Hungarian's feeling about music. The congregants of Ohab Zedek had "a real and sincere love" of "*Chazanuth,* the traditional chanting of the synagogue service." They paid their cantors far more than their rabbis. They employed under the most favorable conditions the famous Joseph Rosenblatt, whom the congregation idolized.

Thus far these generalizations have stressed the Jews' Magyar patriotism, their inclination toward moderation in both politics and religion, their sense of honor, and their tastes in cultural matters. It is this last point that commentators seem to have emphasized—their preference for a particular lifestyle. Edward Steiner, for example, wrote that the Jews "have become convivial like the Magyars, and are not over fond of work. The coffee houses of 'Little Hungary' in New York, draw their revenues largely from these Jews, to whom life without the coffee house would not seem worth the living, and for whom each day must hold its pause for a friendly game of cards or billiards, and a pull at a long and strong black cigar."[26] Again, one wonders how much time the struggling garment workers and cigar makers had for these pursuits, but the large number of Hungarian cafes does attest to the validity of part of this picture.

Remarks by the immigrants and their families frequently allude to their fondness for "fine things" and "good manners." They had, so went the conventional description, a love of theater and "the finer things in life," including fancy clothes, such as those Maurice Amsel bought in Hamburg for his trip to America—a three-quarter coat, spats, cane, and gloves. Quite an outfit for a seventeen-year-old farmhand!

The Jews of Hungary had a distinct style of cooking closely related to that of the Magyars around them. There is this reminiscence: "My mother was convinced that there was no cooking as tasty and succulent as Hungarian cooking. In an era of walk-up tenements, when it was considered socially acceptable for the aroma of delicious cooking to permeate the halls of residential buildings, my mother would sniff a delicious odor and say, 'Hungarians live there.'"[27] It may turn out that their recipes will hold on longer among the grandchildren and great-grandchildren of the immigrants than any other feature of Hungarianness.

These observations about lifestyle seem plausible when one recalls that the Jews in Hungary, by comparison with those in the tsarist empire, were in a more comfortable economic position. This seems to have been true of a majority even of the "little people" in the towns and villages. Many of them had access to better clothes and food, to the theater, and to other features of cultural life in Hungary. In short, Hungarian Jews had incorporated a number of cultural elements from their environment in Hungary that did distinguish them from other Jews in Europe. These differences contributed substantially to the tendency toward separatism among the Hungarian Jewish immigrants.

Much like the Magyarized Jews, those from Germany had a three-way identification. In the words of a rabbi speaking in 1901, "Racially I am a Jew . . . Politically I am an American . . . Spiritually I am a German."[28] Jews had been welcomed into Germany in the late 1600s for their capital and their business experience.[29] By the first half of the nineteenth century they were substantially contributing to Germany's capitalist development and its literature, science, and the arts. But the post-Napoleonic reaction created a repressive climate that influenced many Germans, Gentiles and Jews, to leave their homeland for America in the early and middle years of the nineteenth century. The Jews, in addition, faced obstacles to becoming residents in parts of Germany and were subject to onerous "Jewish taxes." They were attracted to America by a combination of political freedoms and economic opportunities. The Jews were poor and most of the men began here as peddlers.

Ultimately about 200,000 German Jews reached America. When they arrived they found two ethnic communities to which they might have attached themselves. There was a very small but well-established community of Sephardic Jews, who neither welcomed nor attracted the German Jews, and there was in the making a community of German Gentiles with whom the German Jews had unusually strong bonds of language, culture, and liberal ideology. German farmers tended to settle in the Midwest, where traveling Jewish peddlers sought them out as customers. The more liberal, "free-thinking" Germans lived in cities, which the German Jews also favored, thereby facilitating much interchange between them.

Our purpose in reviewing this piece of history is to compare it with the experience of the Hungarian Jews. There were important differences. Unlike the Magyar sojourners, the Christian Germans came here to settle and immediately began constructing permanent institutions. The German Jews participated very actively in the cultural life of the Germans. The sense of identification between German Jews and Gentiles was mutual, especially in the early years. "In great things and in small we encounter Jews as the companions of the Germans."[30]

The Germans welcomed their Jewish countrymen into their glee clubs and athletic associations and vereins. While the Jews eagerly joined, they simultaneously created their own literary clubs and dramatic groups, which the Germans actively patronized. The two groups shared liberal ideas, a German press and theater, and tastes in amusements. The Jews joined German units in the Civil War. By accepting the label of "German" the Jews achieved "their goal of integration into German society . . . albeit on alien shores."[31] Conversely, the Germans saw the Jews as strengthening their cultural position in the United States.[32]

It seems reasonable to conclude that German Jews were socially and ideologically closer to their Gentile compatriots in America than was the case among the Hungarians. But this was not so true of the immigrants' feelings toward the governments they had left behind. In Germany, Cohen writes, "by divorcing German thought from the action of its government, the unemancipated Jews overlooked political restrictions and honestly proclaimed their love of Germany." The Jews of Hungary for the most part could look back at the protection they had enjoyed under the Magyars; they felt kindly toward their government and their king-emperor. But in America their social relations with Magyars were more limited and tenuous in comparison with the situation among Germans.

When the Hungarian Jews arrived here in succeeding "waves," their choice of affiliation and identification was more complex than the Sephardic-German choice the German Jews faced. A range of options was available. Some of the '48ers chose to socialize primarily with Hungarian friends and to become active in Magyar organizations. It should be recalled that there were elements of German culture to which certain Hungarian Jews were devoted even more than to Magyarism. In the years 1860 to 1880 they found an already well-established German-Jewish community and many joined its synagogues and social groups. Some, like the Szolds in Baltimore and General Knefler in Iowa, directly affiliated with German Gentile organizations. Still another pattern, most typical of those who came after 1880, was to cling to other Hungarian Jews in associations of their own kind.

So there were differences between the German and Hungarian Jews, but there were also significant similarities. This paragraph could just as validly have been written about Hungarians:

> The common old home, the mutual ties there, the same reasons for emigration, the simultaneous voyage to the new home, the ability to converse with one another in German, the German feeling of being wronged in America—all this was conducive to good-neighborly relations between Jews and Germans on this continent. Both Germans and Jews, like all recent arrivals, were bound by many threads to the old home. This also resulted in an economic interrelationship.[33]

The mention of the Germans' feeling "wronged" in America refers to their initial rejection by native-born Americans, a phenomenon akin to the derision and discrimination heaped on the Hungarian miners and workers.

Other signs of similarity can be found. Despite friendship and companionship, anti-Semitism lived on in both cases.[34] Germans adopted "Aryan" by-laws in a glee club in New York, a close parallel to the "Christian only" provisions of certain Magyar sick benefit societies. On the other hand, there was visiting back and forth between churches and synagogues. This went further among those who abandoned Judaism. "Among a large part of the Jewish intellectuals who came from Germany the very attachment to the German language and culture went hand in hand with the severance of all ties with religion."[35]

Similar tensions—the pull from three worlds—were experienced by Hungarian and German Jews. This is evident in Cohen's statements that "Jewish participation in German social and cultural activities weakened the focus on Jewish institutions" and that "Germans resented those who turned from German to Jewish institutions."[36] For their part, the Jews "relinquished their Germanism and their German contacts as slowly and reluctantly as possible."[37]

When the dust settled, the resolution of these tensions was much the same among Germans and among Hungarians: erosion of connections between the Jews and their Christian countrymen. Various explanations have been offered for this outcome among the German Jews. "The main cause which separated the German-Jewish immigrants from their cultural partners," Rudolph Glanz argues, "was the great wave of Jewish immigration from Eastern Europe. The German Jews gradually became part of the great Jewish community in the United States, insofar as they were not lost to Jewry in the process of adaptation to the non-Jewish environment."[38]

Another explanation for the separation is advanced by Deborah Dash Moore, who says that in the 1870s and 1880s there took place "a decline in contacts between established Jews and German immigrants. Occupational differences separated the two. The latter tended to be farmers and artisans while the former were merchants and storekeepers. Additionally, the revival of anti-Semitism in Germany affected the more recent immigrants to the United States." She adds that as the affluence and assimilation of the Jews increased, they encountered more rejection by the Germans.[39]

A third interpretation, not inconsistent with the others, comes from Cohen: "After 1870 the German-Jewish nexus dissolved rapidly. In both the Jewish and non-Jewish communities the inexorable force of Americanization weakened foreign customs and loyalties." She also points to the shift away from liberalism in the later German arrivals. Cohen identifies another factor that tended to pull all Jews toward each other: "When the mass immigration of east Europeans to the United States began, 'the Jew' became more visible to Americans and racist tracts highlighted the differences between the lowly Jews and the desirable Aryans."[40]

What about the relationship of Russian and Polish Jews to Gentiles from their lands? Simply put, there appears not to have been much of a relationship. To begin with, there were not many Gentile Russian immigrants; the number has been estimated at ninety thousand as of 1910. Hence there was not a large Russian population with which the mass of Russian Jews could interact, even if they had wanted to—a remote possibility for most of those who were fleeing the pogroms of tsarist Russia.

Actually, for a short time, there were among the Russian émigrés some students and intellectuals with whom Russian-Jewish socialists and radicals found common ground.[41] Russian students in 1885 joined with Hungarian and Galician Jews whom they "happened upon" in the German socialist *New York Volkszeitung* and together formed the Jewish Workmen's Society.[42] But such occurrences were rare and short lived. Whatever attraction Russian culture had for Jews from Russia, once they reached America they were first and foremost Jews.

Contemporary sociological research, Morawska writes, reports "on the persistence of negative attitudes toward Jews among American Slavs, par-

ticularly Polish-Americans."[43] In her own study in small-town western
Pennsylvania, she concluded that relations between Jewish and Slavic immigrants rested basically on "economic exchange between commercial
dealers and their customers, expanded during the inter-war period to
include professional services provided by second-generation Jewish doctors, dentists, and lawyers." Only at the edges of this economic relationship
"there developed some contacts of a social nature" but most of these
seemed to be rooted in a service function performed by the Jews. Morawska
reports greater closeness between Hungarian Jews and Gentiles.[44] In sum,
the relationships that were characteristic of German and Hungarian Jews
and their Gentile compatriots do not seem to have developed between the
Russians and Poles and the Jews from those countries.

We turn now to another group for purposes of comparison—the Hungarian Hasidim. As far back as the 1920s the Williamsburg section of Brooklyn
was becoming "an ultrareligious community of Hungarian Jews."[45] This
community, while not Hasidic in character, paved the way for the arrival of
Hungarian Hasidim who had survived the Nazi years. Led by revered and
powerful "rebbes" and growing rapidly through a high birth rate, the
Hasidim established their own communities and now number in the many
thousands in Williamsburg and other parts of New York City and New York
State.

"Some speak English, but it is not an essential factor in their everyday
interaction," writes the author of a study of Williamsburg. "The males
speak mostly Yiddish, while the females, particularly in gossip, use Hungarian . . . They are not anxious to be identified as Hungarians, but only as
'Hungarian Jews.'" Since we have placed so much emphasis on language
in this book, it is appropriate to quote Solomon Poll's analysis of the role
that the Hungarian language plays among the Hasidim.

> In the United States Hungarian has a different role for the Hungarian Jew. Here
> it is no threat to the ultrareligious Hungarian Jews because there is no social
> intercourse between them and other Hungarians . . . Many Hasidic women speak
> Hungarian almost exclusively amongst themselves because they do not know
> Yiddish or speak it very poorly. Some who know Yiddish still prefer to speak
> Hungarian because it reminds them of the olden days and it expresses strong
> primary-group relationships. It brings back memories and has sentimental asso-
> ciations. Hungarian speech denotes a common background, a common interest,
> and a common understanding of things.[46]

A Russian Jew, Orthodox but not Hasidic, reflecting on the clannishness
of the Hasidim in Williamsburg, had this to say: "They would not patro-

nize a store whose owner is not a Hungarian. They talk a great deal of Hungary, especially the women."[47] He added, in a comment that is strangely reminiscent of the epithet used against Hungarian immigrants fifty years earlier, "Why, Williamsburg is becoming Hunksville."

The Hasidim were fiercely determined to preserve their religious and cultural identity from any changes from outside their ranks. They built strong defenses against the wider American culture, for instance banning TV and the radio from their homes as alien influences that threatened their way of life. And their bulwarks against non-Hasidic Jews were just as strong; the reading of Yiddish newspapers other than their own was not countenanced. In time their extreme measures of social control led non-Hasidic Jews to withdraw from Williamsburg and a new Little Hungary, a Hasidic one, was re-created there, with offshoots in other locations.

In their determination to preserve intact every feature of the Hasidic tradition they had brought from Hungary, willy-nilly they transplanted their idiosyncratic version of Jewish-Hungarian culture to the prayer houses and streets of Brooklyn. This extraordinary development stands in sharp relief to the vast majority of Jewish immigrants who came here from Hungary before the First World War and who experienced a continual and rapid erosion of a culture that was part-Magyar and part-Jewish.

In these final comments we focus again on the three worlds that the immigrants inhabited. Their resolution of the tensions inherent in their three-way identification amounted to this: the Hungarian Jews' Magyar connection eroded well before the middle of the twentieth century. Their bonds to the Jewish community grew stronger and over time they became simply American Jews. (It is impossible even to guess at the number who no longer consider themselves Jewish as a result of conversion to other religions, intermarriage, or for other reasons.) Simultaneous with these changes, Hungarian Jews were proceeding briskly along the road to being Americans, mainly through upward movement on the occupational ladder.

From the beginning—and the beginning goes back to Újhely and Miskolc and Bonyhád—there was a certain tension between feeling like a Magyar and self-identification as a Jew. On one side were the forces pulling in the Magyar direction. The political conditions in Hungary before World War I fostered a sense of loyalty and patriotism on the part of the Hungarian Jews. The economics of nineteenth-century Hungary cast the Jews as commercial agents and artisans and the Gentile peasants as customers and suppliers of raw materials. The ties between the two were buttressed by sharing a language, history, and heroes.[48] Living cheek by jowl with Gentiles in the small towns in the Old Country meant close though ambivalent contacts and shared tastes in food, dance, and music.

In America these connections were reinforced by conditions similar to those in Europe. At first the two groups lived close to each other in urban neighborhoods and in small towns. Economic relations that carried over from the Old Country connected the two groups through daily interchanges. The Jews took an active part in cultural activities of the Hungarian communities, often providing financial support for organizations, newspapers, and philanthropic and patriotic projects. In the early years of the immigration, when the Jews were proportionately a larger part of the Hungarian colonies, they served not only as doctors and lawyers and journalists to the Magyars, but also as community leaders. In those roles they helped to make connections between the Gentile Magyars and elements of the American system, such as its political organizations.

Pulling the Jews away from these ties to their countrymen was another set of forces. Commitment to Judaism as a religion and involvement in its institutions drew most of them toward each other first and ultimately toward Jews from other lands. A whole set of beliefs, values, and life goals separated the Jewish and Gentile groups. This gap was exacerbated by anti-Semitism and anti-intellectualism among some of the immigrants. These divisive forces also had their origins in the Old Country. The anti-Semitism which existed among the peasants was not dropped at the edge of the Atlantic, any more than the hostilities and fears of the Jews toward the Gentiles. Indeed, in assessing the nature of the Magyarization of Jews, one must recall that they had "remained essentially outside the 'native' social structure, despite their evident acculturation and fervent magyarism."[49]

Other things being equal, these positive and negative influences might have approximately balanced each other in the process of settling in the United States, thereby preserving the fragile but workable equilibrium that had existed in Hungary for many decades. Of course that equilibrium in Hungary came to a crashing end in the late 1930s and 1940s, but while it lasted the Jews apparently felt fairly comfortable as participants in Magyar society. In this country the Jewish immigrant generation did in fact manage for much of their lives to bridge the three worlds. But the passage of time progressively upset the balance and unequivocally resolved the matter for their children.

The process by which the Hungarian Jews shed their Magyar attributes and found their identity as Jews and Americans was similar in its dynamics to the experience of the German Jews, although the German Jews had had closer social relations with their Gentile compatriots. Three explanations were offered for the separation of the German Jews from the other Germans: (1) the overwhelming impact of the immigration of two million East European Jews who, merging with the German Jews, created a new American Jewry; (2) the effect of differences in occupation between the German Gentiles and the German Jews; and (3) the leveling effect that Americanization had on both groups. Do these explanations also fit the Hungarians?

The Jews from Hungary saw themselves as "settlers" in the United States while many of the Gentiles thought of themselves as temporary "sojourners." The settlers' perspective encouraged long-range, unconditional commitments to employment, education, politics, and other aspects of American society. The orientation of the sojourner was to work to save money in the short run, to cling to ethnic solidarity and resist Americanization, and to bide time until his return to Hungary. These patterns were vigorously promoted by the Hungarian government. Thus as permanent settlers the Jews were more accessible to the strong influences of Americanization that emanated from the public schools, the settlement houses, the political system, the American press, and the labor movement. This process was mediated for the early arrivals among the Hungarian Jews through contacts with Germans and German Jews who had preceded them.

By the early 1920s the true sojourners had gone home and there was now a sizable community of Gentile Magyars committed to settling in America. At first the events in Europe following the First World War generated an upsurge in Hungarian identification.[50] Both Gentile and Jewish communities loudly demanded "rectification of the injustices" of the peace treaty that cut off much of Hungary's territory and population. The churches here launched intensive efforts to teach the Hungarian language to the children; Hungarian libraries and drama had a renaissance. But it did not last long and soon the Magyarism that had been so strong gave way to the same influences that were Americanizing the Jews. The common cultural base that had connected them to each other was sinking under the feet of both groups.

Moreover, life in Hungary had given the Jews and the Gentiles quite disparate equipment for finding their way in America. While not all of them fit these categories, by and large the Magyars had been peasants and unskilled workers and the Jews had been artisans and traders. Their experiences set them on divergent trajectories in this country. The Jews, even those from the small towns in Hungary, possessed what we called at the beginning of this book the hallmarks of the international migrant, the result of generations of movement back and forth in Europe. These traits included a capacity for adjusting to new places, a facility with languages, and portable occupational skills. It was the latter particularly that prepared the Jews for rapid movement toward middle-class status. They came as precursors of the "service economy" that now characterizes much of America's economic activity.

Many of the Jews had commercial skills that not only fit the developing capitalism in Hungary but were ready-made for the same situation here. This was reinforced by the Jews' knowledge of German, Yiddish, and other non-Magyar languages which permitted communication with groups with whom the Hungarian Gentiles could not or would not interact. The Jews' movement into the middle class likewise influenced inter-group relations, for as they opened stores and acquired professional training and incomes, they moved away from the Little Hungaries, thus weakening the tie of proximity to their Gentile countrymen.

As the Jews moved further into the mainstream of American life, they were less and less middlemen and bridge-makers for the Magyars. The "immigrant industries" in which many Jews had been engaged on behalf of the Hungarian Gentiles—handling remittances to the Old Country, selling steamship tickets, writing for the Hungarian language press, serving as community leaders and representatives—diminished in importance in the first decades of this century and further eroded this connecting link between the groups.

An aspect of the Jewish community that had a significant impact on the resolution of the Magyar-Jewish dilemma was the strong institutional framework that existed here. As newcomers in a strange land, the Christians from Hungary had no strong group to which they could turn for support and guidance. The divisions and hostilities among the "nationalities" from the Kingdom of Hungary exacerbated the Magyars' aloneness. Relationships with Catholic and Protestant churches in this country, which were complicated by the Hungarian government's policies of intervention, were as much of a problem as a help. There was no Hungarian base on which to rely or to build.

By contrast, the Hungarian Jews found an already flourishing Jewish community here. And while it was ambivalent in its welcome, it nevertheless was an anchor, a model, and a source of practical assistance during the demanding process of adjustment. Lloyd P. Gartner observed that among the immigrant groups flooding into Cleveland only the Jews "possessed a native wing that could provide social and philanthropic leadership" to aid the newcomers. This undoubtedly strengthened the pull toward their fellow Jews. At the same time, philanthropy itself was creating Jewish institutions that welded Jews together. "It was charitable activity which became the binding force in making disparate sections into one conscious community."[51]

Thus, on balance, there were resemblances between the processes the German Jews had gone through and the experiences of the Hungarians. Occupational differences with Gentiles and the impact of Americanization had similar impacts. But there were also marked differences between the Hungarians and the German Jews. The German Jews became the dominant component in the American Jewish community of the late 1800s by dint of status, leadership, and financial resources. They went on to establish a formidable array of durable organizations and institutions for American Jewry. The Hungarian Jews left no such legacy.

We come now to the Hungarian Jews qua Jews. Freedom of religious worship was a right in the United States for which the Jewish immigrants did not have to fight as they had in Europe. Nor were they pressed to alter their religious practices, as in Hungary, in order to attain political emancipation. While the proponents of an American "melting pot" tried to smelt all the ethnics down into an Anglo-Saxon mold, they did not object to religious diversity. Social acceptance was something else. There were the strident nativists who abhorred all foreigners. More direct were the anti-Semites who singled out the Jews for special treatment as undesirables. Hungarian Jews experienced their share of this, but overall they found a country where their right to live as Jews was accepted.

The Hungarian Jews and the Jews they found here were not quite ready to accept each other fully at first contact, except for the early '48ers. In part as a result of language and other cultural differences, the bulk of the immigrants chose to go through a period of separatism in Hungarian synagogues, *landsmanschaften*, and other organizations before they were ready for merger. It was to a great extent these organizations that both defined and perpetuated Hungarian Jews as a distinct group at the turn of the century. By the 1930s Hungarian-Jewish organizations, whether religious or secular, had all but disappeared.

Steadily the newcomers were drawn closer to an evolving American Jewish community.[52] The differences among German and Russian and Polish Jews were lessening. And this was true of the Hungarians as well. Joshua Fishman saw this clearly when he wrote that Hungarian Jews were ceasing to be a recognizable group in any linguistic or cultural sense. "Although there are some small Hungarian-Jewish groups that zealously maintain their separate identity on the American-Jewish scene, neither the Hungarian language nor association with non-Jewish immigrants from Hungary are particularly valued among them."[53]

Doctrinal and liturgical differences were settling into a framework of Orthodox, Conservative, and Reform branches of Judaism. Although the people of the Big Migration were essentially Orthodox, in the ensuing decades Hungarian Jews exercised their choice on an individual basis— including the option of secularism—and there is no evidence that they gravitated as a group in one direction or another.

Finally there was a measure of flexibility and openness on the part of those immigrants who chose to come to America, and this eased their adjustments to a new land. "East Europeans who were the most traditionalistic and localistic in outlook (as, for example, the Hungarian Hasidim), did not come to the United States in the period before World War I," according to Marshall Sklare. "Also, those who were the most assimilationist, in the sense of being closely attached to the nationalism and emerging culture of the surrounding people (as were, for example, some Hungarian as well as Polish Jews) generally remained in Eastern Europe."[54] It is interesting that in his parenthetical comments Sklare refers twice to Hungarian Jews. Those who were most Orthodox and most nationalistic and acculturated stayed behind. The Hasidic Hungarians, with their intense attachment to their particular tradition, came here in the 1940s and their adjustment to America has been precisely the opposite of the vast numbers of Jews who immigrated from Hungary earlier.

A recent study of language and ethnicity speaks of two examples of "di-ethnia" in America—the Old Order Amish and the Hasidim.[55] Both groups stringently enforce limits on their members' participation in American society. They maintain their own languages (Luther German and Pennsylvania Dutch among the Amish and Loshn koydesh and Yiddish among the Hasidim). The community structure of the Hasidim, their control of their residential patterns, and their concentration in certain areas of economic activity reinforce their identity and their isolation.

In terms of the story that has unfolded in the pages of this book, the Hungarian Hasidim have succeeded in maintaining exactly that "separatism" that characterized the Jewish immigrants from Hungary during the initial period of their adjustment to America. But that phase of separatism was of short duration. In the Big Migration of 1880 to 1914 the Jews with the strongest Magyarism and those with a tenacious attachment to Hasidism stayed in Hungary. Those who did emigrate were relatively freer to make choices of their way of life here, in both religious and secular terms.

The ultimate outcome is clear. Except for the Hasidim, the connection that the Hungarian Jews once had with the Magyar world has long since disappeared. Nor can they any longer be recognized as a distinct group among the Jews. If, as one writer put it, they were "a group apart," that was long ago. They stand today—quite invisible—in each of two apparently compatible worlds as Jews and Americans.

Appendixes

★

Tables

Table 1 Occupational Distribution of All Earners and Jewish Earners in Hungary, 1910

	All Earners[a]	Jewish Earners	
	%	Number	%
Commerce and credit			
Self-employed	1.6	67,576	19.5
Employees	1.9	60,670	17.5
Industry			
Self-employed	5.7	54,857	15.8
Employees	11.8	71,367	20.6
Transport & communication	2.4	11,064	3.2
Professions, civil service, clergy			
Lawyers	.09	3,049	.9
Doctors	.07	2,721	.8
Editors, journalists	.002	515	.01
Other professions and other white-collar occupations	3.1	21,370	6.2
Agriculture[b]			
Owners & laborers with under 5 holds	12.4	3,272	1.0
Agricultural workers	15.7	2,852	.8
Landowners 100 or more holds	.3	2,271	.7
Other	31.7	14,109	4.1
Miscellaneous			
Pensioners, stockholders, owners of rental property	2.5	12,225	3.5
Armed forces	1.2	3,617	1.0
Other	9.5	15,221	4.4
Total	100.0	346,756	100.0

[a]The total number of earners was 7,750,973.
[b]In the original this included agriculture, horticulture, forestry, and related occupations.
SOURCE: *Magyar Statisztikai Közlemények*, Uj sorozat, 56. Kötet. Az 1910. évi népszámlálás. Hungarian Statistical Publications, New Series, vol. 56. The 1910 Population Census, Pest, 1915.

Table 2 Regional Distribution of Jewish Population of Hungary, 1910, and of Jewish Immigrants, 1885–1924

Region[a]	Jewish Population	Jews as % of Total Popul.	% of Jews in Hungary	% of Immigrants
Northeast (D)	142,286	8.1	15.3	53.5
East Central (E)	197,384	7.6	21.2	17.1
Central (C)	294,254	7.8	31.6	14.1
(Budapest)	(203,687)	(23.1)	(21.9)	(12.5)
Northwest (B)	87,360	4.0	9.3	6.4
West (A)	89,895	2.9	9.6	5.5
South (F)	34,007	1.8	3.7	1.6
East (G)	64,074	2.4	6.9	1.7
Croatia-Slovenia (H)	22,927	0.9	2.4	0.1
Total	932,187	4.5	100.0	100.0

[a]The counties that make up each region are listed in *Magyar Statisztikai Közlemények*, 1910 data, vol. 56. 1915, p. 372, according to the alphabetical designation following the name of the region.

NOTE: Based on samples of 409 passengers, 1885–1905, and 357 applicants for citizenship in New York and Cleveland, 1906–1924. The birthplaces of fifteen passengers and fifty-seven citizenship applicants are not known.

While constitutionally Croatia-Slovenia was not part of the Kingdom of Hungary, it has been included here to indicate that its small Jewish population was a negligible factor in emigration.

Table 3 Geographic Distribution of Passengers and Applicants for Citizenship for Selected Areas

	Passengers			Citizenship Applications		
	1885	1895	1905	Cleveland	NYC	Total
Northeast	85.6	62.5	36.6	52.2	40.8	53.5
Borsod, Abaúj, and Zemplén	50.0	31.7	21.3	25.3	17.2	27.8
East Central	1.6	15.8	34.8	10.2	20.1	17.1
Central	2.3	7.5	16.5	17.7	21.3	14.1
Budapest	1.6	7.5	16.5	14.0	18.9	12.5

Table 4 Regional Distribution of Jewish Earners in Hungary for Selected
Occupations, 1910 (in percent)

	Landowners >1000 holds[a] N = 315	Renters <5 holds N = 3,272	Lawyers N = 3,043	Commerce, credit[b] N = 128,246	Indep. industry, crafts[c] N = 54,857
West	9.8	3.4	10.8	12.4	10.4
Northwest	5.7	5.4	9.4	9.7	11.9
Central	39.4	2.2	48.6	38.3	28.8
Northeast	8.6	33.8	10.3	12.0	17.2
East Central	27.6	51.4	10.0	16.1	20.5
South	5.1	0.6	7.0	5.1	3.1
East	3.8	3.2	4.0	6.1	8.1
	100.0	100.0	100.1	99.7	100.0
National totals	1,657	958,855	6,743	275,030	440,021

[a]70 holds = 100 acres.
[b]Self-employed and employees in commerce and credit.
[c]Self-employed only in industry and crafts.
SOURCE: *Magyar Statisztikai Közlemények*, 1910 data, vol. 56, 1915, pp. 436–765.

Table 5 Birthplaces of 1885, 1895, and 1905 Passengers by Size of Jewish Population as of 1910

City or town	No. of Jews	County	Jews as % of total population	No. of passengers
Budapest	203,000	—	21.9	38
		Places of 5,000–10,000		
Debrecen	8,406	Hajdú	9.0	12
Győr	5,808	Győr	13.6	2
Kassa	6,723	Abaúj-Torna	15.2	14
Miskolc	10,291	Borsod	20.0	12
Munkács	7,675	Bereg	44.4	6
Sziget	7,981	Máramaros	28.0	2
Temesvár	6,727	Temes	9.8	4
Sátoraljaújhely	5,730	Zemplén	28.7	15
Ungvár	6,000	Ung	40.0	27
		Places of 2,500–4,999		
Beregszász	2,770	Bereg	21.3	3
Kisvárda	3,036	Szabolcs	30.2	9
Nyíregyháza	3,882	Szabolcs	10.2	2
		Places of 1,500–2,499		
Eperjes	2,106	Sáros	16.6	7
Eszék	2,340	Verőce	7.4	1
Kispest	1,652	Pest-Pilis-	5.5	2
Lugos	1,878	Solt-Kiskún		
		Krassó-Szörény	9.5	4
Places under 1,500				433
No birthplace recorded				15
Total				608

SOURCE: Ernest László, "Hungarian Jewry: Settlement and Demography," in *Hungarian Jewish Studies*, ed. Randolph L. Braham. New York: World Federation of Hungarian Jews, 1966, pp. 61–136.

Table 6 Family Roles of Jewish Immigrants, 1880–1905 (in percent)

	N	Head of Fam. or Single	Wives with Husbands	Children	Other
1880	327	34.3	17.4	45.9	2.4
1885	198	62.4	5.1	24.9	7.6
1895	205	60.0	2.9	31.7	5.3
1905	212	56.6	8.5	32.5	2.3
Total	942	50.8	9.7	35.4	4.1

Table 7 Hungarian-born Population of New York City, 1870–1930

	1870	1880	1890	1900	1910	1920
Manhattan				28,007	58,907	40,644
Bronx				550	6,256	10,644
Brooklyn				2,449	8,947	8,795
Queens & Richmond				510	2,505	4,310
Total	521	4,101	15,555	31,516	76,615	64,393
Jewish Population of New York City			300,306	597,674	1,252,135	1,643,012

SOURCES: For 1870 and 1880, Ira Rosenwaike, *Population History of New York City*, Syracuse University Press, 1972, p. 67. For 1890, 1900, and 1930, *Population of the City of New York, 1890–1930*, Cities Census Committee, Walter Laidlaw, ed., 1932, p. 247. For 1910, *Statistical Sources for Demographic Studies of Greater New York, 1910*, New York Federation of Churches, Walter Laidlaw, ed., 1912, vol. 1. For 1920, *Statistical Sources for Demographic Studies of Greater New York, 1920*, p. xxiv. The data on Jewish population are from Laidlaw, *Population of the City of New York, 1890–1930*, p. 275.

Table 8 Comparison of Foreign-born, Hungarian, and Jewish Population in New York City and Cleveland, 1910

	New York City	Cleveland
Total population	4,766,883	560,663
Foreign-born	1,927,703	195,703
Born in Hungary	76,625	31,503
Jewish	1,000,000	75,000
Hungarian Jews	53,000	10,000

NOTE: The estimate of 75,000 Jews in Cleveland is for 1920 and comes from Gartner, p. 101. The figure of 53,000 Hungarian Jews in New York is for 1900 and is based on the estimate that they constituted 70 percent of all people born in Hungary; see Rosenwaike, p. 123. The estimate of 10,000 Hungarian Jews in Cleveland assumes they constituted one-third of the Hungarians.
SOURCE: 1910 U.S. Census, except for those noted above and Rosenwaike's estimate that New York's Jewish population was one million in 1910; see Rosenwaike, p. 111.

In New York City those born in Hungary constituted 4.0 percent of all foreign-born, in contrast to 16.1 percent in Cleveland. Hungarian Jews in New York have been estimated to be 70 percent of all those born in Hungary. This would mean that they constituted 5.3 percent of all Jews in New York City. Unlike New York, there are no estimates of the size of the Hungarian-Jewish population in Cleveland. A conservative guess would be one-third of all the Hungarian-born and therefore about 15 percent of all Jews in Cleveland.

Table 9 Occupational Distribution of Hungarian Jews, 1880–1929, in New York, Cleveland, and Nashville (in percent)

	1880 Census N.Y. City N = 133	New York N = 115	Cleveland N = 115	1900 Census Nashville N = 62
Garment Workers	57.9	20.9	10.4	—
Skilled	13.2	30.4	39.1	19.4
Selling	14.3	19.1	16.5	64.5
Unskilled	13.7	13.0	15.7	4.8
Service Jobs	—	9.6	15.7	8.1
Professional	1.0	7.0	—	3.2
Other	—	—	2.6	—

NOTE: The New York and Cleveland data are based on the citizenship papers from those two cities for the years 1906–1929. The information for Nashville comes from the working papers of Fedora S. Frank made available by the Archives of the Jewish Federation of Nashville and Middle Tennessee.

Table 10 Hungarian-Jewish Religious, Welfare, and Social
Societies in New York City, 1865–1914

Date of establishment	Religious	Sick/benefit	Social	Total
1865–1879				
New York	3	4	0	7
Cleveland	1	2	0	3
Chicago	0	1	0	1
Other	0	1	1	2
Total	4	8	1	13
1880–1899				
New York	14	22	9	45
Cleveland	3	3	1	7
Chicago	2	1	0	3
Other	5	6	2	13
Total	24	32	12	68
1900 and later				
New York	12	15	12	49
Cleveland	5	1	0	6
Chicago	1	5	5	11
Other	7	1	1	9
Total	25	32	18	75
Total				
New York	29	51	21	101
Cleveland	9	6	1	16
Chicago	3	7	5	15
Other	12	8	4	24
Total	53	72	31	156

NOTE: The methodology used in assembling this information is described in
Appendix 4.

Table 11 U.S. Cities with More than 5,000
Persons Born in Hungary, 1910, and Number of
Hungarian Organizations

City	Hungarian-born population	No. of organizations
New York City	76,625	78
Cleveland	31,503	81
Chicago	28,938	41
Philadelphia	12,495	22
St. Louis	8,758	
Pittsburgh	6,576	25
Cincinnati	6,344	—
Newark	6,029	18
Detroit	5,935	—
Milwaukee	5,571	—

SOURCES: The population data are from the U.S. Census 1910
and the organizational data are for 1911 from Géza Hoffmann's
work quoted in Géza Kende, *Magyarok Amerikaban*, p. 275.

Table 12 Hungarian-Jewish Organizations by Name, Location, and Year
of Establishment

Before 1880

Cleveland: Hungarian Aid Society, 1863; B'nai Jeshurun, 1866; Hungarian Jewish Ladies Aid Society, 1868.
Atlanta: Concordia Association, 1866 (with Germans).
New York: First Hungarian Congregation Ohab Zedek, 1871; two other synagogues and four sick benefit societies.
Chicago: Oestreich-Ungarisher Kranken Unterstitzung Verein, 1879–1880.
Nashville: Hungarian Benevolent Association (Ungarischer Unterstitzung Verein), 1871.

1880–1889

Philadelphia: Congregation Emunath Israel, 1880; Oheb Sholom, 1884.
Pittsburgh: Austro-Hungarian Poale Zedek, 1881.
Cleveland: Hungarian Social and Benevolent Union, 1881.
Chicago: Agudas Achim Anshei Ungarn, 1884; two chevrot, Osah Chesed veEmeth and Sheveth Achim, merged (1885) to form B'nai David Ohave Zedek.
McKeesport: Gemilas Chesed, 1886.
Poughkeepsie: Shomre Hadath, 1888.

Cleveland: Deak Lodge, Knights of Pythias, 1889.
New York: five synagogues; twelve sick benefit / social societies.

1890–1899

New York: twelve synagogues; seventeen sick benefit / social societies.
Boston: Austro-Hungarian Benevolent Association, 1891; First Hungarian Society, 1892.
Philadelphia: Austro-Hungarian Charity Society, 1890; Austro-Hungarian Volkfest Verein; Petőfi Beneficial Society; Francis Joseph Beneficial Society; Anshe Hungaria Beneficial Society.
Chicago: Hungarian Charity Society, 1893.

1900 and later

Cleveland: Sherit Jacob, 1901; Oheb Zedek, 1904; Shomrei Shaboth, 1905; Shomrei Hadath, 1910; Anshe Marmarasher B'Nai Jacob, 1910; Hungarian-Jewish Sick Benefit Society Testverigseg (date not known).
Yonkers: Ohab Zedek, 1903.
Fairfield, Connecticut: Ahavath Achim, 1905.
Nashville: Shereth Israel, 1905.
St. Louis: Brith Sholom Kneseth Israel, 1908.
Atlanta: Hungarian Benevolent Association, 1910.
Poughkeepsie: Children of Israel (Anshe Ungarn), 1912.
Wharton, Texas: Shearith Israel, 1913.
Highland Park, New Jersey: Ohav Emeth, 1918.
Chicago: Dr. Herzl Vereins, early 1900s; Hungarian Charity Society, Woman's Auxiliary, 1905; Congregation Ahavas Achim, 1925–1943.
New York: nine synagogues; twenty-eight sick benefit / social societies.

NOTE: The organizations established in New York after 1880 are presented above in terms of numbers rather than names. This was done partly because there were so many of them and partly because the information came from incorporation papers and it is therefore not known how long they lasted.

★

Estimating the Number
Who Came to America

For our purpose of determining how many Hungarian Jews reached America, useful statistics are hard to come by. Statistics of the Austro-Hungarian Empire combined Hungarian Jews with Jews from other parts of the empire, including Galicia with its dense Jewish population.[1] Probably more than half of the Jewish emigrants registered between 1899 and 1924 were from Galicia. For example, in 1910–1914 only 22 percent of the Austro-Hungarian Jewish emigrants were from Hungary. In 1900 Hungary had a bit more than 40 percent of the Jews in the Dual Monarchy. In other words, Austro-Hungarian data are not helpful.

The Hungarian government did not register and classify emigrants until 1899 and then did not count Jews separately except for a thirteen-year period as noted below. The United States between 1892 and 1904 counted immigrants from Hungary as part of the total from the Austro-Hungarian Empire; at no time were Jews counted separately from other Hungarian nationals. Other sources of information proved less than helpful. The comprehensive work on Jewish immigration by Samuel Joseph sheds little light on our problem, since his data do not distinguish Hungarian Jews from those from Austria proper or Galicia.[2]

The Dillingham Commission established by the United States government to investigate immigration states that from 1899 to 1910 180,802 Jews emigrated from the Austro-Hungarian Empire, but again it is not known how many came from Austria.[3]

An estimate of net emigration by Jews from Hungary for the period 1870–1910 was made by Alajos Kovács in 1922. Kovács was assembling information to support a political move to limit the proportion of Jews at Hungarian universities, the *numerus clausus*. He based his calculations on an indirect method, since neither the number of Jewish immigrants to

Hungary nor that of emigrants from Hungary was known. Kovács compared the natural increase in Jewish population (the balance between registered births and deaths) with the actual increase as shown in the decennial census reports. He attributed the difference to out-migration. His data on Jews were presented as follows:

Period	Natural population increase	Actual increase	Difference
1870–1880	95,000	82,500	−12,500
1881–1890	122,300	82,800	−39,500
1891–1900	134,900	117,600	−17,300
1901–1910	124,000	79,500	−44,500
Net emigration			113,800

Kovács's figure of 113,800 appears to have been based on the excess of emigration over immigration, but it is subject to several sources of error, one of which is the inadequacy of data on the registration of deaths. It must also be recalled that Kovács was estimating total emigration from Hungary, not limited to movement to the United States.[4]

Information on language provides the most useful basis for estimating the number of Jewish immigrants from Hungary. The 1910 United States Census found that almost twenty thousand Hungarian-born immigrants spoke Yiddish. Some seventy-three thousand spoke German and it is reasonable to assume that many, if not most, of these were Jews.

The most useful information comes from the Hungarian government's estimate of the number of emigrants to the United States who gave Yiddish as their mother tongue. *For the years 1900 to 1913, there were 54,453 Yiddish-speaking emigrants.* There are compelling reasons why this must be considered a low estimate of the number of Jews who left during that period: (1) many Jews did not speak Yiddish; (2) some who did were more disposed to say their mother tongue was Magyar; (3) undoubtedly many Jews were among the 218,630 Hungarians who gave German as their mother tongue.[5] It must also be borne in mind that these figures omit all Jews who entered the United States from Hungary between 1848 and 1900—a considerable number. We can now proceed to construct a minimum estimate covering the whole period of Jewish immigration.

In 1900–1901, Yiddish speakers constituted 6.3 percent of all Hungarian immigrants. In 1901–1902, they were 4.1 percent and in the following two years the percentages were 5.3 and 7.4. This information—plus the fact that "speaking Yiddish" seriously undercounts the number of Jews—suggests strongly that the Jewish proportion of all Hungarian emigration was well above the 3.7 percent reported for the period 1899–1913 by Puskás.[6]

We shall assume a rate of 7 percent for the pre-1900 period, a time when all the evidence suggests that Jews formed a higher percentage of total Hungarian emigration than was the case after 1900. For the period 1871–1899, total immigration from Hungary amounted to 351,484 according to United States statistics and 433,395 according to the seaport authorities.[7] Applying our assumed rate of 7 percent, the number of Jews who came before 1900 would then be between 24,604 and 30,338. Taking a figure of 28,000 for this period and the figure of 54,500 for the years 1900 to 1913, we arrive at 82,500 Jewish immigrants for 1871 through 1913. This estimate does not deduct as Puskás does, for multiple trips made by individuals back and forth between America and Hungary. There was some movement back and forth on the part of Jews visiting their families, but since the vast majority of them settled in the United States, it is reasonable to suppose that there was much less trans-Atlantic traffic than among the Gentile Hungarians. Nor can we assume that a significant portion of the Jewish "returnees" remained in Hungary.

Our calculation of 82,500 Jews who left Hungary for the United States rests on estimates concerning those who spoke Yiddish according to Hungarian statistics. Many did not speak that language. On the other hand, many who gave German as their mother tongue were undoubtedly Jewish, as well as some who said they spoke Magyar. Moreover, the estimate does not reflect people who came before 1871 and those who came after 1913. For these reasons I consider 100,000 Hungarian-Jewish immigrants to be a conservative estimate.

★

Passenger Lists, Citizenship Applications, and U.S. Census of 1880

PASSENGERS

Samples of passengers who arrived at the port of New York in 1885, 1895, and 1905 were drawn from ship lists. They include 614 individuals divided approximately equally among the three years. The individuals were selected according to two criteria: (a) they were listed as nationals of Hungary and (b) their family names and/or their first names indicated Jewish origin.[1]

The identification of names is subject to two kinds of errors. When the Jews were ordered to adopt family names many took names of German origin, such as Rosenberg or Schwartz. But there were also Christians of German origin who had become Hungarian nationals. In some instances this could be solved by identifying first names that were unmistakably Jewish. The other error stemmed from the fact that some Jews Magyarized their last names, for example changing Schwartz to Fekete or Wolf to Farkas. Many adopted Hungarian first names, such as János, Béla, Katarina, and Pepi. Thus, some Jews may have been missed and conversely a few Christians of German background may have been erroneously included in the samples. The same must be said about Polish and Slavic names adopted by Jews.

The 1885 and 1905 passenger lists were prepared for the U.S. Immigration Office as ships arrived at the Port of New York. Generally the lists included the name, age, sex, nationality, and place of birth or in a few instances place of last residence, and occupation where applicable. Ships were selected if they had more than a few Hungarian passengers; in 1885, for example, the number of Jewish immigrants on a ship ranged from five to forty-six. Once a ship was selected, all passengers who could be identified as

Hungarian Jews were recorded. Christian Hungarians were counted on some but not all ships.

I commented in the text on the difficulties English-speaking immigration officials had with the spelling and pronunciation of Hungarian names and places. In the hope that the German port authorities might be better attuned to Hungarian place names, the 1885 sample was drawn from ships leaving Hamburg, a main port of embarkation for Hungarians at that time. It turned out, however, that the German authorities were even less successful in writing legible place names and in recording occupations than the Americans.

Places of birth were assigned to one of Hungary's seventy-one counties by reference to *Magyar Statisztikai Közlemények, 1900*, Budapest, 1902, vol. 1, supplemented by examination of Hungarian gazeteers from the years 1828, 1842, and 1851. The place of origin was obtained for 66.9 percent of the individuals in the samples. This varied as follows: 1885, 67.5 percent; 1895, 56.1 percent; and 1905, 79.7 percent.

APPLICANTS FOR CITIZENSHIP

Beginning in 1906 the procedure for becoming a citizen of the United States required (1) the filing of a declaration of intention (first papers); (2) filing a petition for naturalization (second papers) and (3) a hearing on the petition and a decision. At least two years but no more than seven years had to elapse between the filing of first and second papers. The second papers included such information as the date and the city or town in which the petitioner and each member of the family were born, as well as his or her date of arrival in this country. It is interesting that in addition to the renunciation of allegiance to "any foreign prince, potentate, state or sovereignty," the petition used in 1883 contained the statement "I am not an anarchist; I am not a polygamist." The declaration had to be signed by two witnesses who personally knew the prospective citizen.

The information for this study was extracted (1) from records of the Federal District Court for the Southern District of New York, which are kept at the National Archives, New York Branch, and (2) from records of the Cuyahoga County Court of Common Pleas kept at the Cuyahoga County Archives, Cleveland. In New York, data were obtained on 125 petitioners and 253 members of their families. In Cleveland 114 petitioners and 320 family members were studied. Thus data were collected on a total of 812 individuals. The percentage of applicants whose county of birth was identified was 89.6 percent for Cleveland and 91.5 percent for New York applicants. Some of the children of the immigrants and a few wives and husbands were born in the United States. Not until the years just before 1924 were petitions filed by women. Records were not available at these archives for the years before 1906, and petitions filed after 1924 were not examined. In all cases, however, the petitioner arrived in the United States before 1914. The peak years for arrivals in both Cleveland and New York were 1900–1904.

SAMPLE DRAWN FROM 1880 U.S. CENSUS IN NEW YORK CITY

Working from indications in the literature that the northern part of the Lower East Side was a Hungarian enclave, I located buildings in the 1880 census in which many Hungarians with Jewish names were living. The buildings were located in an area bounded by Delancey Street on the south, Rivington Street on the north, Attorney Street on the west, and Willett Street on the east. A few buildings north of Stanton and south of Delancey were also included. In each building selected, I recorded all persons listed as Hungarian. The information consisted of name, age, occupation, family relationships, and notations where someone was a boarder. The sample consisted of 326 Jews and 12 non-Jews in the same buildings.

★

Questionnaires, Organizations, and Historical and Genealogical Societies

Questionnaires were mailed in the spring of 1987 to seventy-six persons registered with the Family Finder of the Jewish Genealogical Society. These people were listed as working on the family histories of relatives from pre-1919 Hungary. There were fifty-two replies, including a few people suggested by those on the original list.

The questionnaire asked the respondent to focus on one family member who had come to America before 1925 and to answer a series of questions about that person's experiences in Hungary and in America. A few of the replies were not relevant (e.g., the person actually came from Poland or reached the United States after 1925), but there were a number of lengthy responses, including newspaper clippings, documents concerning the family, and in one instance an undergraduate term paper. Several respondents sent data on two family members. In all, there were forty-nine usable replies. The immigrants tended to be somewhat earlier arrivals than those applying for citizenship. Their occupations in Hungary closely followed the distribution among the passengers. These responses do not constitute a sample of any clearly defined universe. Nevertheless, they provided useful impressions, albeit seen through the recollections of relatives, of a cross section of immigrants.

ORGANIZATIONS

Information on Hungarian-Jewish organizations, summarized in Table 12, was drawn from many sources. Data on New York City came primarily from the American Jewish Historical Society in Waltham, Massachusetts, which houses a collection of articles of incorporation, annual reports, and financial records of several thousand *landsmanschaften*, synagogues, sick benefit societies, and other Jewish organizations incorporated in Manhattan in the years 1850–1920. In selecting from this collection, only organizations with "Hungarian" in the title and filed under "Hungary" or "Austria" were included in the analysis.

A few New York organizations were added to the list from the American Jewish Year Books; the Jewish Communal Register of New York City published by the Kehillah (Jewish Community), 1917–1918; and YIVO. Several entries were extracted from the Federal Writers' Project, Yiddish Writers' Group, WPA (Works Progress Administration), *The Jewish Landsmanschaften of New York*, 1938. Dates of founding were not given in the WPA list; these organizations were placed in the post-1900 category. Several organizations of Jewish and non-Jewish members were not included in this count, but are discussed in the text.

Information on organizations outside of New York came from local Jewish historical and genealogical societies throughout the United States. Inquiries were sent in 1989 to seventy-five of these societies and archives to request materials on Hungarian Jewish immigrants. Some forty replies were received containing valuable accounts of local studies, specific events, and individuals.

With regard to Hungarian organizations in general, as distinct from Hungarian-Jewish organizations, in 1911 some 1,339 Hungarian fraternal societies were counted and classified as being either religious (382), secular (766), or socialist (191). They were further categorized according to their function and 888 of the 1,339 organizations were sick and death benefit associations. The others were essentially benefit associations with social and cultural activities added. This information was compiled by Géza Hoffmann and tabulated by Julianna Puskás. See Puskás, *From Hungary to the United States*, p. 162. Géza Kende counted 2,092 Hungarian societies in existence before World War I. Kende accounted for 1,046 sick benefit associations; 317 religious bodies; 638 social organizations, and 91 political clubs. See Joshua Fishman, *Hungarian Language Maintenance in the United States*, p. 6.

★

Notes

1. The People of This Book

1. Russia had 5,215,805 Jews; Austria, primarily Galicia, had 1,233,213; and Hungary had 851,378. The Jewish population in the United States was 1,777,185 and in Germany 607,862. The figures are from *The American Jewish Year Book*, 1909–1910, p. 193.

2. Jacob Katz, "The Uniqueness of Hungarian Jewry," pp. 49–50.

3. Harold S. Himmelfarb, "Research on American Jewish Identity and Identification: Progress, Pitfalls, and Prospects," p. 59.

4. Illés Kaczér, *The Siege*, pp. 145–46.

5. Arnold A. Wieder, *The Early Jewish Community of Boston's North End*, p. 18.

6. Zoltán Kramar, *From the Danube to the Hudson: U.S. Ministerial and Consular Dispatches on Immigration from the Habsburg Monarchy, 1850–1900*, p. 69.

7. Joshua A. Fishman, *Hungarian Language Maintenance in the United States*, p. 22.

8. Celestine Sibley, *Dear Store: An Affectionate Portrait of Rich's*, p. 23.

9. See Steven Bela Vardy, *Clio's Art in Hungary and in Hungarian-America*, pp. 249–81. This books contains an extensive bibliography.

10. In the Bibliography see Glazer, Handlin, Howe, Rischin, Rosenberg, Sklare, *America's Jews*, Benkart, "Hungarians," Brown and Roucek, Lengyel, Puskás, *From Hungary*, Fishman, Grozza, and Vardy, *The Hungarian-Americans*.

11. Uri D. Herscher, ed., *The East European Jewish Experience in America: A Century of Memories, 1882–1982*, p. 11.

12. Naomi Cohen, *Encounter with Emancipation: The German Jews in the United States, 1830–1914*, p. 58.

13. *Szabadság*, 15 September 1892.

14. Géza Kende, *Magyarok Amerikanbán* (Hungarians in America), pp. 439–40.

15. Sylvia Golden, *Neighbors Needn't Know.*

16. See John Kosa, *Land of Choice: The Hungarians in Canada.*

17. See George Barany, "Magyar Jew or Jewish Magyar: Reflections on the Question of Assimilation."

18. These excerpts are from a tape recording made April 22, 1983, and are reproduced here with the permission of the Amsel family.

19. Edward A. Steiner, *Against the Current: Simple Chapters from a Complex Life*, p. 182.

20. Ibid., p. 96.

261

2. A Very Short History of Hungary

1. For a comprehensive account, see C. A. Macartney, *Hungary: A Short History.*
2. A useful and lucid description of the origins of the Magyars and of their language can be found in Lóránt Czigány, *The Oxford History of Hungarian Literature.*
3. For descriptions of Hungary's economic development and problems, see I. T. Berend and György Ránki, *Hungary: A Century of Economic Development,* pp. 13ff., and Andrew C. János, *The Politics of Backwardness in Hungary.*
4. Paula Benkart, "Religion, Family, and Community among Hungarians Migrating to American Cities, 1880–1930," p. 464.
5. Randolph L. Braham, *The Politics of Genocide,* pp. 1–2. See also Oscar Jászi, *The Dissolution of the Habsburg Monarchy,* p. 171.
6. Benkart, "Religion, Family, and Community," p. 462.
7. Howard M. Sachar, *Diaspora: An Inquiry into the Contemporary Jewish World,* pp. 339ff.
8. See Braham, *The Politics of Genocide,* and Braham, ed., *Hungarian Jewish Studies,* vol. 3; also Lucy S. Davidowicz, *The War against the Jews, 1933–1945,* pp. 379–83.
9. Ezra Mendelsohn, *The Jews of East Central Europe between the World Wars,* p. 94.

3. Jews and Magyars

1. For informative accounts of the history of Hungarian Jews see Nathaniel Katzburg, "The History of the Jews in Hungary"; Mendelsohn; and "Hungary" in the *Encyclopaedia Judaica,* vol. 8. On Pannonia, see Shmuel Safra, "The Era of the Mishnah and Talmud, 70–640," pp. 364–65.
2. Meir Sas, *Vanishing Communities in Hungary,* p. 23.
3. Information on Jewish life in the Middle Ages can be found in Raphael Patai, *Apprentice in Budapest,* pp. 30ff.; István Végházi, "The Role of Jewry in the Economic Life of Hungary"; and Bitton, *A Decade of Zionism in Hungary,* pp. 2–4.
4. Livia Rothkirchen, "Deep-Rooted yet Alien: Some Aspects of the History of the Jews in Subcarpathian Ruthenia," p. 154.
5. Bitton, p. 25, and Sas, p. 20.
6. This description is based on Ernest Marton, "The Family Tree of Hungarian Jewry," pp. 39–53. Unless otherwise noted the quotations below are from Marton.
7. Yehuda Don and George Magos, "The Demographic Development of Hungarian Jewry," pp. 189–216. They point out that the Hungarian population grew between 1720 and 1910 from 2.5 million to 18.2 million. During the same period, the Jewish population increased at a much faster rate, from 12,000 to 910,000.
8. George Gabori, *Where Evils Were Most Free,* p. 3.
9. Almost all of the increase between 1880 and 1910 is accounted for by the growth in the Jewish population in the central region (from 135,950 to 294,454); in the northeast (from 117,255 to 142,286), and in the east central region (from 122,303 to 197,384).
10. Personal communication from Yeshayahu Jelinek.

11. Katzburg, "History" (unnumbered pages).

12. Nathaniel Katzburg, "Hungarian Jewry in Modern Times," pp. 138ff.

13. Victor Karady and István Kemény, "Les Juifs dans la Structure des Classes de Hongrie" (summary in English), p. 77.

14. *Encyclopaedia Judaica*, s.v. "Hungarian Literature."

15. The following description of the political attitudes taken toward the Jews after 1850 is based on Nathaniel Katzburg, "Assimilation in Hungary during the Nineteenth Century: Orthodox Positions," pp. 13–22.

16. See Steven Bela Vardy, *The Origins of Jewish Emancipation in Hungary: The Role of Baron Joseph Eötvös*.

17. István Deák, *The Lawful Revolution: Louis Kossuth and the Hungarians, 1848–1849*, p. 114.

18. János, p. 80.

19. Cecil Roth, "The Jews of Western Europe," pp. 276ff.

20. I. Deák, *Lawful Revolution*, p. 102.

21. Ibid., p. 115.

22. A discussion of the complexities of emancipation, assimilation, and conversion at this time is provided by Barany, "Magyar Jew or Jewish Magyar," pp. 70–71.

23. This discussion of the events of 1848 and of 1867 owes much to a personal communication from Professor Victor Karady.

24. Philip J. Adler, "The Introduction of Public Schooling for the Jews of Hungary (1849–1860)," p. 118.

25. I. Deák, *Lawful Revolution*, p. 51.

26. Personal communication from Professor Nathaniel Katzburg, 27 July 1988.

27. Andrew Handler, *Blood Libel at Tiszaeszlár*.

28. I. Deák, *Lawful Revolution*, pp. 113–14.

29. Macartney, *Hungary*, p. 193.

30. Jászi, p. 173.

31. John Lukács, *Budapest 1900: A Historical Portrait of a City and Its Culture*, pp. 188–96.

32. Katzburg, "History" (unnumbered pages).

33. Randolph L. Braham, "Hungarian Jewry: An Historical Retrospect," p. 4.

34. István Deák, "Revolution, Progress, and Decline: Hungary between 1848 and 1918," p. 15.

35. Personal communication from Professor Karady.

36. Berend and Ránki, pp. 40–41.

37. I. Deák, *Lawful Revolution*, p. 51.

38. S. Ettinger, "The Modern Period," pp. 870–76.

39. Nathaniel Katzburg, *Hungary and the Jews: Policy and Legislation, 1920–1943*, pp. 19–22.

40. Kaczér, p. 513.

41. Peter Hanák, in "The Hungarian Jewry in the Twentieth Century," pp. 410–11. For further discussion of anti-Semitism see Emil Lengyel, *Americans from Hungary*, p. 223; Livia Rothkirchen, "Slovakia: I., 1848–1918," pp. 72–84; Aron Moskovitz, *Jewish Education in Hungary*; and "Hungary" in *Encyclopaedia Judaica*.

4. The Quid pro Quo Arrangement

1. Steiner, *Against the Current*, p. 7.

2. For a full treatment of the intense conflicts and competition for supremacy—both military and political—among Hungary's minorities, see Robert A. Kann, *The Multinational Empire*.

3. Robert A. Kann, "Hungarian Jewry during Austria-Hungary's Constitutional Period, 1867–1918," pp. 374–78.

4. Braham, *Politics of Genocide*, pp. 2–9.

5. George Barany, "Hungary: From Aristocratic to Proletarian Nationalism," pp. 279ff.

6. Emily Greene Balch, *Our Slavic Fellow Citizens*, pp. 110–11.

7. This view was presented in "The Jews from Hungary in the Old Country and in the USA," an unpublished paper written in 1972 by Yeshayahu Jelinek and in personal discussions with Dr. Jelinek. Quite a different point of view is presented in Mendelsohn, p. 100.

8. William O. McCagg, Jr., "Jewish Conversion in Hungary in Modern Times," p. 151.

9. Kann, "Hungarian Jewry," p. 364.

10. Benkart, "Religion, Family, and Community," p. 463.

11. Shlomo Avineri, *The Making of Modern Zionism*, p. 48.

12. Bitton, *A Decade of Zionism in Hungary*, p. 14.

13. Patai, p. 97.

14. Louis Finkelstein, ed., *The Jews: Their History, Culture, and Religion*, p. 283.

15. Robert William Seton-Watson, *Racial Problems in Hungary*, pp. 173–74.

16. Jászi, p. 174.

17. The statement was made by Anton Stefanek before he became a minister in the Czechoslovakian government and is quoted in Kann, "Hungarian Jewry," p. 375, and in Jászi, p. 175.

18. Rothkirchen, "Slovakia," p. 73.

19. I. Deák, "Revolution, Progress, and Decline," p. 18.

20. Macartney, *Hungary*, p. 191. See also Jászi's chapter "Capitalism and the Jews."

21. Végházi, pp. 35–84.

22. McCagg, "Jewish Conversion," p. 130.

23. For a detailed account of Jewish artists and writers see Erzsébet Balla, "The Jews of Hungary: A Cultural Overview."

24. *Encyclopaedia Judaica*, s.v. "Hungarian Literature."

25. Czigány, pp. 279–80.

26. Ibid., pp. 475–76.

27. Moshe Carmilly-Weinberger, *The Rabbinical Seminary of Budapest, 1877–1977*, p. xi.

28. *Encyclopaedia Judaica*, s.v. "Péter Ujvári."

29. Andrew Handler, Introduction to Péter Ujvári's *By Candlelight*, pp. 10ff.

30. *Encyclopaedia Judaica*, s.v. "Péter Ujvári."

31. János, p. 114.

32. *Encyclopaedia Judaica*, s.v. "Hungary."

33. Alajos Kovács, *A zsidóság térfoglalása Magyaroszágon*.

34. Rothkirchen, "Deep-Rooted yet Alien," pp. 147–91, and Rothkirchen, "Slovakia," pp. 72–84. Her data are for 1930. For descriptions of the ethnic character of this area, see Herman Dicker, *Piety and Perseverance: Jews from the Carpathian Mountains*, and Paul Robert Magocsi, *The Shaping of a National Identity: Subcarpathian Rus', 1848–1948*.

35. Kann, "Hungarian Jewry," p. 377.

36. Ibid., p. 376.

37. Magocsi, *Shaping of a National Identity*, p. 19.

38. Ibid., p. 66.

39. Aryeh Sole, "Subcarpathian Ruthenia: 1918–1938," pp. 126–27.

40. Rothkirchen, "Deep-Rooted yet Alien," p. 149.

41. Sas, pp. 85–86.

42. Ewa Morawska, "A Replica of the 'Old Country' Relationship in the Ethnic Niche: East European Jews and Gentiles in Small-town Western Pennsylvania, 1880s–1930s," pp. 33–39.

43. Balch, p. 61.

44. Ibid., p. 95.

45. Morawska, pp. 40–53.

46. Oral History Project #1, National Council of Jewish Women, Pittsburgh Section.

47. Steiner, *Against the Current*, foreword and pp. 57, 73, 120–23.

48. Kann, "Hungarian Jewry," pp. 374–77.

49. Mendelsohn, p. 91.

5. Religion, Languages, and Folklore

1. Readers interested in works of fiction, biography, and social history in English that give the flavor of those times and those people may find rewarding these authors, listed in the Bibliography: Andrew Handler, Illés Kaczér, Rebekah Kohut, John Lukács, Raphael Patai, and Victor David Tulman.

2. McCagg, "Jewish Conversion," p. 144.

3. Ettinger, pp. 825–47.

4. McCagg, "Jewish Conversion," pp. 147–59. The estimate of 2 percent erosion is from Jacob Katz, "The Identity of Post Emancipatory Hungarian Jewry," p. 26.

5. Cohen, *Encounter with Emancipation*, pp. 4–5.

6. Patai, pp. 62–63.

7. *Encyclopaedia Judaica*, s.v. "Chorin."

8. Mendelsohn, p. 90.

9. Alexander Scheiber, "Jewish Studies in Hungary" (unnumbered pages).

10. David Ellenson, "The Orthodox Rabbinate and Apostasy in Nineteenth-Century Germany and Hungary," p. 184. See Adler, p. 121, on the extent of the break between the modernist and conservative factions.

11. Mendelsohn, p. 90.

12. Solomon Poll, "The Role of Yiddish in American Ultra-Orthodox and Hasidic Communities," p. 127.

13. Armin Harry Friedman, *Major Aspects of Yeshivah Education in Hungary, 1848–1948*, pp. 48ff.

14. Sas, pp. 108–9.

15. Michael K. Silber, "The Historical Experience of German Jewry and Its Impact on Haskalah and Reform in Hungary," pp. 107–57.

16. Elie Wiesel has written on these themes in *Souls of Fire: Portraits and Legends of Hasidic Masters*. See also Friedman, pp. 34ff.

17. For a description of the Hasidim in Hungary, see Poll, *The Hasidic Community of Williamsburg*, pp. 16–18.

18. Handler, *Rabbi Eizik*, pp. 12–13.

19. Personal communication from Sarah Landesman of McKeesport.

20. Zvi Spiron, "The Yiddish Language in Hungary," p. 200.

21. Katz, "The Identity of Post Emancipatory Hungarian Jewry," p. 20. See also Poll, *Williamsburg*, p. 14.

22. The account in this and the following paragraph is based on a personal communication with Michael Silber.

23. This description is drawn from the study by Armin Friedman, pp. 2–3, 126, 224, 274, 281, 306.

24. Julian Krawcheck, "Temple on the Heights: B'nai Jeshurun . . ." (29 April 1966), p. 15.

25. Lengyel, *Americans from Hungary*, p. 193. See also Sachar, *Diaspora*, p. 347, and Friedman, p. 288.

26. *Encyclopaedia Judaica*, s.v. "Hungary."

27. Quoted in Bitton, *A Decade of Zionism in Hungary*, p. 26.

28. Bitton, p. vii.

29. Patai, pp. 96 and 125.

30. Wolfdieter Bihl, "Das Judentum Ungarns, 1780–1914," p. 23.

31. McCagg, "Jewish Conversion," p. 153.

32. Paul L. Garvin, "The Dialect Geography of Hungarian Yiddish," pp. 108–9.

33. Poll, "The Role of Yiddish," p. 127.

34. C. A. Macartney, *Hungary and Her Successors: The Treaty of Trianon and Its Consequences, 1919–1937*, p. 79n.

35. Bihl, p. 24.

36. Macartney, *Hungary and Her Successors*, p. 203.

37. Thirteenth Census of the United States, 1910, Population, table 8, p. 968.

38. Bihl, p. 24.

39. Spiron, pp. 195–200. For additional material, also in Yiddish, see Y. Taglikht, "Songs of Hungary and Slovakia," in YIVO—Philological Series 1, Vilno, 1929. See also R. Stalek, "Materials Concerning the Yiddish of Burgenland," YIVO, 1928.

40. The definitions are from Leo Rosten, *The Joys of Yiddish*.

41. Patai, pp. 24–25.

42. Sas, p. 58.

43. Patai, p. 50.

44. Benzion C. Kaganoff, *A Dictionary of Jewish Names and Their History*, pp. 22–24.

45. Rebekah Kohut, *His Father's House: The Story of George Alexander Kohut*, pp. 15–16.

46. The difficulties of untangling German, Hungarian, and Jewish names for purposes of identifying Hungarian Jews are discussed in Appendix 3.

47. The quotation from Robert Seton-Watson appears in Mendelsohn, p. 89.

48. Lukács, p. 95.

49. Patai, p. 28.

50. This project and the research prospectus of the Folklore Commission are described in A. First, "Folkloristic-Linguistic Materials from Hungary," pp. 436–52. First describes in detail the articles that appeared in the *Hungarian Jewish Review* over many years as a result of the efforts of this group of scholars.

51. The quotations are from "Folklore," *Magyar Zsidó Szemle*, 18, Budapest, 1901.

52. Ibid., pp. 58, 80, 84–86, 148–52, 158, 291–92.

53. Meyer Denn, "From Certizne to Wharton: A Jewish Journey to the New World," p. 4.

54. Patai, p. 21.

6. Two Jewries

1. Jászi, p. 175. Note that Jacob Katz uses the concept of two Jewries to refer primarily to the division between the Orthodox and the Neologs, though he also discusses the social and economic correlates of the religious split. Katz, "The Identity of Post Emancipatory Hungarian Jewry," pp. 13–31.

2. Ervin Y. Galantay, "Budapest: Eclectic Metropolis, 1867–1919," pp. 20–30.

3. Lukács, p. 95.

4. Andrew Handler, *Dori: The Life and Times of Theodor Herzl in Budapest, 1860–1878*, p. 23.

5. See Steve J. Heims, *John Von Neumann and Norbert Wiener: From Mathematics to the Technologies of Life and Death*, pp. 26–57.

6. McCagg, *Jewish Nobles*.

7. György Ránki, "Can the Holocaust Be Understood? A Hungarian Noble Jew's Papers."

8. Benjamin Balshone, *Determined!*, p. 3.

9. National Council of Jewish Women, Oral History Project #1, Pittsburgh Section.

10. This account comes from letters provided by Robert Morris.

11. Victor David Tulman, *Going Home*.

12. This description is taken from the memoir by May Loveman Sobel, courtesy of the American Jewish Archives, Cincinnati Campus, Hebrew Union College, Jewish Institute of Religion. The house is that of the Loveman family in Somos in Sáros County.

13. See Appendix 3 for a description of this sample of ship passengers.

14. Morawska, p. 37.

15. Leopold Greenwald, *Toiznt Yor Idish Lebn in Ungarn* (A Thousand Years of Jewish Life in Hungary), chap. 9.

16. Ibid., pp. 233–34.

17. Krawcheck, 29 April 1966.

7. The '48ers

1. This information on immigration before 1850 is based on Joseph Széplaki, *The Hungarians in America, 1583–1974*; Eugene Pivány, *Hungarians in the American Civil War*, pp. 31ff.; and Leslie Könnyü, *Hungarians: An Immigration Study*, p. 8.

2. Max J. Kohler, "The German Jewish Migration to America," p. 88.

3. Guido Kisch, *In Search of Freedom: A History of American Jews from Czechoslovakia*, p. 42, and Albert M. Friedenberg, "Austro-Hungarian Movement to Encourage Migration of Jews to America, 1848," pp. 187–88.

4. Leo Goldhammer, "Jewish Emigration from Austria-Hungary in 1848–49," p. 340.

5. Barany, "Magyar Jew or Jewish Magyar," pp. 70–71.

6. Ibid., p. 76.

7. Goldhammer, p. 346.

8. Ibid., p. 357.

9. Mark Wischnitzer, *To Dwell in Safety: The Story of Jewish Migration since 1800*, pp. 20–21.

10. Leibmann Hersch, "International Migration of the Jews," p. 472.

11. Steven Bela Vardy, *The Hungarian-Americans*, p. 13.

12. Julianna Puskás, *From Hungary to the United States*, p. 18.

13. "California for Hungarian Readers," in *California Historical Society Quarterly*, June 1949.

14. Korn, p. 3.

15. Ibid., p. 13.

16. Edmund Vasváry, *Lincoln's Hungarian Heroes: The Participation of Hungarians in the Civil War, 1861–1865*, pp. 31–32.

17. Ibid., p. 58.

18. I am indebted to Lois Hechinger England of Washington, D.C., for this information about her great-great grandfather, Emanuel Lulley. He was variously known by the first names of Menno, Meno, Mano, and Mino and by the last names of Lullay, Lulie, Lulei, and Lully.

19. *Intermountain Jewish News*, Denver, 15 September 1939.

20. Goldhammer, p. 357.

21. Carl Wittke, *Refugees of Revolution: The German Forty-Eighters in America*, p. 88.

22. Oscar Handlin, "The American Scene," pp. 26–42.

23. Pivány, pp. 6ff.

24. Ida Libert Uchill, *Pioneers, Peddlers, and Tsadikim: The Story of the Jews in Colorado*, p. 200.

25. This account is based on Könnyü, pp. 13–14; Kende, pt. 2, pp. 56ff.; Papp, p. 86; Gustav Pollak, *Michael Heilprin and His Sons*, pp. 170–71; and Vardy, *The Hungarian Americans*, p. 39.

26. Emil Lengyel, "Hungarian Americans," p. 221.

27. Cohen, *Encounter with Emancipation*, p. 139.

28. *Asmonean*, 19 December 1851.

29. Oscar Handlin, *Boston's Immigrants 1790–1865: A Study in Acculturation*, pp. 34 and 145.

30. Marcus Braun, *Immigration Abuses: Glimpses of Hungary and Hungarians*, p. 74.

31. This information was provided by Maurice Richter, the great-grandson of Morris Richter.

32. Joseph Lovitz, *Jewish Historical Society of New York Newsletter*, September 1988, p. 4.

33. *Publications of the American Jewish Historical Society* 20 (1911), p. 116.

34. Goldhammer, p. 357.

35. András Csillag, "Joseph Pulitzer's Roots in Europe: A Genealogical History," pp. 48–68.

36. Lengyel, *Americans from Hungary*, pp. 85–86.

37. R. G. Dun and Company Records, Ohio, vol. 42, p. 185.

38. Ibid., p. 177.

39. For more on this point, see Cohen, *Encounter with Emancipation*, pp. 24–25.

40. Lengyel, *Americans from Hungary*, p. 63.

41. Mary Howard Schoolcraft, "The Fire at the Central Hotel," *New York Daily News*, undated, about 1867. This account of the Lulley family was taken from this article and other materials provided by Mrs. Lois Hechinger England.

42. Memorandum of the Arizona-Sonora Historical Society, c. 1905.

43. Louis Wirth, *The Ghetto*, p. 142.

44. Leopold Wintner, "Dr. S. H. Sonneschein: An Appreciation," reprinted from *The Jewish Voice*, St. Louis, and printed in New York, 1909.

45. Stuart E. Rosenberg, *The Jewish Community of Rochester, 1843–1925*, p. 22.

46. Abraham J. Karp, "Simon Tuska's *The Stranger in the Synagogue*."

47. This account is drawn from Jonathan D. Sarna, "From Necessity to Virtue: The Hebrew-Christianity of Gideon R. Lederer."

48. Steven Hertzberg, *Stranger within the Gate City: The Jews of Atlanta, 1845–1915*, pp. 36, 50.

49. Wittke, pp. 88–89.

50. Korn, p. 21.

8. Three Families

1. This account of the Heilprins is based primarily on Pollak; Sas, pp. 96–97; and Lengyel, *Americans from Hungary*, pp. 65–72.

2. Pollak, p. 533.

3. Ibid., pp. 170–71.

4. Much of this account is taken from a memoir written by May Loveman Sobel and was obtained through the courtesy of the American Jewish Archives.

5. *Cleveland News*, 14 January 1928.

6. *Jewish Review and Observer*, 31 October 1913.

7. Géza Kende, in *The Peoples of Cleveland*, Western Reserve Historical Society.

8. Frederic Howe, *The Confessions of a Reformer*, pp. 80–84.

9. Ibid., p. 83.

10. Lloyd P. Gartner, *History of the Jews of Cleveland*, p. 99.

11. Fedora Small Frank, *Beginnings on Market Street: Nashville and Her Jewry, 1861–1901*, p. 6.

12. Letter by Albert H. Morehead to "Dear Mary" dated Christmas 1957, provided by Bernard E. Loveman of Indianapolis.

13. Talk given by Adele Mills Schweid, 14 January 1976; one of the papers on the Loveman-Black families at the American Jewish Archives.

14. Pollak, p. 539.

15. See Sibley, *Dear Store*.

16. Letter by Albert H. Morehead cited above.

17. Both documents were obtained from the Archives of the Jewish Federation of Nashville and Middle Tennessee.

18. May Loveman Sobel, *Family Black and Family Loveman*, pp. 37ff.

19. See Frank, pp. 126–27 for additional names.

20. Letter by Albert H. Morehead cited above.

9. The Big Migration

1. John Bodnar, *The Transplanted: A History of Immigrants in Urban America*, p. 2.

2. *Cleveland Plain Dealer*, 7 September 1964.

3. James MacGregor Burns, *The Workshop of Democracy*, pp. 246–47.

4. Bodnar, p. xix.

5. Balch, pp. 238–39.

6. Arthur A. Goren, "Jews," pp. 579–81.

7. Lloyd P. Gartner, *The Great Migration, 1881–1914: Myths and Realities*, p. 3.

8. Handlin, *Adventure in Freedom*, pp. 81–82.

9. Irving Howe, "Pluralism in the Immigrant World," p. 2.

10. Jonathan Frankel, "The Crisis of 1881 as a Turning Point in Modern Jewish History," p. 13.

11. Puskás, *From Hungary to the United States*, pp. 56–61.

12. Ibid., p. 33; see also Magocsi, "The Shaping of a National Identity," p. 66.

13. Paula Benkart, "Religion, Family, and Community," p. 17.

14. Paula Benkart, "Hungarians," p. 464.

15. Ibid.

16. See Table 4, which shows a concentration of Jewish farm renters and owners in the two northeastern regions.

17. Puskás, *From Hungary to the United States*, p. 34.

18. Marshall Sklare, "Jewish Acculturation and American Jewish Identity," p. 175.

19. The immigrants shown on Map 3 were passengers arriving in New York on ships between 1885 and 1905 and applicants for citizenship in New York and Cleveland. Appendix 3 describes how these immigrants were selected.

20. Table 2 compares the geographic distribution of Jews in 1910 with the distribution of emigrants by region. Table 3 compares, for selected regions, the distribution of immigrants in the sample according to year of arrival and city of citizenship in the United States. See Appendix 1.

21. Finkelstein, p. 1230.

22. The data are drawn mainly from *The American Jewish Year Book* of 1903, which was devoted to "Biographical Sketches of Rabbis and Cantors." The editors had sent out 694 inquiries and published 363 replies. They emphasized that their list was far from complete and certainly not a random sample. From this list, supplemented by other sources, we identified sixty Hungarian-born rabbis; we did not include six cantors. Nine of the rabbis were '48ers and were discussed in Chapter 7. The remaining fifty-one are described in this chapter.

23. In Chapter 13 we discuss the identification of these rabbis as Orthodox, Conservative, or Reform.

24. Among the forty-seven immigrants described by their relatives in response to

a questionnaire, some twenty-seven of them came from the two northeast regions; nine emigrated from Budapest. See Appendix 4 concerning the questionnaire. Other information from this source tends to confirm the picture of the typical Jewish immigrant. Thus, twenty-five of them were characterized as Orthodox and only six as either "conservative" or "secular." Interestingly and not unexpectedly, four of the six non-Orthodox people came from Budapest.

25. Kramar, p. 69.

26. Joel Margareten, *Directory and Genealogy of the Horowitz-Margareten Family*, pp. 8–9.

27. Steiner, *Against the Current*, p. 107.

28. Kramar, pp. 27 and 57.

29. József Gellén, "Geographical Origin and Community in Emigration from Hungary as Reflected in Parish Records in Early 20th Century," pp. 39ff.

30. The figures are based on the 1905 passenger list and 1900 population data from *Magyar Statisztikai Köslemények*, vol. 10.

31. See Appendix 2 for the calculations that led to this estimate.

32. Balch, p. 438.

33. See Johann Chmelar, "The Austrian Emigration, 1900–1914," for the Austro-Hungarian data.

34. Based on data in Raphael Mahler, "The Economic Background of Jewish Emigration from Galicia to the United States," pp. 257 and 266, and on Gartner, *The Great Migration*, p. 3.

35. Howard Morley Sachar, *The Course of Modern Jewish History*, p. 309.

36. Avraham Barkai, "German-Jewish Migration in the Nineteenth Century, 1830–1910," p. 208.

37. Joseph Kissman, "The Immigration of Rumanian Jews up to 1914," pp. 160 and 176–79.

38. See Puskás, *From Hungary*, p. 22 for data on total Hungarian emigration.

39. Balch, pp. 236–37.

40. I was not able to include every ship, but a complete count was made on every ship examined for this purpose. The ships that arrived in 1885 brought 197 Jews and 150 non-Jews from Hungary. Ten years later the two groups were almost exactly equal: 205 Jews and 208 Christians. By 1905 the balance had shifted to 75 Jews and 174 non-Jews.

41. Puskás, *From Hungary*, pp. 64–115.

42. United States Immigration Commission, vol. 4, p. 385.

43. Puskás, *From Hungary*, p. 93.

44. Reed Ueda, "Naturalization and Citizenship," p. 137.

45. Pamela Susan Nadell, "The Journey to America by Steam: The Jews of Eastern Europe in Transition," pp. 73–75. This includes a detailed account of the ill-fated deal between the Hungarian government and the Cunard Line which was related to the development of the port of Fiume.

46. The Germans kept careful records of each departing passenger. Records for Hamburg are now accessible through the Mormon collection in Utah. See "The Hamburg Passenger Lists," the Genealogical Department of the Church of Jesus Christ of Latter-Day Saints, Salt Lake City, 1976.

47. Moses Rischin, *The Promised City: New York's Jews, 1870–1914*, p. 33.

48. Edward A. Steiner, *From Alien to Citizen: The Story of My Life in America*, pp. 30–37.

49. Steiner, *On the Trail of the Immigrant*, p. 35.

50. Steiner, *From Alien to Citizen*, p. 37.

51. National Council of Jewish Women, Oral History Project #1, Pittsburgh Section.

52. Denn, pp. 5–6.

53. Harry Golden, *Forgotten Pioneer*, p. 107.

54. Oral History Project #1, Interview #178.

55. *Long Island Daily Press*, 1 February 1951.

56. Steiner, *On the Trail*, p. 64.

57. Deborah Dwork, "Immigrant Jews on the Lower East Side of New York: 1880–1914," p. 103.

58. Steiner, *On the Trail*, pp. 72–79.

59. Denn, p. 6.

60. Recorded by Louis Perlman, c. 1948.

10. Urban Colonies

1. Rischin, pp. 81 and 294.

2. The quotation is from family records provided by Robert Morris.

3. Barkai, p. 209.

4. Simon Kuznets, quoted in Ira A. Glazier and Luigi De Rosa, eds., *Migration across Time and Nations*, p. 224. See also Samuel Joseph, *Jewish Immigration to the U.S. 1881–1910*, pp. 127–29, and Goren, p. 58.

5. Jonathan Sarna, "The Myth of No Return: Jewish Return Migration to Eastern Europe, 1881–1914," pp. 256ff.

6. This account is drawn from Sarna's book, *People Walk on Their Heads: Moses Weinberger's Jews and Judaism in New York*.

7. *Encyclopaedia Judaica*, s.v. "Hasidism."

8. Personal communication from Rabbi Herman Dicker, author of *Piety and Perseverance*.

9. Some 80 percent of the immigrants in 1898–99 and 1912–13 went to Pennsylvania, New York, New Jersey, and Ohio; 30 percent went to Pennsylvania alone. If one adds Illinois, Michigan, and Indiana, these seven states account for 90 percent of the immigrants in those years. Puskás, *From Hungary*, p. 128.

10. Ibid., p. 129.

11. I am indebted to Norman D. Schwartz of the Chicago Jewish Historical Society for much help in collecting this information.

12. Morris A. Gutstein, *A Priceless Heritage: The Epic Growth of Nineteenth Century Chicago Jewry*, pp. 43–46.

13. From a private communication from Sidney Sorkin of Chicago, who has made a study of six hundred landsmanschaften in that city.

14. The Chicago Community Blue Book, 1917–1918, p. 88.

15. Allen Meyers of Sewell, New Jersey, was most helpful in assembling the information on Philadelphia.

16. Henry Samuel Morais, *The Jews of Philadelphia*, pp. 231–32.

17. Wieder, p. 18.

18. Albert Ehrenfried, *A Chronicle of Boston Jewry: From the Colonial Settlement to 1900*, p. 480.

19. *Boston Herald,* 17 March 1903.

20. Ira Rosenwaike, *Population History of New York City,* p. 123.

21. Louis Pink, "The Magyars in New York."

22. Burns, p. 255. This Hungarian enclave is also described in Ira Rosenwaike, *Population History of New York City,* p. 67. Rischin located the Hungarian Jews just after 1900 in an area from the East River to Avenue B and from Houston Street to 10th Street. See Rischin, map on page 77.

23. See Appendix 3 for the method of selecting this sample. The 1880 census did not report the year of the immigrant's arrival, but for those families in which a child had been born in the United States, it was possible to estimate the latest date the family could have come to America. At least twelve of the total of fifty-seven families arrived between 1859 and 1878 and eight more came in 1879.

24. Rischin, pp. 81ff.

25. This information is part of a study I made of organizations whose incorporation papers are held in the archives of the American Jewish Historical Society. See Appendix 4 for a description of the AJHS collection.

26. Pink, pp. 262–63.

27. The figures are from unpublished data obtained through the courtesy of the Population Analysis Unit of the City Planning Commission of New York City.

28. Pink, p. 262.

29. Sachar, p. 317.

30. Rischin, p. 73.

31. This information is based on a conversation with Frank Vardy of the New York City Planning Commission.

32. *New York Times,* 14 May 1987.

33. Sylvia Golden, *Neighbors Needn't Know,* 1953. The reader will recall that this novel is based on a Hungarian-Jewish family, which happens to be that of the author of this book. The general picture of family life and economic differences among families seems to be reasonably accurate in the novel in the light of interviews with family members.

34. This account is based on an interview 28 June 1987 with Jennie Mandelbaum Cohen, daughter of Morris and Lena Spiegel.

35. Based on an interview with Sadie Gold on 28 June 1987.

36. Steiner, *From Alien to Citizen,* pp. 70ff.

37. *Evening World,* 27 February 1925.

38. Agnes Primes, "The Hungarians in New York: A Study in Immigrant Cultural Influences," chap. 4.

39. Gartner, pp. 106 and 347. See Karl Bonutti and George Prpic, "Analysis of Ethnic Communities of Cleveland," p. 29.

40. Gartner, pp. 116 and 65.

41. Daniel E. Weinberg, "Ethnic Identity in Industrial Cleveland: The Hungarians, 1900–1920," p. 174. From 1874 through 1907 some twenty-three thousand Hungarian immigrants arrived in Cleveland. The flow from the Kingdom of Hungary to Cleveland began slowly, averaging only 76 a year from 1874 through 1879 and 401 yearly from 1880 to 1899. From 1900 through 1907 the annual average immigration rose to 1818, making a total of 23,022 for the whole period 1874–1907. See David D. Van Tassel and John J. Grabowski, *The Encyclopedia of Cleveland History,* pp. 542–43.

42. For descriptions of the Hungarian settlements in Cleveland, see *The Peoples of*

Cleveland, pp. 3–5, Western Reserve Historical Society; Wellington Fordyce, "Immigrant Colonies in Cleveland," pp. 325 and 337–39; and Pap, p. 157.

43. Weinberg, p. 173.

44. Gartner, pp. 106–7.

45. Susan M. Papp, "Hungarian Americans and Their Communities of Cleveland," p. 166.

46. Interview with Rev. Matyas Daroczy, undated, in *The Peoples of Cleveland*, Western Reserve Historical Society.

47. Géza Hoffmann, *Csonka Munkásosztály* (Hungarians in America), pp. 36–37.

48. Hulda Florence Cook, *The Magyars of Cleveland*.

49. H. A. Liebovitz and Mihály Parlagh, *A Clevelandi Magyarok Története* (History of Cleveland's Hungarians), pp. 114–15.

50. Donald Levy, "A Report on the Location of Ethnic Groups in Greater Cleveland," p. 25.

51. This quotation is from the English translation and summary of the book by Liebovitz and Parlagh. The Hungarian text adds at this point that some assimilated Hungarians also lived in the Jewish-Hungarian section.

52. Ibid., pp. 127–28 and 45–46, in Hungarian.

53. Vilma M. Goodman, "Boulevard Reminiscences," p. 18.

54. The information covers 1906–1929 in New York and 1906–1924 in Cleveland, though in both cities the bulk of the applications were made before World War I.

55. Based on an examination of the working papers of Fedora S. Frank made available to me by the Archives of the Jewish Federation of Nashville and Middle Tennessee.

11. *Small Town Diaspora*

1. Nathan Glazer, *Social Characteristics of American Jews*, p. 18.

2. Caroline Golab, *Immigrant Destinations*, pp. 34–35.

3. Morawska, pp. 27–86.

4. Uchill, pp. 42, 50, 200.

5. Frank, pp. 154–56.

6. Courtesy of the Archives of the Jewish Federation of Nashville and Middle Tennessee.

7. Based on examination of Frank's working papers I found 142 Hungarian-born individuals, which was twenty fewer than her total.

8. Frank, p. 103.

9. Personal communication from Robert Doochin of Nashville, 19 November 1989. I am indebted to Mr. Doochin for sharing much information about Nashville and the Loveman family.

10. János Makár, *The Story of an Immigrant Group in Franklin, New Jersey*, pp. 84–85.

11. Personal communication from Jacob S. Feldman, author of *The Jewish Experience in Western Pennsylvania*.

12. This history was written in 1954 with the title "The Beginnings of the McKeesport Jewish Community" and was published in 1986 by Congregation Gemilas Chesed of that city.

13. This information was provided by Matilda H. Brand of Pittsburgh.

14. Rischin, p. 54.

15. Denn, pp. 7ff.

16. Farther north in Dallas, another Hungarian, Martin Weiss, arrived in 1911. See *Hungary Sends a Dallas-Builder: The Story of Martin Weiss* by Carolyn Holmes Moses, published by Weiss in 1948.

17. This account was provided by Louis Holitser's granddaughter, Kaye Kole of Savannah, Georgia.

18. This information is taken from an account written by Janet S. Cynkus of Syracuse.

19. Morawska, pp. 72–73.

20. This explanation, among others, was advanced by Morawska in a lecture at Harvard University, 20 April 1988. See also her article cited above.

12. The Magyar Connection

1. Stuart E. Rosenberg, *The New Jewish Identity in America*, p. 58.

2. Rischin, p. 129.

3. Kende, p. 139.

4. The newspaper articles ran from 25 July to 12 September, 1887.

5. Liebovitz and Parlagh, pp. 134, 213, and 235–38.

6. *The Hungarian Jew*, vol. 1, no. 2 (24 May 1932).

7. Cleveland *Plain Dealer*, 3 September 1883.

8. Gartner, p. 106.

9. See Julianna Puskás, "The Differentiation of the Hungarian Newspapers, Reflecting Some Aspects of Acculturation, 1854–1914"; Vardy, *The Hungarian-Americans*, chap. 6; Lengyel, *Americans from Hungary*, pp. 194–205; Otto Árpád Taborsky, "The Hungarian Press in America"; Liebovitz and Parlagh, p. 140.

10. Robert E. Park, *The Immigrant Press and Its Control*, pp. 73ff.

11. Concerning Előre, see Zoltán Deák, ed., *This Noble Flame: An Anthology of a Hungarian Newspaper in the U.S.A.*

12. A dour and unflattering essay was written by a former staff member of the newspaper who complained that the staff was unprofessional and incompetent. See Lengyel, *Americans from Hungary*, pp. 197–99.

13. *Cleveland Foreign Language Newspaper Digest*, 1942, Western Reserve Historical Society.

14. The author is indebted to Martha Herskovits for the translation.

15. Sarna, *People Walk on Their Heads*, pp. 67–68.

16. Liebovitz and Parlagh, p. 140.

17. Taborsky, p. 86.

18. For a full account of this cultural activity, see Puskás, *From Hungary*, pp. 169ff., and Benkart, "Hungarians," p. 468.

19. Thomas Szendry, "Hungarian-American Theatre," pp. 191–95.

20. Papp, p. 134.

21. Árpád Gerster, *Recollections of a New York Surgeon*.

22. Lengyel, *Americans from Hungary*, p. 170, and also Primes, pp. 97–98.

23. Joseph Balogh, "Analysis of Cultural Organizations of Hungarian Americans in Pittsburgh and Allegheny County," pp. 25–46.

24. Cleveland *Plain Dealer*, 13 September 1887.

25. Puskás, *From Hungary*, pp. 179–81.

26. Ibid., p. 150, n.57.
27. Benkart, "Hungarians," p. 466.
28. Bonutti and Prpic, p. 29.
29. Kende, pp. 439–40.
30. The material was excerpted from interviews conducted by Oral History Project #1, National Council of Jewish Women, Pittsburgh Section.
31. For descriptions of these and other issues, see Puskás, *From Hungary*, pp. 182–215; Vardy, *Hungarian-Americans*, pp. 52ff.; and Benkart, "Hungarians," p. 467.
32. Benkart, "Hungarians," pp. 466ff.
33. For other discussions of these associations, see Puskás, *From Hungary*, pp. 155–69; Vardy, *Hungarian-Americans*, pp. 38–41; Lengyel, *Americans from Hungary*, pp. 158–68.
34. Géza Kende, "First Hungarians in Cleveland of Jewish Race," in "Peoples of Cleveland."
35. Puskás, *From Hungary*, 1982, pp. 162–69.
36. Primes, p. 98.
37. Yeshayahu Jelinek, "Self-Identification of First Generation Hungarian Jewish Immigrants," p. 220, n.19.
38. Balogh, p. 43.
39. Lengyel, *Americans from Hungary*, pp. 159–60.
40. Vardy, *Hungarian-Americans*, p. 40.
41. OL K26, 1909, XXII, 1935, Országos Levéltár Miniszterelnökségi Levéltár Records, Immigration History Research Center, University of Minnesota. The translation was done with the kind assistance of Professor Harry Zohn.
42. Benkart, "Religion, Family, and Community," p. 117.
43. OL K26, 1909, XXII, 1170, Cleveland, 15 July 1906, Országos Levéltár Miniszterelnökségi Levéltár Records, Immigration History Research Center, University of Minnesota.
44. Yeshayahu Jelinek, "The Jews from Hungary in the Old Country and in the USA," p. 221.
45. *Encyclopedia of Cleveland History*, p. 533.
46. Benkart, "Hungarians," p. 470.
47. *Cleveland Press*, 23 January 1935.
48. Primes, p. 89.
49. Puskás, *From Hungary*, pp. 206ff.
50. Michael S. Pap, "The Hungarian Community of Cleveland," p. 157; Géza Szentmiklosy Éles, "Hungarians in Cleveland," p. 38; Benkart, "Hungarians," p. 119; Jelinek, "Jews from Hungary," p. 15.
51. Papp, p. 121.
52. Jelinek, "Self-Identification," p. 219.
53. Benkart, "Hungarians," p. 466.
54. Burns, p. 256.

13. The Jewish Bond

1. Sachar, *The Course of Modern Jewish History*, p. 315.
2. Fishman, *Hungarian Language Maintenance*, p. 22.

3. See Rischin, *The Promised City,* and Howe, *World of Our Fathers.*

4. This period of separatism was analogous to the stage of "self-segregation" that Jews as a whole went through in America. See Sklare, "Jewish Acculturation," p. 167.

5. Personal communication from Professor Walter Ehrlich, University of Missouri–St. Louis.

6. Lengyel, *Americans from Hungary,* p. 168.

7. *American Jewish History* devoted its September 1986 volume, 76, no. 1, primarily to the *landsmanschaften.*

8. Ibid.; see Nathan Kaganoff, pp. 60–61, and Daniel Soyer, *American Jewish History,* 77, no. 1, pp. 5–6.

9. Dicker, p. 108.

10. See Table 10 for a detailed breakdown of these 156 organizations categorized by city.

11. These papers are in the archives of the American Jewish Historical Society. For a description of these records see Appendix 4 and Nathan Kaganoff, "The Jewish Landsmanshaftn in New York City in the Period Preceding World War I." Appendix 4 also describes the other sources of information on organizations. For more on the typology of *landsmanschaften* see Hannah Kliger, "Traditions of Grass-Roots Organization and Leadership: The Continuity of Landsmanshaftn in New York."

12. Rischin, pp. 104ff. A 1917 study of 365 Lower East Side congregations showed that 90 percent of them owned cemetery plots; nearly half had free loan provisions; and one-third incorporated sick benefit functions. See Goren, p. 582.

13. Nathan Kaganoff, p. 62.

14. Goren, p. 582.

15. Brith Abraham, "History of the Independent Order Brith Abraham, 1887–1937," p. 24.

16. See, for example, Deborah Dash Moore, *B'nai B'rith and the Challenge of Ethnic Leadership.*

17. These were examined in the Jewish Archives of the Western Reserve Historical Society.

18. Ibid.

19. Jelinek, "Self-Identification," p. 218.

20. *History of the Knights of Pythias,* Cleveland, 1892.

21. Steiner, *On the Trail of the Immigrant,* pp. 168–69.

22. Irving Howe, quoted in Soyer, p. 5. In the same edition of *American Jewish History* Nathan Kaganoff discusses the *landsmanschaften* in New York, based on his study of the incorporation papers from which we drew much of our information about Hungarian societies.

23. Irving Howe, p. 153.

24. Federal Writers' Project, Yiddish Writers' Group, Works Progress Administration, "The Jewish Landsmanschaften of New York."

25. Cohen, *Encounter with Emancipation,* p. 159.

26. Gartner, *History of the Jews of Cleveland,* p. 146.

27. Peter Wiernik, *History of the Jews in America,* p. 283.

28. Cohen, *Encounter with Emancipation,* p. 171.

29. Sarna, *People Walk on Their Heads.*

30. See the following essays in Jacob Rader Marcus and Abraham J. Peck, eds., *The*

American Rabbinate: A Century of Continuity and Change, 1883–1983; Jeffrey S. Gurock, "Resisters and Accommodators: Varieties of Orthodox Rabbis in America, 1886–1983"; Abraham J. Karp, "The Conservative Rabbi—'Dissatisfied but Not Unhappy'"; and David Polish, "The Changing and the Constant in the Reform Rabbinate."

31. Ann Catherine McCullough, *A History of B. W. Huebsch, Publisher.*

32. Karp, "The Conservative Rabbi," p. 105.

33. Benny Kraut, "A Unitarian Rabbi? The Case of Solomon H. Sonneschein," pp. 272–308.

34. Ibid., p. 286.

35. See W. Gunther Plaut, *The Jews in Minnesota,* pp. 70–72.

36. Moshe Davis, *The Emergence of Conservative Judaism: The Historical School in 19th Century America,* p. 329. See also Myron Berman, *Richmond's Jewry, 1769–1976,* p. 212.

37. Rebekah Kohut, *My Portion,* pp. 10–11.

38. See Davis; Berman, pp. 212–13.

39. Davis, p. 144.

40. Ibid., p. 366.

41. Robert Chazan and Marc Lee Raphael, eds., *Modern Jewish History: A Source Reader,* pp. 218–19.

42. This account of the Szolds is drawn from Irving Fineman, *Woman of Valor: The Life of Henrietta Szold, 1860–1945*; Marvin Lowenthal, *Henrietta Szold: Life and Letters*; and Joan Dash, *Summoned to Jerusalem: The Life of Henrietta Szold.*

43. Davis, p. 360.

44. Isaac Fein, *The Making of an American Jewish Community: The History of Baltimore Jewry from 1733 to 1920,* p. 89.

45. Davis, pp. 360–61.

46. Polish, p. 182.

47. Davis, pp. 345–46.

48. Ibid., p. 201.

49. Cohen, *Encounter with Emancipation,* p. 184.

50. Kohut, *My Portion,* p. 190.

51. Gurock, "Resisters and Accommodators," p. 10. See also Davis, pp. 329–66.

52. Kohut, *My Portion.*

53. The data are drawn primarily from "Biographical Sketches of Rabbis and Cantors," in *American Jewish Year Book,* 1903.

54. Morris M. Feuerlicht of Indiana is the subject of one book. The book about Morris Newfield in Birmingham, Alabama, covers a somewhat later period than we have been discussing, as does an article on Bernard Ehrenreich. Brief mention is made of Hungarian rabbis in Gutstein's history of Jews in Chicago and in Raphael's work on Columbus, Ohio. See Mark Cowett, *Birmingham's Rabbi: Morris Newfield and Alabama, 1895–1940*; Byron L. Sherwin, "Portrait of a Romantic Rebel: Bernard C. Ehrenreich, 1865–1955"; Indiana Jewish Historical Society, *Morris M. Feuerlicht: A Hoosier Rabbinate*; Marc Lee Raphael, *Jews and Judaism in a Midwestern Community: Columbus, Ohio, 1840–1975*; and Gutstein, pp. 107, 119, 122.

55. Wiernik, p. 283. See also Jeffrey S. Gurock, "From Exception to Role Model: Bernard Drachman and the Evolution of Jewish Religious Life in America, 1880–1920," p. 476.

56. Gurock, "Resisters and Accommodators," p. 31.

57. Nancy Isaacs Klein, *Heritage of Faith: Two Pioneers of Judaism in America,* p. 23.

58. Bernard Drachman, *The Unfailing Light: Memoirs of an American Rabbi*, pp. 278–82.

59. Gurock, "From Exception to Role Model," p. 476.

60. Jeffrey S. Gurock, *The Men and Women of Yeshiva: Higher Education, Orthodoxy, and American Judaism*, pp. 25ff.

61. Wiernik, p. 371.

62. Gurock, "Resisters and Accommodators," p. 29.

63. Klein, pp. 41–42.

64. Gurock, "From Exception to Role Model," pp. 460ff.

65. Ibid., p. 462.

66. Joseph Kaminetsky and Alex Gross, "Shraga Mendlowitz," pp. 551–72.

67. Hertzberg, pp. 62–64.

68. Jelinek, "Self-Identification," p. 220, and "The Jews from Hungary," pp. 17–19.

69. Helen F. Wolf, "The Evolution of a Synagogue—B'nai Jeshurun Congregation."

70. *American Israelite*, 16 January 1880.

71. Congregation Oheb Zedek was established in 1904 in a dispute over mixed seating of men and women. In 1905 Shomrei Shaboth Congregation was set up, and five years later Anshe Marmaresher B'nai Jacob. In 1910 people from Sziget organized Marmaresh B'nai Jacobo Society, and in 1922 Jews who "wished to retain the associations and religious customs of their European homeland" founded Shomrei Hadath Congregation. This information comes from the WPA Church Records Inventory at the Western Reserve Historical Society and from *Encyclopedia of Cleveland History*, pp. 734–35.

72. Cleveland *Plain Dealer*, 1 and 5 September 1887.

73. *American Israelite*, 16 September 1887.

74. Cleveland *Plain Dealer*, 13 September 1887.

75. Ibid., 31 December 1888.

76. Gartner, *History of the Jews of Cleveland*, p. 168.

77. Ibid., p. 170.

78. Ibid., 199.

79. Cohen, *Encounter with Emancipation*, chap. 3.

80. Gartner, *History*, 162–63.

81. Jo Renee Fine and Gerald R. Wolfe, *The Synagogues of New York's Lower East Side*, p. viii. See also Oscar Israelowitz, *Synagogues of New York City*.

82. Hertzberg, p. 123.

83. This congregation, not to be confused with Beth Hamidrash Hagadol founded by Russian and Polish Jews, developed into one of the larger Hungarian congregations. It was still located on the Lower East Side in 1917, with 110 members and seating capacity of 500. *Kehillah Register*, New York, 1917–1918.

84. From a five-page history written about 1965.

85. Kaufman as quoted in Kende, p. 349.

14. The American Door

1. Benkart, "Hungarians," p. 469.

2. Archives of the Prime Minister, 1 September 1902, No. 49 res., obtained from the Immigration History Research Center, University of Minnesota.

3. Papp, p. 227, and Vardy, *The Hungarian-Americans*, p. 94. This percentage rose to 30 percent in the decade following the First World War.

4. Puskás, *From Hungary to the United States*, pp. 174–75.

5. Steven Bela Vardy, "Hungarians in America's Ethnic Politics," pp. 171–96.

6. Burns, p. 205.

7. H. Armin Weltner, "Hungarians in American Politics," pp. 80–83.

8. The information on the 1899 meeting with Governor Roosevelt and on the later banquet with President Roosevelt comes from the proceedings of the banquet, 14 February 1905, and from Antoinette Feleky, *Charles Feleky and His Unpublished Manuscript*.

9. Rischin, p. 129.

10. Ibid., p. 229.

11. *New York Times*, 8 December 1957.

12. Wellington Fordyce, "Nationality Groups in Cleveland Politics," p. 110.

13. Cohen, *Encounter with Emancipation*, pp. 329–36.

14. Ibid., p. 335.

15. Kohut, *My Portion*, p. 175.

16. Ida Cohen Selavan, "Adolph Edlis: A Hungarian Jew in Pittsburgh Politics."

17. Ibid., p. 3.

18. Rischin, p. 224.

19. Burns, p. 176.

20. I. Howe, "Pluralism in the Immigrant World," pp. 151–52.

21. Elias Tcherikower and Aaron Antonovsky, *The Early Jewish Labor Movement in the United States*, pp. 275–77.

22. Ibid., pp. 279–80.

23. Ibid., p. 278.

24. Judith Greenfeld, "The Role of the Jews in the Development of the Clothing Industry in the United States," pp. 199–200.

25. Samuel Gompers, *Seventy Years of Life and Labor—An Autobiography*, pp. 109–10.

26. Rischin, p. 174.

27. Ibid., p. 145.

28. Burns, pp. 178–79.

29. Ibid., p. 178.

30. Tcherikower and Antonovsky, p. 279.

31. Gerald Sorin, *The Prophetic Minority: American Jewish Immigrant Radicals, 1880–1920*.

32. Lengyel, *Americans from Hungary*, pp. 292–93.

33. Edward P. Hutchinson, *Immigrants and Their Children, 1850–1950*, pp. 265 and 277.

34. Ibid., p. 178.

35. Goren, p. 588.

36. See, for example, Cohen, *Encounter with Emancipation*, pp. 19–30; *Jewish Encyclopedia*, 1925, vol. 6, pp. 267–69; H. Golden, *Forgotten Pioneer*.

37. *The Hungarian American*, Millennial Festival Edition, May, 1896.

38. Oral History Project #1, National Council of Jewish Women, Pittsburgh Section, Interview #240.

39. Ibid.

15. Flickers and Reflections

1. Benkart, "Hungarians," p. 470.
2. Lengyel, *Americans from Hungary*, pp. 172 and 221.
3. JDC General Files 1921–31, Files 210–14.
4. *Universal Jewish Encyclopedia*, s.v. "Hungarian Jews in America, Federation of."
5. *American Hungarian Jewish Review*, 15 May 1922.
6. *The Hungarian Jew*, 24 May 1932.
7. Group Record 869 at YIVO Institute for Jewish Research.
8. Federal Writers' Project, *New York Panorama*, p. 110.
9. *Amerikai Magyar Népszava*, Golden Jubilee Album, 1950, p. 65.
10. MSS 3653, Western Reserve Historical Society.
11. Ruth Marcus Patt, *The Jewish Scene in New Jersey's Raritan Valley, 1698–1948*, p. 48.
12. Oscar Z. Rand, ed., *Toldoth Anshe Shem*, vol. 1.
13. Vardy, *The Hungarian-Americans*, p. 114.
14. See Vardy, *The Hungarian-Americans*, p. 47, and Lengyel, *Americans from Hungary*, p. 171.
15. Zoltán Neumark, "Summary History of Our 75 Years."
16. *Jewish Independent*, Cleveland, 14 December 1928.
17. *The Encyclopedia of Cleveland History*, s.v. "HBSU."
18. There are today a number of Hungarian Jewish organizations in the Hasidic communities mostly in and around New York. These are not the outgrowths of earlier turn-of-the-century immigration and therefore are not included in this study.
19. Vardy, *The Hungarian-Americans*, pp. 115–33.
20. S. Alexander Weinstock estimates the number of 1956 refugees at thirty-eight thousand and describes them as middle-class people. *Acculturation and Occupation: A Study of the 1956 Hungarian Refugees in the United States*, pp. 39–43.
21. James Paul Allen and Eugene James Turner, "People of Eastern European Origin—Hungarian Ancestry," unpaged.
22. I am indebted to Sherry Israel of the Combined Jewish Philanthropies of Greater Boston for making these calculations.
23. (1) Alexander Boros, "Comparative Study of Assimilation Patterns of Four Waves of Hungarian Immigrants," pp. 46ff.; (2) Primes, p. 3, where she quotes Edward Alsworth Ross's book (*The Old World in the New*), p. 173; (3) *Hungarian American Federation Bulletin*, Cleveland, 1906, article by Joseph Turk; (4) Konrad Bercovici, *Around the World in New York*, pp. 347–48; (5) Pink, pp. 262–63.
24. From a speech by J. C. Bloch at the Hungarian Festival in Cleveland in 1887, reported in the Cleveland *Plain Dealer*, 12 September 1887.
25. Drachman, pp. 279–81.
26. Steiner, *On the Trail of the Immigrant*, p. 149.
27. Joseph Lovitz, "Jewish Historical Society of New York," p. 4.
28. Cohen, *Encounter with Emancipation*, p. 63. In addition to the sources cited in this discussion of the German Jews, see also Goren, pp. 571–76, and Louis J. Swichkow and Lloyd P. Gartner, *The History of the Jews of Milwaukee*, pp. 59–64.
29. *Encyclopaedia Judaica*, s.v. "Germany."
30. Rudolph Glanz, *Studies in Judaica Americana*, p. 206.
31. Cohen, *Encounter with Emancipation*, pp. 58–59.

32. Glanz, pp. 230–32.
33. Ibid., p. 216.
34. Ibid., pp. 143, 246, 227, 231.
35. Ibid.
36. Cohen, *Encounter with Emancipation*, pp. 58 and 60.
37. Sachar, *The Course of Modern Jewish History*, p. 171.
38. Glanz, p. 248.
39. Moore, p. 37.
40. Cohen, *Encounter with Emancipation*, p. 62.
41. Magocsi, "Russians," p. 890.
42. Rischin, p. 176.
43. Morawska, p. 30.
44. Ibid., pp. 69–73.
45. This description of Williamsburg is drawn from Poll, *The Hasidic Community of Williamsburg*, pp. 29–30. See also George Kranzler, *Williamsburg: A Jewish Community in Transition*, and Arthur A. Cohen and Philip Garvin, *A People Apart: Hasidism in America*.
46. Poll, "The Role of Yiddish," p. 135.
47. Kranzler, p. 219.
48. Barany, "Magyar Jew or Jewish Magyar," pp. 77–78.
49. Mendelsohn, p. 91.
50. Fishman, *Hungarian Language Maintenance*, pp. 9–10.
51. Gartner, *History of the Jews of Cleveland*, pp. 216–17.
52. See Fishman, *Hungarian Language Maintenance*, p. 22, and Sklare, *America's Jews*, pp. 14–15.
53. Fishman, *Hungarian Language Maintenance*, p. 43.
54. Sklare, *America's Jews*, p. 15.
55. Joshua A. Fishman, *The Rise and Fall of the Ethnic Revival*, p. 49.

Appendix 2: Estimating the Number Who Came to America

1. Hersch, p. 479.
2. Joseph, p. 110.
3. Immigration Commission, vol. 4, p. 375.
4. Kovács.
5. *A Magyar Szent Korona Országainak Kivándorlása és visszavándorlása, 1899–1913*, "Immigrants and Remigrants of the Hungarian Kingdom, 1899–1913," Magyar Statisztikai Közleméneyek, n.s., 1918, vol. 67, table 46.
6. Puskás, p. 28.
7. Ibid., p. 18.

Appendix 3: Passenger Lists, Citizenship Applications, and U.S. Census of 1880

1. See Glanz, p. 88, who used the same approach in examining ship lists to identify German Jews.

★

Bibliography

Adler, Philip J. "The Introduction of Public Schooling for the Jews of Hungary (1849–1860)." *Jewish Social Studies* 36 (1974): 118–33.

Allen, James Paul, and Eugene James Turner. "People of Eastern European Origin—Hungarian Ancestry." In *We the People: An Atlas of America's Ethnic Diversity.* New York: Macmillan, 1988.

American-Hungarian Jewish Review. Vol. 1, Nos. 4 and 5 (15 May 1922). Jewish Publishing Co., 400 East Houston Street, New York. Ernest Lendway and Margaret Foldes, editors.

American Jewish Year Book. "Biographical Sketches of Rabbis and Cantors." 1903.

Amerikai Magyar Népszava. 1 June 1907.

Asmonean. Editorial. 19 December 1851.

Ausabel, Nathan. *A Treasury of Jewish Folklore.* New York: Crown, 1956.

Avineri, Shlomo. *The Making of Modern Zionism.* New York: Basic Books, 1981.

Balch, Emily Greene. *Our Slavic Fellow Citizens.* New York: Charities Publication Committee, 1910.

Balla, Erzsébet. "The Jews of Hungary: A Cultural Overview." In Braham, ed., *Hungarian Jewish Studies,* vol. 2, pp. 85–136.

Balogh, Joseph. "Analysis of Cultural Organizations of Hungarian Americans in Pittsburgh and Allegheny County." Ph.D. diss., University of Pittsburgh, 1945.

Balshone, Benjamin. *Determined!* New York: Bloch, 1984.

Barany, George. "Hungary: From Aristocratic to Proletarian Nationalism." In *Nationalism in Eastern Europe,* edited by Peter Sugar and Ivo Lederer. Seattle: University of Washington Press, 1969.

———. "Magyar Jew or Jewish Magyar: Reflections on the Question of Assimilation." In *Jews and Non-Jews in Eastern Europe, 1918–1945,* edited by Béla Vago and George L. Mosse. New York: Wiley, 1974.

Barkai, Avraham. "German-Jewish Migration in the Nineteenth Century, 1830–1910." In *Migration across Time and Nations,* edited by Ira A. Glazier and Luigi DeRosa. New York: Holmes and Meier, 1986.

Benkart, Paula. "Hungarians." In *Harvard Encyclopedia of American Ethnic Groups,* edited by Stephan Thernstrom. Cambridge: Harvard University Press, 1980.

———. "Religion, Family, and Community among Hungarians Migrating to American Cities, 1880–1930." Ph.D. diss., Johns Hopkins University, 1975.

Bercovici, Konrad. *Around the World in New York.* New York: Century, 1924.

Berend, I. T., and György Ránki. *Hungary: A Century of Economic Development.* New York: Barnes and Noble, 1974.

Berger, David. *The Legacy of Jewish Migration: 1881 and Its Impact.* New York: Brooklyn College Press, 1983.

Berman, Myron. *Richmond's Jewry, 1769–1976.* Charlottesville: Published for the Richmond Jewish Community Council by the University Press of Virginia, 1978.

Bihl, Wolfdieter. "Das Judentum Ungarns, 1780–1914." In *Studia Judaica Austriaca,* vol. 3, *Studien zum Ungarischen Judentum.* Eisenstadt: Roetzer, 1976.

Bitton, Livia Elvira. *A Decade of Zionism in Hungary, The Formative Years–The Post-World War I Period: 1918–1928.* Ph.D. diss., New York University, 1968.

Bodnar, John. *The Transplanted: A History of Immigrants in Urban America.* Bloomington: Indiana University Press, 1985.

Bonutti, Karl, and George Prpic. "Analysis of Ethnic Communities of Cleveland." Cleveland: Urban Observatory, 1974.

Boros, Alexander. "Comparative Study of Assimilation Patterns of Four Waves of Hungarian Immigrants." Ph.D. diss., Kent State University, 1959.

Braham, Randolph L. "Hungarian Jewry: An Historical Retrospect." *Journal of Central European Affairs* 2 (1960).

———. *The Politics of Genocide: The Holocaust in Hungary.* New York: Columbia University Press, 1981.

———, ed. *Hungarian Jewish Studies.* New York: World Federation of Hungarian Jews, vol. 1, 1966; vol. 2, 1969; vol. 3, 1973.

Braun, Marcus. *Immigration Abuses: Glimpses of Hungary and Hungarians.* New York: Pearson, 1906.

Brith Abraham, Independent Order. "History of the Independent Order Brith Abraham, 1887–1937." Golden Jubilee publication. New York: 1937.

Burns, James MacGregor. *The Workshop of Democracy.* New York: Knopf, 1985.

Carmilly-Weinberger, Moshe. *The Rabbinical Seminary of Budapest, 1877–1977.* New York: Sepher-Hermon, 1986.

Carpenter, Niles. *Immigrants and Their Children, 1920.* Bureau of the Census, 1927.

Chazan, Robert, and Marc Lee Raphael, eds. *Modern Jewish History: A Source Reader.* New York: Schocken, 1974.

Chmelar, Johann. "The Austrian Emigration, 1900–1914." In *Perspectives in American History: Dislocation and Emigration—The Social Background of American Immigration,* vol. 7, edited by Donald Fleming and Bernard Bailyn. Cambridge: Harvard University Press, 1973.

Cleveland Foreign Language Newspaper Digest. "Hungarian 1891–1892," Annals of Cleveland Newspaper Series. Works Projects Administration in Ohio, District Four, Cleveland, January 1942.

Cleveland News. Article by Dan Gallagher. 14 January 1928.

Cohen, Arthur A., and Philip Garvin. *A People Apart: Hasidism in America.* New York: Dutton, 1970.

Cohen, Naomi W. *Encounter with Emancipation: The German Jews in the United States, 1830–1914.* Philadelphia: The Jewish Publication Society of America, 1984.

———. "The Ethnic Catalyst: The Impact of the East European Immigrant on the American Jewish Establishment." In *The Legacy of Jewish Migration: 1881 and Its Impact,* edited by David Berger. New York: Brooklyn College Press, 1983.

Cook, Hulda Florence. *The Magyars of Cleveland.* Cleveland Americanization Committee, 1919.

Cowett, Mark. *Birmingham's Rabbi: Morris Newfield and Alabama, 1895–1940.* Tuscaloosa: University of Alabama Press, 1986.

Csillag, András. "Joseph Pulitzer's Roots in Europe: A Genealogical History." *American Jewish Archives* 39 (1987): 48–68.

Czigány, Lóránt. *The Oxford History of Hungarian Literature.* Oxford: Clarendon Press, 1984.

Dash, Joan. *Summoned to Jerusalem: The Life of Henrietta Szold.* New York: Harper and Row, 1949.

Davis, Moshe. *The Emergence of Conservative Judaism: The Historical School in 19th Century America.* Philadelphia: The Jewish Publication Society of America, 1963.

Dawidowicz, Lucy S. *The War Against the Jews, 1933–1945.* New York: Holt, Rinehart, and Winston, 1975.

Deák, István. *The Lawful Revolution: Louis Kossuth and the Hungarians, 1848–1849.* New York: Columbia University Press, 1979.

———. "Revolution, Progress, and Decline: Hungary between 1848 and 1918." *Swissair Gazette,* June 1986.

Deák, Zoltán, ed. *This Noble Flame: An Anthology of a Hungarian Newspaper in the U.S.A.* New York: Heritage, 1982.

Denn, Meyer. "From Certizne to Wharton: A Jewish Journey to the New World." University of Texas at Austin, 1985. Typescript.

Dicker, Herman. *Piety and Perseverance: Jews from the Carpathian Mountains.* New York: Sepher-Hermon, 1981.

Dillingham Commission. See United States Immigration Commission.

Don, Yehuda, and George Magos. "The Demographic Development of Hungarian Jewry." *Jewish Social Studies* 45 (1983).

Drachman, Bernard. *The Unfailing Light: Memoirs of an American Rabbi.* New York: The Rabbinical Council of America, 1948.

Dun, R. G., and Company Records, Ohio, vol. 42. Baker Library, Harvard Business School.

Dwork, Deborah. "Immigrant Jews on the Lower East Side of New York, 1880–1914." In *The American Jewish Experience,* edited by Jonathan Sarna. New York: Holmes and Meier, 1986.

Ehrenfried, Albert. *A Chronicle of Boston Jewry: From the Colonial Settlement to 1900.* N.p., 1963.

Éles, Géza Szentmiklosy. "Hungarians in Cleveland." Master's thesis, John Carrol University, 1972.

Ellenson, David. "The Orthodox Rabbinate and Apostasy in Nineteenth-Century Germany and Hungary." In *Jewish Apostasy in the Modern World,* edited by Todd M. Endelman. New York: Holmes & Meier, 1987.

Encyclopedia of Cleveland History. See Van Tassel.

Ettinger, S. "The Modern Period." In *A History of the Jewish People,* edited by H. H. Ben-Sasson. Cambridge: Harvard University Press, 1976.

Federal Writers' Project. *New York Panorama: A Comprehensive View of the Metropolis.* New York: Random House, 1938.

Fein, Isaac M. *The Making of an American Jewish Community: The History of Baltimore Jewry from 1733 to 1920.* Philadelphia: Jewish Publication Society of America, 1971.

Feldman, Jacob. *The Jewish Experience in Western Pennsylvania: A History 1755–1945.* Pittsburgh: Historical Society of Western Pennsylvania, 1986.

Feleky, Antoinette. *Charles Feleky and His Unpublished Manuscript.* New York: Representative Press, 1938.

Fine, Jo Renee, and Gerald R. Wolfe. *The Synagogues of New York's Lower East Side.* New York: Washington Mews, 1978.

Fineman, Irving. *Woman of Valor: The Life of Henrietta Szold, 1860–1945.* New York: Simon and Schuster, 1961.

Finkelstein, Louis, ed. *The Jews: Their History, Culture, and Religion.* Philadelphia: The Jewish Publication Society of America, 1949.

First, A. "Folklore and Language Materials from Hungary" (in Yiddish). YIVO Bletter 14 (1939): 436–52.

Fishman, Joshua A. *Hungarian Language Maintenance in the United States.* Bloomington: Indiana University Press, 1966.

———. *The Rise and Fall of the Ethnic Revival.* Berlin: Mouton, 1985.

Fordyce, Wellington. "Immigrant Colonies in Cleveland." *Ohio State Archaeological and Historical Quarterly* 45 (1936).

———. "Immigrant Institutions in Cleveland." *Ohio State Archaeological and Historical Quarterly* 47 (1938).

———. "Nationality Groups in Cleveland Politics." *Ohio State Archaeological and Historical Quarterly* 46 (1937).

Frank, Fedora Small. *Beginnings on Market Street: Nashville and Her Jewry, 1861–1901.* Nashville: Jewish Community of Nashville and Middle Tennessee, 1976.

Frankel, Jonathan. "The Crisis of 1881 as a Turning Point in Modern Jewish History." In *The Legacy of Jewish Migration: 1881 and Its Impact,* edited by David Berger. New York: Brooklyn College Press, 1983.

Friedenberg, Albert M. "An Austro-Hungarian Movement to Encourage the Migration of Jews to America, 1848." *Publications of the American Jewish Historical Society* 23 (1915).

Friedman, Armin Harry. "Major Aspects of Yeshivah Education in Hungary, 1848–1948 (with emphasis on the role of the Yeshivah of Pressburg)." Ph.D. diss., Yeshiva University, 1971.

Gabori, George. *When Evils Were Most Free.* Ottowa: Deneau Publishers, 1981.

Galantay, Ervin Y. "Budapest: Eclectic Metropolis, 1867–1919," *Swissair Gazette,* June 1986, pp. 20–30.

Gartner, Lloyd P. *The Great Migration, 1881–1914: Myths and Realities.* Cape Town: Kaplan Centre, University of Cape Town, 1984.

———. *History of the Jews of Cleveland.* Cleveland: Western Reserve Historical Society, 1978.

Garvin, Paul L. "The Dialect Geography of Hungarian Yiddish." In *The Field of Yiddish: Studies in Language, Folklore, and Literature—Second Collection,* edited by Uriel Weinreich. The Hague: Mouton, 1965.

Gellén, József. "Geographical Origin and Community in Emigration from Hungary as Reflected in Parish Records in Early 20th Century." *Magyar Történeti Tanulmányok* 19 (1986).

Gerster, Árpád. *Recollections of a New York Surgeon.* New York: Hoeber, 1917.

Glanz, Rudolf. *Studies in Judaica Americana.* New York: Ktav Publishing House, 1970.

Glazer, Nathan. *Social Characteristics of American Jews.* New York: Jewish Education Committee, 1965.

Glazier, Ira A., and Luigi De Rosa, eds. *Migration across Time and Nations*. New York: Holmes and Meier, 1986.

Golab, Caroline. *Immigrant Destinations*. Philadelphia: Temple University Press, 1977.

Golden, Harry. *Forgotten Pioneer*. Cleveland: World Publishing, 1963.

Golden, Sylvia. *Neighbors Needn't Know*. New York: Macmillan, 1953.

Goldhammer, Leo. "Jewish Emigration from Austria-Hungary in 1848–49." *YIVO Annual* 9 (1954).

Goldmark, Josephine. *Pilgrims of '48*. New Haven: Yale University Press, 1930.

Gompers, Samuel. *Seventy Years of Life and Labor—An Autobiography*. New York: Dutton, 1925.

Goodman, Vilma M. "Boulevard Reminiscences." New York: Amerikai Magyar, 1922.

Goren, Arthur A. "Jews." In *Harvard Encyclopedia of American Ethnic Groups*, edited by Stephan Thernstrom. Cambridge: Harvard University Press, 1980.

Gracza, Rezsoe, and Margaret Gracza. *The Hungarians in America*. Minneapolis: Lerner, 1969.

Greenfeld, Judith. "The Role of the Jews in the Development of the Clothing Industry in the United States." *YIVO Annual* vol. 2–3 (1948).

Greenwald, Leopold. *Toiznt Yor Idish Lebn in Ungarn* (A Thousand Years of Jewish Life in Hungary). New York: Paris Press, 1945.

Gurock, Jeffrey S. "From Exception to Role Model: Bernard Drachman and the Evolution of Jewish Religious Life in America, 1880–1920." *American Jewish History* 76 (1987).

———. *The Men and Women of Yeshiva: Higher Education, Orthodoxy, and American Judaism*. New York: Columbia University Press, 1988.

———. "Resisters and Accommodators: Varieties of Orthodox Rabbis in America, 1886–1983." In *The American Rabbinate: A Century of Continuity and Change, 1883–1983*, edited by Jacob Rader Marcus and Abraham J. Peck. Hoboken, N.J.: Ktav Publishing Company, 1985.

Gutstein, Morris A. *A Priceless Heritage: The Epic Growth of Nineteenth Century Chicago Jewry*. New York: Bloch Publishing Company, 1953.

Hanák, Peter. As reported in Lászlo Váradi, "The Hungarian Jewry in the Twentieth Century." *Acta Historica Academiae Scientiarum Hungaricae* 31 (1985).

Handler, Andrew. *Blood Libel at Tiszaeszlár*. New York: Columbia University Press, 1980.

———. *Dori: The Life and Times of Theodor Herzl in Budapest, 1860–1878*. Tuscaloosa: University of Alabama Press, 1983.

———. *Péter Ujvári's "By Candlelight."* Introduction and translation by Andrew Handler. Cranbury, N.J.: Associated University Presses, 1977.

———. *Rabbi Eizik: Hasidic Stories about the Zaddik of Kálló*. Rutherford, N.J.: Associated University Presses, 1978.

Handlin, Oscar. *Adventure in Freedom: Three Hundred Years of Jewish Life in America*. New York: McGraw Hill, 1954.

———. "The American Scene." In *The Forty-Eighters: Political Refugees of the German Revolution of 1848*, edited by A. E. Zucker. New York: Columbia University Press, 1950.

———. *Boston's Immigrants 1790–1865: A Study in Acculturation*. Cambridge: Harvard University Press, 1941.

Heims, Steve J. *John Von Neumann and Norbert Wiener: From Mathematics to the Technologies of Life and Death.* Cambridge: MIT Press, 1980.

Hersch, Leibmann. "International Migration of the Jews." In *International Migrations*, edited by Walter F. Wilcox, vol. 2. New York: National Bureau of Economic Research, 1931.

Herscher, Uri D., ed. *The East European Jewish Experience in America: A Century of Memories, 1882–1982.* Cincinnati: American Jewish Archives, 1983.

Hertzberg, Steven. *Strangers within the Gate City: The Jews of Atlanta, 1845–1915.* Philadelphia: Jewish Publication Society of America, 1978.

Himmelfarb, Harold S. "Research on American Jewish Identity and Identification: Progress, Pitfalls, and Prospects." In *Understanding American Jewry*, edited by Marshall Sklare. New Brunswick, N.J.: Transaction Books, 1982.

Hoffmann, Géza. *Csonka Munkásosztály—The Incomplete or Broken Working Class* (Hungarians in America). Budapest: Az Amerikai Magyarság, 1911.

Howe, Frederic C. *The Confessions of a Reformer.* New York: Scribner's, 1925.

Howe, Irving. "Pluralism in the Immigrant World." In *The Legacy of Jewish Migration: 1881 and Its Impact*, edited by David Berger. New York: Brooklyn College Press, 1983.

———. *World of Our Fathers.* New York: Harcourt, Brace, Jovanovich, 1976.

Hungarian-American. Millennial Festival Edition, May 1896.

Hungarian American Federation Bulletin. Cleveland: Eisele Printing Company, c. 1906.

Hungarian Jew (A Magyar Zsidó). 24 May 1932.

Hungarian Republican Club, Banquet for Theodore Roosevelt. New York: Schlesinger Press, 14 February 1905.

Hutchinson, Edward P. *Immigrants and Their Children, 1850–1950.* New York: Wiley, 1956.

Hutturer, C. J. "The Phonology of Budapest Yiddish." In *The Field of Yiddish, Second Collection*, edited by Uriel Weinreich. The Hague: Mouton, 1965.

Immigration Commission (Dillingham Commission. See United States Immigration Commission.)

Independent Order Brith Abraham. See Brith Abraham.

Indiana Jewish Historical Society. *Morris M. Feurlicht: A Hoosier Rabbinate.* Fort Wayne, 1974.

Irwin, William Henry. *The House That Shadows Built.* New York: Arno and the New York *Times*, 1970.

Israelowitz, Oscar. *Synagogues of New York City.* New York: Dover, 1982.

János, Andrew C. *The Politics of Backwardness in Hungary, 1825–1945.* Princeton: Princeton University Press, 1982.

Jászi, Oscar. *The Dissolution of the Habsburg Monarchy.* Chicago: University of Chicago Press, 1929.

Jelinek, Yeshayahu. "The Jews from Hungary in the Old Country and in the USA." 1972. Typescript.

———. "Self-Identification of First Generation Hungarian Jewish Immigrants." *American Jewish Historical Quarterly* 61 (1972).

Joseph, Samuel. *Jewish Immigration to the U.S., 1881–1910.* New York: Columbia University Press, 1914.

Kaczér, Illés. *The Siege.* New York: Dial, 1953.

Kaganoff, Benzion C. *A Dictionary of Jewish Names and Their History.* New York: Schocken, 1977.

Kaganoff, Nathan. "The Jewish Landsmanshaftn in New York City in the Period Preceding World War I." *American Jewish History* 76 (1986).

Kahn, Hans. "Before 1918 in the Historic Lands." In *The Jews of Czechoslovakia: Historical Studies and Surveys*, vol. 1. Philadelphia: The Jewish Publication Society of America, 1968.

Kaminetsky, Joseph, and Alex Gross. "Shraga Mendlowitz." In *Men of the Spirit*, edited by Leo Jung. New York: Kymson Publishing Company, 1964.

Kann, Robert A. "Hungarian Jewry During Austria-Hungary's Constitutional Period, 1867–1918." *Jewish Social Studies* 7 (1945).

———. *The Multinational Empire*. New York: Octagon Books, 1977.

Karady, Victor, and István Kemény. "Les Juifs dans la structure des classes en Hongrie" (Summary in English). *Actes de la Recherche de Sciences Sociales* 22 (1978)

Karp, Abraham J. "The Conservative Rabbi—'Dissatisfied But Not Unhappy.'" In *The American Rabbinate: A Century of Continuity and Change, 1883–1983*, edited by Jacob Rader Marcus and Abraham J. Peck. Hoboken, N.J.: Ktav Publishing Company, 1985.

———. "Simon Tuska's *The Stranger in the Synagogue*." *University of Rochester Library Bulletin* 14 (1958).

Katz, Jacob. "The Identity of Post Emancipatory Hungarian Jewry." In *A Social and Economic History of Central European Jewry*, edited by Yehuda Don and Victor Karady. New Brunswick: Transaction Publishers, 1990.

———. "The Uniqueness of Hungarian Jewry." *Forum* 27 (1977).

Katzburg, Nathaniel. "Assimilation in Hungary During the 19th Century: Orthodox Positions." In *Jewish Assimilation in Modern Times*, edited by Béla Vago. Boulder, Colo.: Westview Press, 1981.

———. "The History of the Jews in Hungary." In *The Story of the Jews in Hungary*. Tel Aviv: Beth Hatefutsoth, the Nahum Goldmann Museum of the Jewish Diaspora, 1984.

———. "Hungarian Jewry in Modern Times." In *Hungarian Jewish Studies*, edited by Randolph L. Braham. New York: World Federation of Hungarian Jews, 1966.

———. *Hungary and the Jews: Policy and Legislation, 1920–1943*. Tel Aviv: Bar-Ilan University Press, 1981.

Kende, Géza. *Magyarok Amerikanbán* (Hungarians in America). Cleveland: Szabadság Kiadása, 1927.

Kisch, Guido. *In Search of Freedom: A History of American Jews from Czechoslovakia*. London: Edward Goldston, 1949.

Kissman, Joseph. "The Immigration of Rumanian Jews up to 1914." *YIVO Annual* 2–3, 1947–1948.

Klein, Nancy Isaacs. *Heritage of Faith: Two Pioneers of Judaism in America*. Hoboken, N.J.: Ktav Publishing House, 1987.

Kliger, Hannah. "Traditions of Grass-Roots Organization and Leadership: The Continuity of Landsmanshaftn in New York." *American Jewish History* 76 (1986).

Kohler, Max J. "The German Jewish Migration to America." *Publications of the American Jewish Historical Society* 9 (1901).

Kohut, Rebekah. *His Father's House: The Story of George Alexander Kohut*. New Haven: Yale University Press, 1938.

———. *My Portion*. New York: Albert & Charles Boni, 1927.

Könnyü, Leslie. *Hungarians: An Immigration Study.* St. Louis: The American Hungarian Review, 1967.

Korn, Bertram Wallace. *Eventful Years and Experiences: Studies in Nineteenth Century American Jewish History.* Cincinnati: American Jewish Archives, 1954.

Kosa, John. *Land of Choice: The Hungarians in Canada.* Toronto: University of Toronto Press, 1957.

Kovács, Alajos. *A zsidóság térfoglalása Magyarországon.* Budapest: Aszeso Kiadása, 1922.

Kramar, Zoltán. *From the Danube to the Hudson: U.S. Ministerial and Consular Dispatches on Immigration from the Habsburg Monarchy, 1850–1900.* Atlanta: Hungarian Cultural Foundation, 1978.

Kranzler, George. *Williamsburg: A Jewish Community in Transition.* New York: Philipp Feldheim, 1961.

Kraut, Benny. "A Unitarian Rabbi? The Case of Solomon H. Sonneschein." In *Jewish Apostasy in the Modern World,* edited by Todd M. Endelman. New York: Holmes & Meier, 1987.

Krawcheck, Julian. "Temple on the Heights: B'nai Jeshurun . . ." *Cleveland Jewish News:* 29 April and 13 May 1966.

László, Ernő. "Hungarian Jewry: Settlement and Demography, 1735–38 to 1910." In *Hungarian Jewish Studies,* edited by Randolph L. Braham. New York: World Federation of Hungarian Jews, 1966.

Lengyel, Emil. *Americans from Hungary.* Philadelphia: Lippincott, 1948.

————. "Hungarian Americans." In *One America,* edited by Francis J. Brown and Joseph S. Roucek. Englewood Cliffs, N.J.: Prentice-Hall, 1945.

Levy, Donald. "A Report on the Location of Ethnic Groups in Greater Cleveland." Cleveland: Institute of Urban Studies, 1972.

Liebovitz, H. A., and Mihály Parlagh. *A Clevelandi Magyarok Története* (History of Cleveland's Hungarians). Cleveland: Published by H. A. Liebovitz, c. 1917.

Lovitz, Joseph. In "Jewish Historical Society of New York." September 1988. Newsletter.

Lowenthal, Marvin. *Henrietta Szold: Life and Letters.* New York: Viking Press, 1942.

————. *The Jews of Germany: A Story of Sixteen Centuries.* Philadelphia: The Jewish Publication Society of America, 1944.

Lukács, John. *Budapest 1900: A Historical Portrait of a City and Its Culture.* New York: Weidenfeld & Nicolson, 1988.

Macartney, C. A. *Hungary: A Short History.* Chicago: Aldine, 1962.

————. *Hungary and Her Successors: The Treaty of Trianon and Its Consequences, 1919–1937.* London: Oxford University Press, 1937.

Magocsi, Paul Robert. *Our People: Carpatho-Rusyns and Their Descendants in North America.* Toronto: Multicultural History Society of Ontario, 1984.

————. "Russians." In *Harvard Encyclopedia of American Ethnic Groups,* edited by Stephan Thernstrom. Cambridge: Harvard University Press, 1980.

————. *The Shaping of a National Identity: Subcarpathian Rus', 1848–1948.* Cambridge: Harvard University Press, 1978.

Magyar Statisztikai Közlemények (Hungarian Statistical Reports). Budapest, 1902.

Mahler, Raphael. "The Economic Background of Jewish Emigration from Galicia to the United States." *YIVO Annual* 7 (1952).

Makár, János. *The Story of an Immigrant Group in Franklin, New Jersey.* Published by the author, 1969.

Marcus, Jacob Rader, and Abraham J. Peck. *The American Rabbinate: A Century of Continuity and Change, 1883–1983*. Hoboken, N.J.: Ktav Publishing House, 1985.

Margareten, Joel. *Directory and Genealogy of the Horowitz-Margareten Family*. 1955.

Marton, Ernest (Ernő). "The Family Tree of Hungarian Jewry." In *Hungarian Jewish Studies*, edited by Randolph L. Braham. New York: World Federation of Hungarian Jews, 1966.

McCagg, William O., Jr. "Jewish Conversion in Hungary in Modern Times." In *Jewish Apostasy in the Modern World*, edited by Todd M. Endelman. New York: Holmes & Meier, 1987.

——. *Jewish Nobles and Geniuses in Modern Hungary*. Boulder, Colo.: East European Quarterly, 1972.

McCullough, Ann Catherine. "A History of B. W. Huebsch, Publisher." Ph.D. diss., University of Wisconsin–Madison, 1979.

Mendelsohn, Ezra. *The Jews of East Central Europe between the World Wars*. Bloomington: Indiana University Press, 1983.

Moore, Deborah Dash. *B'nai B'rith and the Challenge of Ethnic Leadership*. Albany: State University of New York Press, 1981.

Morais, Henry Samuel. *The Jews of Philadelphia*. Philadelphia: Levytype Co., 1894.

Morawska, Ewa. "A Replica of the 'Old Country' Relationship in the Ethnic Niche: East European Jews and Gentiles in Small-town Western Pennsylvania, 1880s–1930s." *American Jewish History* 77 (1987).

Moskovitz, Aron. *Jewish Education in Hungary*. New York: Bloch, 1964.

Nadell, Pamela Susan. "The Journey to America by Steam: The Jews of Eastern Europe in Transition." Ph.D. diss., Ohio State University, 1982.

National Council of Jewish Women, Pittsburgh Section. *Oral History Project #1*. Archives of Industrial Society, Hillman Library, University of Pittsburgh.

Neumark, Zoltán. "Summary History of Our 75 Years." Seventy-fifth Anniversary Album. New York: First Hungarian Literary Society, 1964.

Pap, Michael S. "The Hungarian Community of Cleveland." In *Ethnic Communities of Cleveland*. Glasgow University, Institute for Soviet and East European Studies, 1973.

Papp, Susan M. "Hungarian Americans and Their Communities of Cleveland." Ph.D. diss., Cleveland State University, 1981.

Park, Robert E. *The Immigrant Press and Its Control*. New York: Harper, 1922.

Patai, Raphael. *Apprentice in Budapest: Memories of a World That Is No More*. Salt Lake City: University of Utah Press, 1988.

Patt, Ruth Marcus. *The Jewish Scene in New Jersey's Raritan Valley, 1698–1948*. New Brunswick: Jewish Historical Society of Raritan Valley, 1978.

"Peoples of Cleveland." Work Projects Administration, Ohio. 1942, unpublished. Courtesy of the Western Reserve Historical Society.

Pink, Louis. "The Magyars in New York." *Charities and Commons* 13 (1904).

Pivány, Eugene. "Hungarian-American Historical Connections." Budapest: Royal Hungarian University Press, 1927.

——. *Hungarians in the American Civil War*. Cleveland, 1913.

Plaut, W. Gunther. *The Jews in Minnesota*. New York: American Jewish Historical Society, 1959.

Polish, David. "The Changing and the Constant in the Reform Rabbinate." In *The American Rabbinate: A Century of Continuity and Change, 1883–1983*, edited by Jacob Rader Marcus and Abraham J. Peck. Hoboken, N.J.: Ktav Publishing Company, 1985.

Poll, Solomon. *The Hasidic Community of Williamsburg.* New York: The Free Press of Glencoe, 1962.

———. "The Role of Yiddish in American Ultra-Orthodox and Hasidic Communities." *YIVO Annual* 13 (1965).

Pollak, Gustav. *Michael Heilprin and His Sons.* New York: Dodd, Mead, 1912.

Primes, Agnes. "The Hungarians in New York: A Study in Immigrant Cultural Influences." Master's thesis, Columbia University, 1940.

Puskás, Julianna. "The Background of Migration and Its Role in Shaping Magyar Communities in the U.S.A., 1880–1914." In *The Dynamics of East European Ethnicity Outside of Eastern Europe,* edited by Irene Portis Winner and Rudolph M. Susel. Cambridge: Schenkman, 1982.

———. "The Differentiation of the Hungarian Newspapers, Reflecting Some Aspects of Acculturation, 1853–1914." In *The Press of Labor Migrants in Europe and North America 1880s to 1930s,* edited by Christiane Harzig and Dirk Hoerder. Bremen: Labor Newspaper Preservation Project, 1985.

———. *From Hungary to the United States (1880–1914).* Budapest: Akadémiai Kiadó, 1982.

———. "Hungarian Migration Patterns, 1880–1930: From Macroanalysis to Microanalysis." In *Migration across Time and Nations,* edited by Ira A. Glazier and Luigi DeRosa. New York: Holmes and Meier, 1986.

———. "Transatlantic Migration from a Hungarian Village on the Basis of Oral Testimonies." In *The Press of Labor Migrants in Europe and North America 1880s to 1930s,* edited by Christiane Harzig and Dirk Hoerder. Bremen: Labor Newspaper Preservation Project, 1985.

Rand, Oscar Z., ed. *Toldoth Anshe Shem.* Vol. 1. New York: Toldoth Anshe Shem, 1950.

Ránki, György. "Can the Holocaust Be Understood? A Hungarian Noble Jew's Papers." *Elet és Irodalom* (Life and Literature). Budapest, 25 July 1986.

Raphael, Marc Lee. *Jews and Judaism in a Midwestern Community: Columbus, Ohio, 1840–1975.* Columbus: Ohio Historical Society, 1979.

Rischin, Moses. *The Promised City: New York's Jews 1870–1914.* Cambridge: Harvard University Press, 1962.

Rosenberg, Stuart E. *The New Jewish Identity in America.* New York: Hippocrene, 1985.

———. *The Jewish Community of Rochester, 1843–1925.* New York: Columbia University Press, 1954.

Rosenwaike, Ira. *Population History of New York City.* Syracuse: Syracuse University Press, 1972.

Rosten, Leo. *The Joys of Yiddish.* New York: McGraw-Hill Book Company, 1968.

Roth, Cecil. "The Jews of Western Europe." In *The Jews: Their History,* edited by Lewis Finkelstein. New York: Schocken, 1972.

Rothkirchen, Livia. "Deep-Rooted yet Alien: Some Aspects of the History of the Jews in Subcarpathian Ruthenia." *Yad Vashem Studies* (Jerusalem) 12 (1977).

———. "Slovakia: I., 1848–1918." In Society for the History of Czechoslovak Jews, *The Jews of Czechoslovakia,* vol. I. Philadelphia: The Jewish Publication Society of America, 1968.

Sachar, Howard Morley. *The Course of Modern Jewish History.* New York: Dell, 1977.

———. *Diaspora: An Inquiry into the Contemporary Jewish World.* New York: Harper & Row, 1985.

Safra, Shmuel. "The Era of the Mishnah and Talmud, 70–640." In *A History of the Jewish People,* edited by H. H. Ben-Sasson. Cambridge: Harvard University Press, 1976.

Sarna, Jonathan D. "From Necessity to Virtue: The Hebrew-Christianity of Gideon R. Lederer." *Iliff Review* 37 (1980).

———. "The Myth of No Return: Jewish Return Migration to Eastern Europe, 1881–1914." *American Jewish History* 71 (1981).

———. *People Walk on Their Heads: Moses Weinberger's Jews and Judaism in New York.* New York: Holmes and Meier Publishers, 1982.

Sas (Szász), Meir. *Vanishing Communities in Hungary: The History and Tragic Fate of the Jews in Újhely and Zemplén County.* Willowdale, Ontario: Memorial Book Committee, 1986.

Scheiber, Alexander. "Jewish Folklore, a bibliography." In *The Rabbinical Seminary of Budapest, 1877–1977,* by Moshe Carmilly-Weinberger. New York: Sepher-Hermon, 1986.

———. "Jewish Studies in Hungary." In *The Story of the Jews in Hungary.* Beth Hatefutsoth. Tel Aviv: The Naham Goldmann Museum of the Jewish Diaspora, 1984.

Schopflin, George. "Jewish Assimilation in Hungary: A Moot Point." In *Jewish Assimilation in Modern Times,* edited by Béla Vago. Boulder, Colo.: Westview Press, 1981.

Selavan, Ida Cohen. "Adolph Edlis: A Hungarian Jew in Pittsburgh Politics." *American Jewish Archives* 36 (1984).

Seton-Watson, Robert William. *Racial Problems in Hungary.* New York: Howard Fertig, 1982.

Sherwin, Byron L. "Portrait of a Romantic Rebel: Bernard C. Ehrenreich, 1865–1955." In Nathan M. Kaganoff and Melvin I. Urofsky, eds., *"Turn to the South": Essays on Southern Jewry.* The University Press of Virginia for the American Jewish Historical Society, 1979.

Sibley, Celestine. *Dear Store: An Affectionate Portrait of Rich's.* Garden City: Doubleday, 1967.

Silber, Michael K. "The Historical Experience of German Jewry and Its Impact on Haskalah and Reform in Hungary." In *Toward Modernity: The European Jewish Model,* edited by Jacob Katz. New Brunswick, N.J.: Transaction, 1987.

Sklare, Marshall. *America's Jews.* New York: Random House, 1971.

———. "Jewish Acculturation and American Jewish Identity." In *Jewish Life in America,* edited by Gladys Rosen. Hoboken, N.J.: KTAV, 1978.

Sobel, May Loveman. *Family Black and Family Loveman.* American Jewish Archives. Cincinnati, undated.

Sole, Aryeh. "Subcarpathian Ruthenia: 1918–1938." In *The Jews of Czechoslovakia,* vol. 1. Philadelphia: The Jewish Publication Society of America, 1968.

Sorin, Gerald. *The Prophetic Minority: American Jewish Immigrant Radicals, 1880–1920.* Bloomington: Indiana University Press, 1985.

Souders, David Aaron. *The Magyars in America.* New York: Doran, 1922.

Soyer, Daniel. "Between Two Worlds: The Jewish Landsmanshaftn." In *American Jewish History* 76 (1986): 5–24.

Spiron, Zvi. "The Yiddish Language in Hungary." *Philological Series 1*. Vilno: YIVO, 1926.

Steiner, Edward A. *Against the Current: Simple Chapters from a Complex Life*. New York: Revell, 1910.

———. *From Alien to Citizen: The Story of My Life in America*. Boston: Pilgrim Press, 1914.

———. *On the Trail of the Immigrant*. New York: Revell, 1906.

Swichkow, Louis J., and Lloyd P. Gartner, *The History of the Jews of Milwaukee*. Philadelphia: Jewish Publication Society of America, 1963.

Szász, Meir. See Sas.

Szendry, Thomas. "Hungarian-American Theatre." In *Ethnic Theatre in the United States*, edited by Maxine Schwarts Seller. Westport, Conn.: Greenwood Press, 1983.

Széplaki, Joseph. *The Hungarians in America, 1583–1974: A Chronology and Fact Book*. Dobbs Ferry, N.Y.: Oceana Publications, 1975.

Taborsky, Otto Árpád. "The Hungarian Press in America." Master's thesis, Catholic University of America, 1955.

Tcherikower, Elias, and Aaron Antonovsky. *The Early Jewish Labor Movement in the United States*. New York: YIVO, 1961.

Tulman, Victor David. *Going Home*. New York: Times Books, 1977.

Uchill, Ida Libert. *Pioneers, Peddlers, and Tsadikim: The Story of Jews in Colorado*. Boulder: Quality Line Printing Co., 1957.

Ueda, Reed. "Naturalization and Citizenship." In Robert A. Easterlin, David Ward, William S. Bernard, and Reed Ueda, *Immigration*. Cambridge: Harvard University Press, Belknap Press, 1982.

Ujvári, Péter. *By Candlelight*. See Andrew Handler.

United States Immigration Commission. *Abstracts of Reports*, with an introduction by Oscar Handlin. New York: Arno and The New York Times, 1970.

Van Tassel, David D., and John T. Grabowski. *The Encyclopedia of Cleveland History*. Bloomington: Indiana University Press, 1987.

Vardy, Steven Bela. *The Hungarian-Americans*. Boston: Hall, 1985.

———. "Hungarians in America's Ethnic Politics." In *America's Ethnic Politics*, edited by Joseph C. Roucek and Bernard Eisenberg. Westport, Conn.: Greenwood, 1982.

———. *The Origins of Jewish Emancipation in Hungary: The Role of Baron Joseph Eötvös*. Pittsburgh: Duquesne University, 1978.

——— (with Agnes Huszar Vardy). "Research in Hungarian-American History and Culture: Achievements and Prospects." In Steven Bela Vardy, *Clio's Art in Hungary and in Hungarian-America*. New York: Columbia University Press, 1985.

Vasváry, Edmund. *Lincoln's Hungarian Heroes: The Participation of Hungarians in the Civil War, 1861–1865*. Washington, D.C.: Hungarian Reformed Federation of America, 1939.

Végházi, István. "The Role of Jewry in the Economic Life of Hungary." In *Hungarian-Jewish Studies*, edited by Randolph L. Braham. New York: World Federation of Hungarian Jews, 1969.

Weinberg, Daniel E. "Ethnic Identity in Industrial Cleveland: The Hungarians, 1900–1920." In *Ohio History* 86, no. 3 (Summer 1977): 174.

Weinstock, S. Alexander. *Acculturation and Occupation: A Study of the 1956 Hungarian Refugees in the United States*. The Hague: Martinus Nijhoff, 1969.

Weltner, H. Armin. "Hungarians in American Politics." *The Hungarian-American Festival Edition,* May 1896, pp. 80–83. Copy in New York Public Library.

Wieder, Arnold A. *The Early Jewish Community of Boston's North End.* Waltham: Brandeis University, 1962.

Wiernik, Peter. *History of the Jews in America.* New York: The Jewish Press Publishing Company, 1912.

Wirth, Louis. *The Ghetto.* Chicago: The University of Chicago Press, 1928.

Wischnitzer, Mark. *To Dwell in Safety: The Story of Jewish Migration Since 1800.* Philadelphia: The Jewish Publication Society of America, 1948.

Wittke, Carl. *Refugees of Revolution: The German Forty-Eighters in America.* Philadelphia: University of Pennsylvania Press, 1952.

Wolf, Helen F. "The Evolution of a Synagogue—B'nai Jeshurun Congregation." Cleveland, 1985. Mimeo.

Work Projects Administration, Ohio. "Peoples of Cleveland." Cleveland, 1942. Typescript.

INDEX

943.9004 Perlman, Robert.
PER
        Bridging three
        worlds.

$39.95

<table>
<tr><td></td><td></td><td></td></tr>
<tr><td></td><td></td><td></td></tr>
<tr><td></td><td></td><td></td></tr>
<tr><td></td><td></td><td></td></tr>
<tr><td></td><td></td><td></td></tr>
<tr><td></td><td></td><td></td></tr>
<tr><td></td><td></td><td></td></tr>
<tr><td></td><td></td><td></td></tr>
</table>

943.9004 Perlman, Robert.
PER   743
        Bridging three
        worlds.

$39.95

31743

DATE	BORROWER'S NAME	